50p

GW00982795

"THAT BOUNTY BASTARD"

«*THAT BOUNTY BASTARD*»

THE TRUE STORY OF CAPTAIN WILLIAM BLIGH

Kenneth S. Allen

LONDON
ROBERT HALE & COMPANY

Robert Hale & Company
Clerkenwell House
Clerkenwell Green
London EC1R 0HT

Filmset by Specialised Offset Services Limited, Liverpool
and printed in Great Britain by
Lowe & Brydone Limited
Thetford, Norfolk

Contents

Illustrations

Breadfruit

[1]

Expedition to the South Seas

DEPTFORD, and a miserable, rain-laden March wind ruffling the grey water of the Thames, making the anchored ships jerk uneasily at their cables and whipping across the open acres of the 'King's Yard' where an army of men were busy building, repairing and fitting out the warships of His Majesty, King George III.

On board H.M.S. *Resolution* of 462 tons, Lieutenant John Williamson huddled miserably in the lee of the mizzen-mast, hands thrust deep in his pockets, staring with unseeing eyes across the river to the huddle of wet roofs on the opposite bank. Eleven days earlier the ship had been hauled out of dock into the river and now, with her pendant flapping limply at her masthead, was entering men and taking on stores and provisions for a voyage that was expected to last at least three years.

For the past week, lighters had bobbed alongside, swaying up the amazing variety of stores necessary for such a long voyage. At first it had been back-breaking work for the small ship's company but as more men came on board the work had gone along faster and with better co-ordination. On this wet afternoon, Lieutenant Williamson had the deck and from time to time he would leave the scanty shelter of the mast to stare moodily down from the quarter-deck rail at the men working in the waist. He was just turning from one of these reluctant excursions when there came a shout from the seaman stationed at the entry port.

"Boat ahoy!"

At the call Williamson glanced hurriedly towards Deptford Hard from which a wherryman's boat had pushed off, its bows pointing straight at the *Resolution*. He then walked across to the starboard bulwark, his eyes half-closed against the rain, staring at a single figure hunched in the thwarts. The boat was soon alongside and as its passenger had made no move to open his cloak to reveal the distinguishing buttons of an officer, Williamson did not move but watched with mild interest as the newcomer paid off the boatman and spoke to the man at the entry port who, with one of his mates, heaved up a chest which they thumped on the deck to await further orders. Williamson shrugged. Such arrivals had been commonplace during the past few days and there would be more before the ship's company of over a hundred men had signed on to show that they were willing to serve in the *Resolution*, for there were no 'pressed' men, this being 1776 with Britain at peace with Europe.

The latest member of the *Resolution*'s crew had already stepped onto the quarter-deck and Williamson, ostentatiously tucking the telescope of his office under his left arm, moved forward to meet him. He raised his chin and the other replied to the unspoken question with, "William Bligh, sir. Reporting for duty as master".

After a few words, Bligh thanked him and walked aft into the sudden twilight beneath the poop to arrive at the door of the captain's cabin. He raised his hand, hesitated, then rapped twice with his knuckles. Almost immediately a voice from within answered, "Come in!"

He entered diffidently, blinking in the light of several lanterns which illuminated the cabin and saw before him, seated at a desk, a man whose name was already famous, not only in Britain, but throughout Europe. It was Captain James Cook, already considered the finest navigator of the century and one who was destined to become the greatest of all time. He looked up from his work and waited whilst the other said, "William Bligh, sir. Reporting for duty," then in a voice that plainly revealed his Yorkshire origin, asked the other to be seated.

The young man did so, perching himself on the edge of his chair, overawed at being so close to one whom he had admired for the five years that had passed since Cook had returned from his first great voyage of discovery. Of Cook's second and most recent voyage he knew very little, for he himself had only just returned from a voyage as a midshipman in the *Ranger* sloop, and having only been paid off three days previously, had not been able to learn of the other's fresh triumphs.

For a while there was silence in the cabin as the captain studied his new master then, seeing the growing embarrassment on the other's face said, "William Bligh, eh? Now, let me see ..." and he ruffled through some of the papers that littered his desk until he found the one he sought. It was obviously a resumé of Bligh's naval career for Cook read it through, muttering quietly to himself as he did so. He then rose to his feet, walked across to a table and returned with several rolls of parchment. He spread them out on the desk before him and Bligh realized with pleasure that the charts which Cook was displaying were his own. His new captain pointed to them and stated that he had never seen such well-prepared and well executed charts. It was obvious that Bligh was a born cartographer, one who could usefully be employed under his direction in the preparation of similar charts of the places it was Cook's intention to discover.

On his first two voyages, Cook explained, he had carried astronomers – good men but no sailors. In Bligh, he considered, he had the best of both worlds, a man whose map-making skill was exceptional and who had achieved nearly six years active service. He had been looking for such a man and once he had seen the examples of Bligh's skill, he knew instinctively that his search was over.

Bligh's duty was to work with the second lieutenant, James King, who also had considerable skill in navigation. Both would be employed in preparing charts, in making views of the coasts and headlands near which the expedition might pass and in drawing plans of the bays and harbours in which it anchored.

Holding down a large map of the two hemispheres, Cook began to explain his orders for the coming voyage. They were to find a shorter passage to the East other than by way of the Cape of Good Hope, making their way along the western coast of North America of which nothing was then known, determine its distance from Asia and then search for a shorter route back to Europe – the elusive North-West Passage, in fact. As he spoke, both men bent over the chart, the dark hair of Bligh and the greying hair of Cook, as their common interest and enthusiasm brought them closer together. During that hour at dusk of 20th March 1776, a bond of mutual respect and understanding was born, a bond that was to strengthen until it was tragically broken nearly three years later.

The *Resolution* remained at anchor for another two months and it was not until the afternoon of 26th May that she moved down-river to arrive at Long Reach to take in powder, shot and guns. She was closely followed by the *Discovery* which was to sail with her on the voyage. This 300-ton vessel was commanded by Charles Clerke who had already been with Cook on his previous two voyages and who had been promoted from master's mate, to second lieutenant, and now to captain.

During the next week, the *Resolution* and the *Discovery* settled lower in the water as stores were taken on board. On 8th June work stopped for a while and the crews of both ships were mustered in their best uniforms – tarpaulin hats, short jackets, chequered shirts and white trousers. The officers, too, were in their best, the commissioned officers in blue frock-coats with white facings, white breeches and stockings, Bligh and the other warrant officers in blue breeches, with their blue frock-coats lined with white. They waited patiently until, at exactly three o'clock in the afternoon, some smart launches moved away from the shore. As they drew near the ships, there came the flat boom of the first of a seventeen-gun salute, causing hundreds of gulls to rise on beating wings, to mew and scream overhead.

With his blue triangular hat firmly settled on his white wig, Cook stood at the entry port to welcome his guests. As the final gun banged and a thin skein of grey smoke drifted away to leeward, he stepped forward as the pipes shrilled and the first of the visitors set foot on the *Resolution*'s deck. He was the Earl of Sandwich, First Lord of the Admiralty. Behind him came Sir Hugh Palliser, Sir Charles Middleton and other august members of the Board of Admiralty whose presence revealed how important the forthcoming voyage was considered. With Cook leading the way, the party inspected the ship and then, satisfied with what they had seen, stayed to dinner.

After the guests had gone unsteadily ashore, Bligh returned to his tiny cabin to write his last letters before the voyage began. The first was to his father, Francis Bligh, living in Plymouth and working in the Customs Service. His mother had died when he was fifteen and his father had married again but the second wife had also died, some three years previously. Now, from his father's most recent letter, it appeared that he was already considering a third marriage, this time to a widow named Judith Welch.

His duty letters out of the way, Bligh sharpened a new quill and settled down to write a long and romantic epistle to his "dear Betsy". This was Elizabeth Betham whom he had met whilst serving in the *Hunter* which had visited Douglas, in the Isle of Man, where her father, a Scot from Glasgow, was Collector of Customs. He had visited Elizabeth's home with several of his fellow midshipmen in 1771 and again in 1775 when serving in the *Ranger*. She was seventeen when they first met, a year older than young Bligh, but he was completely captivated by her sweet face and charming disposition, and continued to write to her. He was determined, once he was established in the service, to ask her to marry him. If all went well, this voyage to the South Seas would make that possible.

Writing in the flowing and typically elegant script that embellished his charts, he poured out his heart, knowing that it would be at least three years before they met again and he wished her to know exactly how he felt – the thought of returning home and finding that she was promised, or perhaps married to another, was unthinkable.

The last person to come on board before the mud of the Thames was hosed from the ship's anchors was someone whose fame equalled that of Cook. He was Omai, a young native from the Society Islands who had been brought back to England by Captain Furneaux who had commanded the sloop, *Adventure*, which had accompanied the *Resolution* on the second voyage to the South Seas. Omai had been born in Tahiti although at the time of his departure, he was living on the island of Huaheine.

His impact on the sensation loving society of the time was fantastic. He was fêted and lionized but wherever he went – to the opera, stately homes or even into the House of Lords – he behaved with a quiet, calm dignity that impressed all who met him. Even Dr Johnson had pleasant things to say of him.

On 25th June, both ships weighed together but separated soon afterwards, for the *Resolution* had to call in at Deal to collect two boats which had been specially built for her there. A huge crowd of people had gathered at the small port hoping that the legendary Omai would go ashore or at least appear on deck, but they were disappointed – he preferred to stay below.

Five days later, at three o'clock in the afternoon, the *Resolution* arrived in Plymouth Sound and the *Resolution* and *Discovery* remained at anchor for several days, taking in fresh water and final stores and also a number of marines – an officer and nineteen in the former, eleven in her consort.

On the 10th, the commissioner and his pay-clerks came on board, paid the men up to the 30th of the previous month and also gave them two months' wages in advance. This ready money would enable everyone to buy necessaries for a voyage of unusual duration to regions where no further supplies could be purchased. With the typical improvidence of the seamen of the time, most spent their money in one massive debauch ashore. Bligh, carefully advised by Lieutenant James Burney of the *Discovery* who had been to the South Seas before, used a great proportion of his advance in buying items with which to trade with the native – axes, hatchets, mirrors, beads and pocket knives and even medals bearing the likeness of King George III.

At the time of sailing, however, Captain Clerke was detained in London. He had backed a bill for his brother and at the time was actually in the Fleet Prison as he was unable to pay. He finally managed to dodge his creditors and reached Plymouth to take command of the *Discovery*. During his brief stay in prison, however, he had contracted tuberculosis, a disease that was to kill him later in the voyage.

The *Resolution* weighed with the ebb tide on 12th July and after one unsuccessful attempt finally stood out of the Sound and with a fresh westerly wind filling her new canvas, was soon tacking down Channel. A week later, she was past Ushant and the ship's company had shaken down.

Bligh had already realized that the crew was composed of first-class seamen, all volunteers, whose handling of the ship, as well as the performance of their other duties, was first class. Of some of the officers, however, he had reservations. Because of their similar duties he soon came into conflict with James King, the second lieutenant. King had a sneering and supercilious manner which he did not fail to conceal when dealing with his inferior – for a master, however experienced, took rank after all commissioned lieutenants – and Bligh, whose own temper was to lead him into many troubles was continually arguing with him. Occasionally he refused to speak to him at all. Another person Bligh detested was Molesworth Phillips, the lieutenant commanding the marines, King's particular crony and a man whom Bligh was to describe later as one who did nothing "but eat and sleep".

The *Resolution* touched at Tenerife to take in water as well as fodder for the livestock she had on board, the number of which was increased by the purchase of more bullocks, pigs, sheep and goats. Captain Cook also took in a quantity of fresh fruit and vegetables. From the outset he insisted on the lower deck being kept clean, made his men bathe frequently and change their clothing when wet – installing stoves to dry their gear – and also made them air their bedding frequently.

More than anyone else, Cook realized the value of fresh fruit and vegetables, and personal cleanliness, to combat that scourge of all mariners – scurvy. At first his men were obstinate, resisting such new-fangled ideas, especially in the matter of diet, protesting that they were compelled to eat 'foreign foods' in place of the ration of dried peas and beans to which they were entitled. There was considerable opposition also to a form of sauerkraut made from fermented cabbage, but on seeing that it was served to the officers and presumably enjoyed by them, the men decided that it could not be so bad after all.

Such precautions and innovations had already been justified by Cook during his second voyage when with a company of 118 men, he had sailed some 60,000 miles over a period of three years with the loss of only one man from sickness – and that not from scurvy. This was a fantastic record compared to Anson's circumnavigation of twenty years earlier when, after a voyage of three years and nine months his ship, the *Centurion*, returned alone, with only 145 men out of the thousand and more who had sailed in her and the three escorting vessels.

Towards the end of August the *Resolution* ran into weather that was dark and gloomy and with incessant rain storms. This rain, with close and sultry weather, was the climate that fostered disease, but Cook maintained his high standards of hygiene – a difficult enough task, for the deck seams opened and the rain poured in.

The ceremony of Crossing the Line was carried out on 1st September during a gale from the south-east and the ship raced on, reeling away the miles until two and a half weeks later she anchored beneath the cloud-covered mass of Table Mountain. The *Discovery* had not yet arrived at the rendezvous and Cook passed the time by setting up an observatory and in having his ship caulked and the leaky upperworks repaired.

On the morning of 10th November, the *Discovery* slipped into harbour and Captain Clerke informed Cook that he had been delayed by the heavy storms, his ship having taken a week longer in the passage from England than the *Resolution*. His ship had also to be caulked and it was not until the end of the month that both were finally ready for sea. By 3rd December they were clear of the land and, in a fresh gale from the west-nor'-west, headed south.

Bligh was now immersed in a pleasurable orgy of navigation

taking sights and charting the islands through which they sailed.
He was sublimely happy. This was the work he enjoyed and
which he could do well. Cook was also delighted with someone
who, in effect, was his protégé and when on Christmas Eve 1776
they sighted a high, round rock he expressed his feelings by
naming it Bligh's Cap.

The ships sailed onwards in company. They first visited
Kerguelen Island, anchoring at the entrance to the bay whilst
Bligh went off in a boat to sound the harbour beyond. On his
return he reported it to be a safe anchorage, but with not a stick
of wood anywhere along the shore. The ships moved in on
Christmas Day and their crews were soon busy filling the water-
casks and cutting grass for the cattle. On 27th, as everyone had
worked with a will and to celebrate the festive season, Cook
decreed a day of rest and many of his men went ashore to explore
the area but found it barren and desolate. One group, however,
penetrated as far as the north side of the harbour and discovered a
bottle fastened by wire to a prominent rock. It was brought to
Cook who opened it and found written on a piece of parchment:

Ludovico XV Galliarum
rege, et d. de Boynes
regi a Secretis as res
maritimas annis 1772 et
1773

It was a token of discovery and claim by de Kerguelen, a
Frenchman and a navigator of note. Cook wrote on the reverse
side of the parchment:

Naves Resolution
et Discovery
de Rege Magnae Britanniae,
Decembris 1776

He then replaced it, together with a silver piece of 1772, sealed
the bottle and had it set up on a pile of stones near where it had
been found. Before he left the anchorage he named it Christmas
Harbour.

Soon afterwards the ships ran into thick fog and realizing that
they might easily lose each other, Cook told Clerke that their
next rendezvous would be Adventure Bay in Van Diemen's
Land. Although the ships hardly saw each other for a week, they
kept firing guns at intervals and when they ran into clearer

weather were still in company. At 4 p.m. on 26th January 1777 they anchored in the still waters of Adventure Bay in what is now Tasmania. This island, tucked away below the south-east corner of Australia, was discovered by the Dutch navigator Abel Tasman in 1642. He found it a wildly beautiful place inhabited by a strange black race. Having read of these natives, Cook sent two parties ashore under Lieutenant King with a marine guard for protection, for although none of the local inhabitants had yet been seen, tall columns of smoke rising from the wooded country near the shore proved that they were nearby.

During the afternoon of the following day, a wooding party received a visit from nine natives who casually strolled out of the woods and approached without any signs of fear. The English eyed them with interest, for their visitors were completely naked although their bodies were marked with punctures and ridges which formed intricate patterns. They were given presents of food and Cook, who had joined the party, made signs to one of them to demonstrate the use of a stick that he carried. A mark was set up and the native threw his stick at it from twenty yards, but completely missed it every time. Then Omai came up, fired at the mark with his musket and within seconds, every one of the natives had disappeared into the woods.

The next day another group approached a party under King and it was obvious from their behaviour that the fright had been forgotten or that they realized that no harm was intended. This group included some women and children. Like the men, they were quite naked except that the women wore kangaroo skin over one shoulder as a sling for their babies. They were as dark as the men but their features were not unpleasant, and some of the seamen, grinning broadly, came forward with presents, at the same time making gestures. These were so obvious that an elderly native, who appeared to be their leader, ordered all the women to leave the beach. They obeyed although as King reported later to Cook, some of them appeared to do so with much reluctance.

Bligh also spent some time ashore and was impressed by the bearing and independence of the natives. It was the first time he had met natives such as these for his earlier encounters had been in the West Indies where the coloured people were servile Negro slaves — regarded by their owners as animals — and a far different breed to the proud, independent and essentially *free* peoples of the Pacific. He soon became impressed by Cook's attitude towards these people, an attitude that was friendly and fair and that was intended to create an atmosphere of mutual respect and trust that would be of inestimable value to subsequent European visitors to the Pacific.

At 8 a.m. in the morning of 30th January, a light breeze sprang up – for it had been flat calm since their arrival – and the ships weighed and put to sea where, with the tall peak of Mount Ossa slipping astern, they ran into a full gale during which a second marine fell overboard from the *Discovery* and, like the former, was never seen again.

New Zealand was sighted some days later and the following morning Cape Farewell on the northern tip of South Island. At 10 a.m. on the morning of 12th February both ships anchored in the large harbour which Cook had discovered in 1769 and which he had named Queen Charlotte's Sound.

[2]

Arrival at Otaheite

BLIGH VIEWED the shore with some foreboding for during the recent stay in harbour James Burney, first lieutenant of the *Discovery* had paid a visit to the *Resolution* and one evening on the quarterdeck, re-lived a terrifying experience that had taken place in this very sound three years previously. Burney was then second lieutenant of the *Adventure* which had become separated by bad weather from the *Resolution*, her consort, and which, in fact, never met up with her again. Captain Furneaux took his ship into the sound, which had been named as a rendezvous and on seeing that the anchorage was empty, began to have fear that Cook's ship had run into trouble. A party was sent ashore and soon discovered an old tree stump on which had been carved the words "Look beneath". They did so and found a bottle containing a message from Cook informing them that he had waited for their arrival but had finally decided to sail during the previous week.

Burney and Bligh walked up and down the lee side of the quarterdeck, turning together, whilst Burney continued his story.

"When we realized that Cook had sailed we rushed to get our own ship ready for sea. One of our young midshipmen, a youngster called Rowe, was sent ashore in the cutter with nine men. By nightfall they hadn't returned. The next day I was ordered to find out what had happened. We rowed along the coast, firing guns at intervals, but got no reply. Then we reached a place called Grass Cove and I spotted a number of baskets on the beach. We landed, opened the baskets and found them to be full of half-roasted flesh. We began to search further and found first a shoe, and then a hand which we recognised as belonging to one of our men, for his initials were tattooed on its back. I kept to the beach and was glad that I had a dozen marines with me, for the woods at the edge of the beach were filling with natives. We then moved into a patch of shrub and came across something that haunted me for days."

He paused for a moment, staring seawards, his face reflecting his thoughts then continued, "Strewn all over the place were the heads and organs of our men with wild dogs gnawing at their entrails. The rest of my party came running up at my shout and I had difficulty stopping them from attacking the murderers. Instead, they levelled their muskets and fired several volleys into the woods. There were plenty of yelps and I'm sure that quite a few of the savages were wounded, if not killed."

Barney paused again, to watch the sun disappearing over the western horizon in a breathtaking explosion of gold, orange and yellow. As the disc slowly slid out of sight he went on, "The man responsible for all this was a chief named Kahoora".

The ships anchored and boats began to move towards the shore, some with men with empty watercasks, others with a party who were to set up an observatory. As the boats discharged their crews, a number of canoes drew alongside the *Resolution* and although the natives stood up and waved in a friendly fashion, none would come aboard, although Cook called out to them and even addressed some by name. It was quite obvious they believed that the English had returned to punish them for what had happened to Furneaux's men, a feeling that was strengthened by seeing Omai on deck, for he had been in the *Discovery* when the massacre had taken place.

Cook shouted to them that they need have no fear on that account and finally, although with some reluctance, several clambered up the ship's side and coming onto the quarterdeck, greeted him with great respect.

The next day two tents were set up and observatories placed near them under the command of King and Bligh. The rest of the empty watercasks were trundled up the shore, other men were sent to collect fodder for the animals, whilst those left in the ships were busily refitting and cleaning the holds ready for the fresh provisions. A marine guard patrolled the beach whilst every man on shore was armed.

The shore parties, however, had no trouble with the natives. Indeed, the New Zealanders brought their families along to the cove where the observatories had been set up and were soon living near them in constructed huts. This proved to be a great help for the natives spent much of their time fishing and kept the English supplied with a variety of fish to supplement their already ample diet of celery, soup, wheat and home-brewed spruce beer.

The natives also produced other things for barter — carvings, curiosities ... and women. The seamen were glad to have the former but shied away from having anything to do with the latter. No doubt they had visions of being attacked from behind whilst in a helpless position, or the memory of murder of Rowe and his men still rankled. Whatever it was, despite the fact that they had now been away from England for over a year, not one man left his post to slink off into the woods for a few minutes of doubtful sexual gratification.

By 23rd February both ships were well stocked and Cook decided it was time to continue the voyage. The tents were struck, everything was carried back to the ships and the next morning they weighed. Outside the sound, however, the wind died away to a whisper that scarcely stirred their canvas and as the tide was against them, they anchored off the Island of Motuara before sailing through what is now Cook Strait.

The next few months were the happiest of Bligh's life. There was the continual excitement of sighting new islands that rose out of translucent blue water, islands that were crowned with green fronded palms and fringed with white coral over which the long Pacific swell pounded and broke in sparkling spray, islands with limpid names like the calm lagoons which sheltered them — Mangeea and Wateeoo, Annamooka and Neeneeva. He was doing the work he loved, sounding in boats then delineating the charts in the tiny area of his cabin, working late into the night so that when he straightened from his desk, he became aware that his young body was one great ache from being bent for so long in an unnatural position.

Although they were bound for Tahiti, Cook was in no immediate hurry and kept his two ships cruising amongst the 150 islands that made up the Friendly Islands (now the Tongas) where there was friendship indeed. Three months were spent in the area, during which the officers and men were frequently ashore and living in perfect harmony with the islanders. Although from time to time arguments arose owing to the natives' inveterate habit of stealing, Cook ensured that no violence occurred.

There was a great deal of coming and going between the islands by the natives whose outrigger canoes could travel as fast as the English ships and on going ashore Bligh would frequently be surprised at meeting friends he had left on another island several days before. The various islands, also, became jealous of the hospitality offered by others and did their best to outdo them. Dances by both men and women were put on for their entertainment, dances in which hands, arms and slim bodies performed incredible and frequently provocative gyrations. These '*mai*', or dances, were usually performed in open spaces amongst the tall palms near the shore, with lights set at intervals to illumine the scene and where the lilting voices of the singers and the continual pounding of the distant surf blended into a bewitching and almost hypnotic entity.

If Bligh and his fellow officers found such scenes enchanting, to the seamen this was Paradise itself. Many were men who had come from overcrowded and insanitary homes, whose previous idea of bliss was to herd into a waterside tavern, drink themselves stupid and possibly finish their debauch with some slatternly, coarse-mouthed doxy, and this present existence had the substance of a dream. During these nights on the islands, away from the discipline of shipboard routine, away from the smell of the bilge and rancid food, they became new men – individuals in their own right. Rich meats and luscious fruits were thrust upon them to be washed down with '*kava*', fermented cocoa-nut milk. Then, these basic appetites satisfied, they could easily satisfy others in the arms of warm, scented and willing maidens.

But these Friendly Islands had to be left at last and the two ships, well stocked with water and provisions, continued their voyage. On 8th August, the island of Tubai in the Austral group was discovered and then, sailing northwards, the vast mountains of Tahiti were seen rising majestically from an azure sea. Bligh, standing on the *Resolution*'s quarterdeck could sense his captain's nervous anticipation when the hail came from the mast-head that the island was in sight.

But the weather became contrary, a fresh easterly gale being followed by light winds that seemed to blow from every point of the compass. It was impossible to work in to an anchorage and the ships were compelled to stand out to sea again and lay off until morning.

At first light the ships began to move into Vaitepiha Bay. Staring at the island, Bligh knew that he had never seen anywhere as beautiful. From the shore to the high mountains beyond, everything was a fresh, inviting green but with an infinite number of hues of that colour. Wherever he looked there were peaks and ridges that were touched with the morning sunlight and which threw deep purple shadows into the valleys and ravines. Precipitous waterfalls flashed and sparkled whilst the tall, elephant-grey trunks of the fronded palms swayed and beckoned along the shore. He sniffed appreciatively, for the early offshore breeze brought the heady scent of flowers, of wood smoke from breakfast fires, and the pungent smell of rich, rotting vegetation.

As he watched, several canoes sped out from the land and Omai, obviously excited to be amongst his own people again, called to them in greeting. Soon afterwards a much larger and more elaborate canoe came alongside. It held a chief named Ootee and other important people, one of whom was Omai's brother-in-law. At first there was a strange indifference on the part of the newcomers. Then Omai took them below and showed them a few of his possessions which included some red feathers, highly prized in the islands. At this his brother-in-law became suddenly overwhelmed with delight at being reunited with his relative and even Ootee, who up till then had treated Omai with some disdain, grabbed some of the feathers and insisted that they should be "*taios*" – or close friends.

He then sent some of his men ashore for a pig as a gift and they soon spread the news that the English possessed vast supplies of red feathers. Soon both ships were surrounded by hundreds of bobbing canoes, most of them crowded with excited Tahitians to the point of foundering, who held up pigs, fruits and other objects of barter. Bligh stared down at them from the quarterdeck bulwarks and decided that the natives matched the beauty of their island. They were generally of a much lighter shade than those of the Friendly Islands; some, indeed, were very close to being white skinned. Although most had black hair he was surprised to see that some had brown and a few even red hair. They were more elegantly built than others he had seen during their passage, the men being tall, muscled and well-proportioned whilst the girls, most of whom wore only short skirts about their waists revealed a lithe, high-breasted beauty that made him stare with a great deal of pleasure.

Once the ship had been given her harbour stow and everything secured, Cook appeared quite content for the islanders to come on board his ship and soon the decks, above and below, were filled with an excited, chattering crowd of Tahitians. The sailors' supply of feathers was soon exhausted and the exchanges began to take in other goods, but Bligh was surprised to see that iron nails, which he understood had been in great demand during former voyages, now attracted little interest. He recalled, with a chuckle, the story that Lieutenant Gore had told him of the first visit to Tahiti. Gore was then gunner in Captain Samuel Wallis' ship, the *Dolphin*, which had discovered the island in 1767 and realising Blight's intense interest, he had recalled many incidents which had occurred during their stay.

There had been no iron on the island and nails became for a while the basis of all bartering. They were used particularly to purchase the favours of the island maidens, what was known as a "thirty penny nail" being the standard rate. These nails were also used to buy provisions for the ship and in order that the rate of exchange should not be spoilt, Wallis gave instructions for his carpenter to keep every nail in a safe place. But the men were not to be denied. They had been at sea a long time, the girls were very willing and represented an allurement that could not be resisted. So, in sailor fashion, they set to and found alternatives. Within a few days, a harassed master was reporting to Wallis that every cleat in the ship had been ripped off and the supporting nails taken, whilst a good two-thirds of the crew were sleeping on the deck, for their hammock nails had gone too. Robertson, the master, also reported that prices had gone up. The girls were no longer satisfied with a thirty or even a forty penny nail but were demanding seven-inch spikes!

Remembering this, Bligh was relieved that this 'trade' had to a large extent disappeared. As master himself, he appreciated how Robertson must have felt on realizing that the ship was beginning to fall apart beneath his feet. This time, luckily, there seemed no danger of that happening to the *Resolution*.

A few days after their arrival the ships moved round to Matavai Bay and Cook learned that Otoo, king of the entire island, had arrived at Matavai Point and wished to see him. As soon as this was known, Cook, Bligh and some of the other officers were rowed ashore and saluted the great ruler. Omai, who accompanied them, knelt and embraced the king's legs, then made him a present of feathers and of some gold cloth. Bligh noticed that very little notice was taken of Omai and assumed that the king and his nobles were jealous of one who had gone to live in the white man's country and had returned with so many wonderful possessions.

The next day, some of the animals that had been brought from England were put ashore and two observatories were put up on Venus Point where Cook had observed the transit of Venus during his first visit. A guard, under Lieutenant King, was stationed there to watch the precious instruments. At the same time there was intense activity on both ships. Sails and water-casks were repaired, the ships were caulked and their rigging overhauled.

Bligh was keeping a private journal of all that he saw on the island and took every opportunity to go ashore, meet the islanders, and study their strangely conflicting customs. Although they were basically a happy, lazy and pleasure-loving people, many of these customs were quite barbaric. Cannibalism was not practised, but he discovered that it was usual to slaughter considerable batches of people as a sacrifice to their gods. He visited one of the many 'morais', or holy places, and saw the putrefying bodies of the victims still lying where they had been sacrificed. War was also commonplace in this otherwise earthly paradise for during their stay, Otoo asked their help in putting down an uprising in the island of Morea and was most upset when Cook, understandably, replied that he was not acquainted with the reasons for the dispute and did not feel justified in assisting, despite his great friendship for Otoo and his people.

The *Resolution* and *Discovery*, surrounded by hundreds of canoes filled with waving, singing and crying islanders, slowly moved out of the harbour during the afternoon of 29th September 1777 and anchored some days later on the western side of the island of Huaheine, from which Omai had sailed with Captain Furneaux in 1774 and to which Cook now returned him. Men from both ships were set ashore and a house was built, a garden with vines, water-melons and vegetables laid out, and Omai's diminished store of personal possessions taken ashore and placed in the house. In order that the young man, who had proved invaluable as an interpreter during the voyage should not be harmed because of his apparent wealth, Cook solemnly announced to the chiefs of the island that he would soon be back amongst them to see how his friend was getting on.

Before sailing, Cook had an inscription cut over the door of Omai's house. It read:

Georgius Tertius Rex, 2 Novembris,
1777

Naves ·

Resolution, Jac. Cook, Pr.
Discovery, Car. Clerke, Pr.

At four in the afternoon of the same day, the ships cleared the harbour although Omai stayed on board until the last possible moment. He then took his farewell of all the officers but when he came to Cook he broke down and sobbed. He was taken ashore in one of the ship's boats and wept all the way to the beach. As the *Resolution* and *Discovery* squared away for the open sea, Bligh, looking back over the taffrail, could see a white-clad figure standing alone and miserable on the beach. ...

[3]

The Death of Cook

LEAVING THE Society Islands, the ships headed north as Cook wrote in his journal, "though seventeen months had now elapsed since our departure from England ... I was sensible that, with regard to the principal object of my instructions, our voyage was at this time only beginning".

The search for the North-West Passage had begun. Soon after crossing the Line, a low-lying island, surrounded by the inevitable coral reef, was sighted on Christmas Eve and after Bligh had gone off in the ship's boat to find a suitable anchorage, both ships sent crews ashore to catch some of the many turtles they saw basking on the beach. Later, in the golden flush of a Pacific dawn, the ships weighed and the newly named Christmas Island soon disappeared astern.

The next discovery was probably the most important of the whole voyage for on 18th January 1778, the first of a whole series of islands began to show above the horizon. Cook went ashore and was surprised when all the natives fell flat on their faces and remained in this position worshipping him as a god. The ships were restocked with water and provisions and naming the group the Sandwich Islands, in honour of the First Lord of the Admiralty, Cook gave orders for the course to be continued northwards.

Months passed with the ships making their way along the coast of North America, through the Bering Strait and as far north as Icy Cape, with Bligh busily surveying and mapping as they went, a number of places being possessed in the name of King George III and given appropriate names. As the weather had been very cold for most of their passage along the coast, officers and seamen alike were delighted to find that they could obtain magnificent skins from the natives for a very moderate outlay. They also bought fur clothes, many still warm from the wearer's body.

The ships headed westwards, doubling the great promontory of Alaska to reach the most westerly point of the American continent which Cook named Prince of Wales Cape, and then pushed on into the Northern Ocean where they met an increasing number of ice floes. Finally they arrived at a six-foot wall of solid ice that seemed to stretch away to the horizon, its white surface dotted with hundreds of walruses which kept the crews in fresh meat for a considerable time. They called it "marine beef".

The ships then moved along the coast of Asia, Cook, Bligh and King checking and surveying work done by Vitus Bering, the Danish navigator who had first sailed this area some forty years earlier, and finding it remarkably accurate. They subsequently visited the Russian coast and the Peninsula of Kamchatka where Bering was buried in 1741.

The year was now well advanced and Cook decided to turn back and winter in the Sandwich Islands in order to refit and to rest his men so that they would be ready for another attempt in the following spring. The islands were raised at the end of November but a further one was sighted that had been unaccountably missed on the previous visit – unaccountably for it was so big that, for sheer size, it was only surpassed by New Zealand. From the natives, who were even more trusting and friendly than those of Tahiti, he discovered that the name of the island was Owhyhee (Hawaii). He cruised along its shores for some weeks looking for a suitable harbour, then learned from Bligh that he had found a bay that offered both a good anchorage and fresh water.

The following morning the ships dropped anchor in a bay which, Bligh learned, was called by the natives Karakakooa, on the western side of the island. As the men were unbending the sails and sending down the yards and topmasts, Bligh studied the shore through his telescope. Immediately facing him was a village named Kowrowa and, separated from it by a high rocky cliff and marked by a grove of tall cocoa-nut palms, was the larger village of Kakooa. The shore along the bay was covered with black coral rock which made landing very dangerous except at Kakooa, where there appeared to be a good sandy beach. As soon as the natives saw that the ships intended to anchor, they began to swarm out in their thousands, men, women and children packed into canoes and all singing and shouting and throwing their arms about in gestures of welcome. The canoes were soon alongside and the ships' decks and rigging began to be covered with excited and happy islanders. Others, who had not been able to get into the canoes swam around the ships in shoals, many remaining in the water alongside throughout the day.

An imposing young chief named Pareea came on board and announced that he was attached to Terreeoboo, the king of the island, who was away at the moment but who was expected back within a few days. Pareea soon made himself useful, for the *Discovery* had so many people hanging on to one side that she was heeling over in an alarming manner. The young chief immediately dropped down into his canoe, sped across to the other ship and within minutes had driven away all the canoes that surrounded her. The *Resolution* was also placed in the same danger but another chief named Kaneena shouted out some words of command, everyone ran to the side and, without hesitation, jumped overboard. One man lingered but in a few quick strides Kaneena was across the deck, picked him up and threw him over the side after the rest. Bligh, who as master had been worrying about the alarming heel to his ship, was grateful for this prompt action.

Another important man came on board the *Resolution*. He was named Koah. Although once a great warrior chief he was now the head priest of the island, a little old man, very emaciated and scrofulous. On entering Cook's cabin, he moved forward and with an air of great veneration, threw a red cloth over the captain's shoulders then stepped back and delivered a long prayer, in which he hailed Cook as the great god, Orono. From that moment, whenever he went ashore, Cook was greeted by the natives as if he was indeed this god. They prostrated themselves at his feet, offering gifts of pigs, fruit and vegetables, and when he was being rowed to and from the shore, every man in nearby canoes would stop paddling and lay down on their faces until he had passed.

The ships stayed in Karakakooa until February of the following year when Cook, having decided to finish the survey of Hawaii before visiting the other islands, weighed and with the *Discovery* following in her wake and with a great number of canoes in company, sailed northwards. Two days later they were off a wide bay and Bligh was sent in to examine it and report whether it would afford a good anchorage. Koah went with him as pilot having, out of compliment to the English, changed his name to 'Britannee'. As they sounded in the bay the sky became overcast and soon violent gusts of wind were shipping across the exposed water. Bligh stood up in his boat and saw that the ships had taken in their canvas and were hove to under mizzen-staysails and that the accompanying canoes were speeding for the shore. He therefore decided that it was time to return. On the way back he saw an old woman and two men whose canoe had been overturned by the wind struggling in the water. He dragged them over the gunwale of his boat and took them to the *Resolution*.

The weather worsened considerably and a sudden gale forced them to double reef their topsails and send down the top-gallant yards. The next day a grey dawn revealed that the *Resolution*'s foremast, already weakened, had sprung during the gale and that it was necessary to unstep it for repair. As the ship plunged up and down in the heavy after-gale swell, Cook paced up and down in his cabin, faced with the decision of whether to keep close to the islands and hope to find a better anchorage or return to Karakakooa which, although not very good, at least would serve whilst the mast was unstepped and the repairs made. It was a difficult decision for although he knew that the bay would be sufficient to house his ships, he was also very aware that the district around had been drained of provisions and that their return might prove unpopular. Finally, he decided to return.

The ships struggled back through another vicious storm which nearly drove the *Resolution* onto some rocks, then anchored in Karakakooa again, almost exactly where they had lain before. As they did so, Bligh was disturbed to see that their reception was vastly different to what it had been when they first arrived. Now there were no shouts of welcome, no bustle of excited natives coming alongside, no clustering canoes. Instead there was a deserted bay with, here and there, an isolated canoe stealing furtively along the shore. A boat was sent off to find out the reason for this atmosphere and returned with the disquieting news that the king had laid a tabu on the whole bay.

The damaged mast was taken ashore and as the repairs would obviously take several days, an observatory was set up on a large *morai*, or mound, near the beach, under the guard of a corporal and six marines. The tabu was removed the next day and the natives, generally, appeared to be friendly, but there were many indications that there was an undercurrent of unrest. The god

Orono, it seemed, had outstayed his welcome!

Things came to a head during the morning of 15th February 1779, when Captain Clerke came on board the *Resolution* with the disturbing news that his ship's cutter had been stolen from its buoy during the night. Cook was furious at this theft and ordered away the ship's pinnace and launch, going in the former with Lieutenant Phillips and some marines, whilst Lieutenant Williamson commanded the other. He intended to do what had proved successful in similar situations before – hold the chief and some of his relatives as hostages until the stolen goods were restored. Before the two boats pushed away from the *Resolution* he also ordered Lieutenant Rickman to take the *Discovery*'s launch, and Bligh to take the cutter, and to stop any canoes escaping out to sea.

Whilst Cook and his two boats moved to the shore, the others stationed themselves at the entrance to the bay. Seeing one canoe trying to creep past, young Rickman impulsively ordered his marines to fire. They did so and saw one of the natives standing in the bows of the canoe crumple and fall. There was a moment of panic amongst the rest then the canoe span around and raced back to the shore.

Meanwhile Cook had landed near Kowrowa and with Phillips and an escort of nine marines, walked into the village where they found king Terreeoboo emerging sleepily from his hut. He agreed to accompany them back to their ship but as the party drew near the shore, the crowd began to thicken, and one of Terreeoboo's wives, together with some of his chiefs, begged him not to go. Cook was now in a difficult position. He kept urging the king to come with him and although the old man appeared willing to do so, every time he tried to move forward he was held back by his own people. At last Cook realized that he could do nothing further without using violence and ordered the marines to fall back to the beach. He was walking down to the water's edge to join them when he heard a sudden wild cry behind him. The news had reached the crowd that in the recent shooting out in the bay, the popular Kaneena had been killed.

As Cook hesitated and looked back, the women and children began to draw away and the natives, many of whom were now clad in their primitive armour of war-mats, began to move forward. They were led by a man whom Cook recognized as someone whom he had ordered off the *Resolution* for stealing, and he saw him make a gesture as if to hurl the large stone he held in his hand. Cook turned to face him and ordered him to stop, but the other sidled nearer in a menacing manner and Cook raised his gun and fired one of the barrels. It was loaded with small shot which did not penetrate the other's war-mat but only increased his rage. Several stones were thrown and Lieutenant Phillips narrowly avoided being stabbed, but managed to knock his assailant down with the butt of his musket. Cook, moving backwards, now fired his second barrel. It was loaded with ball which killed one of the natives in the front rank. This provoked a further shower of stones and the marines brought their muskets up and fired. Several of the natives fell, but before the marines could re-load, the rest fell upon them with frightening shouts and yells. Four marines were cut off amongst the rocks near the water's edge and killed, another was struck in the eye with a wooden spear and two others dangerously wounded. Phillips was stabbed between the shoulders, only escaping certain death by shooting his attacker.

The two boats were still lying some way off from the beach and the men in them began to fire at the natives, but Cook, wishing to avoid further bloodshed, turned to shout to them to cease fire. Whilst he had faced the natives, none had actually attacked him but when he turned one sprang forward and stabbed him in the back. He gave a groan and fell forward into the surf, his face in the water. At this, there was a great shout and several natives ran forward, dragged his body up the beach and continued to stab it with their daggers. The surviving English swam off to the pinnace whilst Williamson, during the entire incident, had done nothing except lay off in the launch and allow his men to fire a couple of volleys, whereas a determined landing might possibly have saved his captain's life.

Leaving the bodies on the shores, the two boats rowed back to the *Resolution* to spread the terrible news. It was a nerve-wracking moment for Captain Clerke, to find himself suddenly in command and not sure what was happening. He turned his telescope onto the shore where Lieutenant King and six marines were guarding the *Resolution*'s mast and most of her sails and he knew that they would have to be rescued, together with their precious charge. As he looked, he saw that a large number of natives were already pressing about the *morai* and he gave the order to fire two four-pounders as a warning. One of the balls cut a cocoa-nut palm in half, the other shivered a rock near where a crowd had gathered. As there had been no signs of hostility from any of these particular natives, however, King sent off a boat with orders that the ship should stop firing and not begin again unless he hoisted a flag.

A quarter of an hour of anxiety followed and then to his relief King saw a cutter pulling hard for the shore with Bligh, fully armed, standing in its bows. As it drew near King cupped his hands and shouted "What's happening?'

"The captain has been killed – you must strike the place at once and get everything off the shore."

"Cook, killed?" King repeated, unable to take in the other's meaning. He had known that something was going on further along the beach for he had seen the natives massing and also heard the sound of firing, but this. ...

By now the cutter was grounding on the beach and Bligh jumped ashore and ran forward. King could see by his face that the news was true. "The captain's been murdered by the natives. We have also lost four marines and haven't been able to recover any of the bodies yet. Captain Clerke insists that we get everything off as soon as possible."

King paused, his face showing his indecision then said, "Take command. I'm going back to the *Resolution* to report to Captain Clerke. Things are still quiet here, the natives don't seem to be at all hostile. Keep it that way. Under no circumstances are you to open fire on them. Act only on the defensive, do you understand me? On the defensive," and with that he clambered into the cutter which turned and made for the *Resolution.*

Bligh watched it go then walked slowly up the beach to find the marines, their muskets ready, posted on the top of the *morai* which gave them some protection. Hardly had he joined them, however, than several stones whistled around him. Staring down, he saw that a large number of natives were beginning to move towards them. More stones thudded near and Bligh ordered the marines to fire a volley over the natives' heads. This stopped them for a moment then seeing that none of their number was injured, they began to move forward again. Another order brought down the barrels of the muskets, the marines fired again and several natives fell. The rest retreated for a space to take cover behind huts and trees and as they did so King, who at the sound of firing had come back from the *Resolution*, ran up the beach and began to scream at Bligh for ignoring his orders. Faced with his *bête noir*, his nerves already at

full stretch, Bligh gave as good as he received and whilst the
natives began to creep steadily nearer, there was the ludicrous
situation of both men shouting and yelling abuse at each other.
But King was the senior officer and he swung round and shouted
at the marines to ground their muskets. They did so reluctantly
and watched as the natives, seeing that they were no longer
attacked, kept moving forward.

King looked about him and saw that several large groups of
the enemy were coming towards them from Kowrowa whilst
still more were approaching from Kakooa. It was obvious that
the odds would soon be overwhelming and, as a further hail of
stones began to thud about them, King was forced to order the
marines to begin firing again. This forced the enemy back once
more and during this spell, Bligh looked seawards and was
relieved to see boats pulling towards them carrying
reinforcements from both ships. The men landed and the natives
sullenly drew off to allow the observatory to be dismantled and
the mast and sails to be taken off without further trouble.

As darkness fell over the bay, the men stood-to all night, for
everyone expected a massive attack. None came, however, and
during the next few days an uneasy peace was established
between the ships and the shore, which enabled the English to
complete the repairs to the mast and also negotiate for the return
of Cook's body, for everyone was determined that they would
not leave until it had been given proper burial. The recovery,
however, took a considerable time for it was learned that it had
been cut up and distributed throughout the island.

The repaired foremast was stepped – a dangerous task as some
of the ropes had become so rotten that the hoisting tackle gave
way several times – hardly was it in place and the shrouds and
rigging replaced than mournful singing was heard coming from
the shore. Exhausted from his labours with the mast, Bligh
slumped down on the forecastle head and saw a long procession
winding down a pathway leading to the beach. It was headed by
two drummers who set up a white flag on the shore then sat
down beside it and continued to beat their drums. Others
followed bringing presents of sugar-cane, bread-fruit and other
vegetables which they placed on the beach before withdrawing.
Finally Eappo, one of the principal chiefs, dressed in a ceremonial
feathered cape, and reverently bearing something in his arms
came into view and stood waiting near the white flag. Clerke
realized that he was returning Cook's body and with some of his

officers, went ashore and accepted a box covered with a cloak of black and white feathers. They then returned to the *Resolution* where the cloak was removed to reveal Cook's gruesome remains, the identification being definite by an unusual scar on one of the severed hands. They were then covered again, taken below and a guard placed over them for the night.

The next morning Eappo came on board with the remaining parts of Cook's body, his gun, his shoes and some personal trifles. He then told them that the recent fighting had caused the death of six of their chiefs and a large number of the islanders. He also regretted that he could not return the bodies of the marines who had been killed, explaining their bodies had been cut up and the portions carried off by 'the common people' and were now irrecoverable. He was dismissed with orders to tabu the whole bay and during the afternoon the remains of Captain Cook were committed to the still waters of the bay with full honours. As the hammock containing them spiralled gently down, a volley crackled from the marines' muskets, to be followed by a salute of eleven guns.

The next day Eappo came on board again to be assured that as the 'Orono' had returned to paradise, the whole matter was to be considered something that had never happened. The tabu was removed and soon both ships were surrounded by canoes bringing provisions and gifts, whilst Clerke hurried on with the last of his watering. At eight o'clock in the evening of 22nd February, the ships weighed and stood out of the bay, leaving the shores crowded with natives waving farewell with every mark of affection and goodwill.

Clarke's thin body was racked with the tuberculosis he had picked up before sailing from England and he well knew that he could only be kept alive as long as he stayed in the warm climate of the Pacific. Despite this, he was determined to carry out the orders of his dead captain and took the ships northwards in another attempt to find a passage through the Northern Ocean. He passed the Bering Strait for a second time but as before found the ice barrier quite impassable. The impossibility of any passage by the northern route having been sufficiently proved, he gave orders for the ships to be turned and to set course for home. When they reached Kamchatka, however, the tired, wasted body of the faithful Clarke could stand no more, and he died on 22nd August 1779.

The command of the expedition now fell to the next senior

officer, John Gore, who took over the *Resolution* and gave the command of the *Discovery* to James King. The ships then set course for China, arriving at the Portuguese settlement of Macao on 3rd December. Here they learned what had been going on in Europe since their departure. Britain and France had been officially at war since 11th May 1778, although there had been clashes at sea for some months previously. Despite this state of hostilities, the French Minister of Marine had instructed the captains of all his country's men-of-war that should they meet with Cook they were to treat him with every respect, and regard him as the commander of a neutral and friendly power. This high regard for so eminent a navigator was also echoed by Benjamin Franklin, at that time the ambassador in Paris of the newly created United States of America, who made a similar request.

The ships anchored in Canton River and were immediately surrounded by a cluster of sampans filled with Chinese holding up objects of barter to the sailors who, having traded away most of their spare clothing before leaving the South Seas, were reduced to wearing little more than rags. Some of the things held up in an uncanny silence – so different to the eager chattering of the Tahitians – were so tempting, that many of the seamen ran below to see what they had left to trade. In desperation, one came back on deck with an old skin he had picked up on the north-west coast of America and, somewhat diffidently, dangled it over the side. There was a sudden outcry and many of the sampans thrust forward, the occupants standing up and stretching out eager hands.

Seeing what their shipmate received for his skin, there was a mad rush below by the rest to grab their own. Before many of the skins were sold, however, the seamen began to have second thoughts. If these poor traders alongside were ready to give all they had, what would the richer merchants offer? To the great disappointment of the thickly clustering boats, the rest of the skins and furs were taken below again to see what would happen. Within the hour – for the news had travelled as quickly as that – larger sampans and even junks were coming alongside both ships and the highly delighted seamen, and the officers, were handing over their skins and getting bags of dollars in return.

The prospect of more 'easy money' excited the crews to such an extent that the next day they trooped aft, demanding that they be taken back to America or Russia to collect more furs, and were furious when their request was curtly dismissed. For a while there was every prospect of a mutiny but the officers, together with the elder and more level-headed amongst the men, managed to suppress it.

A few managed to desert and became the first adventurers to cross the Pacific Ocean and begin the fur trade which was later to grow into immense proportions, and which brought hundreds of European ships to these waters. Those that remained underwent a complete and ludicrous change. Now, with plenty of dollars to spend their former rags were thrown away and they strutted about the ships decked out in gaudy silks and other Chinese finery.

Realizing that the men were getting out of hand, Gore curtailed their stay and the two ships squared away for home via the Sundra Straits, the Cape of Good Hope and the Azores.

On 4th October 1779, they anchored at the Nore after an absence of four years, two months and twenty-one days, and were paid off three weeks later. Bligh returned with mixed feelings. The deaths of both captains had meant promotion but he returned as he had gone – a master – although Harvey, one of the midshipmen had been raised to lieutenant as had Lanyan, his own master's mate. This latter promotion, which meant that one of his juniors had been promoted over his head, understandably made him furious, for he was convinced, had Cook survived, that his own promotion from warrant to commissioned rank would have been assured.

On the other hand, he had learned a tremendous amount from the voyage. Apart from the wonderful experience he had gained in surveying and navigation, he also returned a better seaman and with a deeper knowledge of how to handle men. He had also learned how to look after their health for during the voyage, the *Resolution* had only lost five men by sickness, of whom three were ill before leaving England. The *Discovery* did not lose a single man from sickness, a great tribute to Cook's insistence on careful diet and regular cleaning, and definite proof that a voyage of such duration did not necessarily affect the health of the crew. This, in many respects, was a discovery of greater importance than that of a new continent. By banishing the terror that had always existed where a high mortality rate was considered inevitable on long voyages, Cook abolished the limits of any future voyages either in time or distance.

[4]

The Battle of the Dogger Bank

"IN THE MIDST of life we are in death: of whom may we seek for succour, but of thee, O Lord, who for our sins are justly displeased. ..."

A chill December wind blew across the churchyard of St Andrew's, Plymouth, rustling the brown scattered leaves, pulling at the clothes of a small group of mourners, making them shrug deeper into their warm winter cloaks. Bligh stood alone at the head of the open grave and stared with unseeing eyes into the far distance. The mortal remains of his father, Francis, had just been lowered and as he stood there, his thoughts inevitably went back across the years to his younger days. It was because of his father's insistence that he had gone to sea at all, for Francis had entered him on the books of the *Monmouth* as 'Captain's servant' when still a lad of seven in order to give him 'service' against the time when he actually went to sea.

His father was also responsible for his high standard of education, especially in the encouragement of his natural aptitude for mathematics, which was to serve him so well in later years. Not having had any brothers or sisters, he and his father had been very close and now little forgotten incidents were tugging at his abstracted mind. He recalled his father's great patience with a frequently stubborn and at times almost unmanageable child, for even then he had been bedevilled by an uncontrollable temper, although within minutes his rage would disappear as if nothing had happened.

That evening Bligh had to decide about his future. It was 27th December, two months since he had been paid off, and no orders had come from the Admiralty regarding his future. Although his time in Plymouth had been clouded by his father's illness and death, the days had passed quickly enough. He was still on full pay and had spent a great deal of time preparing his charts for the official history of the recent voyage, a story eagerly awaited by a public who regarded Cook as a national hero and to whom such accounts of remote and romantic places made fascinating and almost compulsive reading. Bligh was to receive considerable payment for his work, for it had been agreed by the sponsor, Joseph Banks, that he should receive one-eighth of the profit after one hundred pounds had been paid to Mrs Anderson, widow of the *Resolution*'s surgeon, whose descriptions of places and events contributed a great deal to the work.

Bligh's own part was now finished and his future stretched uncertainly ahead. Until called upon by the navy he had nothing to do and for such an energetic person this enforced rest would be intolerable. He was annoyed that he had not already been ordered to sea, for Britain was fighting for her very existence and, surely, needed every fighting man she possessed. She was at war with America, with France and with Spain and, for the last week, with Holland. Also, because of their long jealousy of Britain's arrogant naval superiority, Russia, Sweden, Denmark, Prussia and the trading states of Italy had entered into a league known as the 'Armed Neutrality' in an endeavour to limit Britain's right to stop and search all neutral vessels.

The country was frantically building new ships and dragging out older ones from 'Rotten Row', press-gangs were scouring the country and large bounties were being paid to volunteers. The navy had already achieved some successes – Admiral Keppel had beaten a French fleet to the westward of Ushant, there had been other victories off Ushant and Grenada, and Sir George (afterwards Lord) Rodney had defeated a powerful French fleet off the Leeward Islands. Recalling these victories, Bligh rose and began to pace impatiently up and down the room. He was now twenty-six, an age when many of his contemporaries were reaching post rank, and the two occasions during the recent voyage when he had been passed over for commissioned rank by men his juniors still nagged at his mind. With his father's death there was nothing now to keep him in Plymouth and he suddenly decided to go north, to the Isle of Man, and find out for himself if Elizabeth Betham really meant what she had hinted about in her letters. ...

Early in January 1781, after a nightmare journey of mired roads and floundering horses, he came at last to Onchan, near Douglas, on the east coast. With a suddenly pounding heart he pulled the bell at the portal of the Betham's home. A month later, on Sunday, 4th February 1781, they were married in the parish church.

It was a big wedding for the Bethams were of considerable importance in the island, and had many family connections. The relatives began to arrive and Bligh was considerably impressed with one of them, Duncan Campbell, who had come from London especially for the wedding of his favourite niece. He was a man of great influence, a wealthy trader with plantations in the West Indies, and a fleet of ships which traded with the islands and which carried his produce back to Britain. He also related to John Campbell who had sailed round the world with Anson and was now a rear-admiral. This was marrying into a family with influence indeed!

Three days after the wedding Bligh received the orders he had been expecting. He was appointed master of the frigate *Belle Poule*, now refitting at Portsmouth, and was to join her without delay.

Bligh signed articles as master of the *Belle Poule* on 14th February and soon realised what a beautiful ship she was. Like all French vessels she had been designed and built with flair and imagination — so different from the English vessels which, it was said, were so badly designed and proportioned that they seemed to have been built by the mile and cut off as required.

After some repairs, the *Belle Poule* sailed northwards under the command of Captain Philip Patton, in company with the *Berwick*, 74, to join the main fleet anchored at Leith. It was a short passage but one which gave Bligh his first taste of action. The ships were running towards their destination with the *Berwick* some distance ahead when the *Belle Poule*'s look-out shouted that the seventy-four was in action with another ship. Patton looked up, nodded in acknowledgement then turning to his first lieutenant said in an over-casual voice, "I'll have the ship cleared for action, if you please".

This order was bellowed through the ship and brought the boy marine drummer up from below, still buckling his drum about him. Soon the staccato rattle and the shrilling of boatswain's pipes threw the *Belle Poule* into a frenzy of controlled confusion. Men swarmed aloft to shake out every possible scrap of canvas and as the sails were sheeted home, the frigate seemed to surge forward, white water mounting under her slim bows. Down below, where men were slacking away the breechings of her guns there came the creaking of tackles as the ports were opened and when the guns captains began to shout, "Run 'em up boys!"

an ominous, dull rumbling was heard as the men heaved on the
tackles and the guns trundled forward to poke their ugly snouts
through the open ports.

Powder boys ran up from below where, in the magazine, the
felt-slippered gunner and his mates handed out the cartridges.
Other seamen wetted and sanded the decks against fire and
slipping feet, then the crews huddled about their guns – and
waited.

This, to Bligh, was the testing time. He forced himself to
appear nonchalant, standing at his post on the quarterdeck, hands
clasped behind his back and very conscious that he was feeling
nervous and that his throat was suddenly dry. The frigate forged
on, slipping past the slower sailing *Berwick*, whose crew leaned
out of her open ports to give her a cheer as she did so. Then the
seventy-four was wallowing astern and the *Belle Poule* was
climbing up the Frenchman's wake until, at 5 p.m., Patton
ordered her to pay off so that her port broadside could bear.
There was a long moment of silence to be shattered by the first
lieutenant's voice. ... "Take your aim! Steady there! FIRE!"

Bligh stared ahead at the Frenchman, his interlaced fingers
moving nervously within each other behind his back and with
the acrid stink of the powder rasping his throat. Sharp points of
light rippled along her sides and for the first time he heard the
nerve-stretching sound of enemy shots passing overhead. *Belle
Poule*'s guns replied independently as they bore and the noise
grew into a rolling, pounding torrent of sound and venom.
Overhead there was a crash as the maintopsail truss was shattered
and Bligh bawled an order that sent men scurrying aloft to draw
the yard in to the mast with temporary lashings. The two ships
were now running closehauled, broadside to broadside. Both had
the same number of guns although those of the frigate were
heavier, for she had twenty-four-pounders on her upper deck
against the privateer's twelve-pounders, whilst on her
quarterdeck and forecastle she carried the navy's latest gun – the
carronade – a devastating weapon at short range and one that
lived up to its popular name of 'the smasher'.

The frigate was manoeuvring closer in order to bring these
carronades into action when the other ship suddenly backed her
topsails and the white flag of France fluttered down from her
ensign staff. There came a final bellow from below, "Belay
there. Cease fire!" then only the slap of the waves against the side

of the ship and the harping of the wind in her taut rigging broke the stillness. As the two ships edged nearer, Patton clambered onto the lee bulwark and, holding on to the mizzen shrouds with one hand shouted across, "Heave to and prepare to take our boats".

The prize was *La Cologne* of Dunkirk and when her captain came on board *Belle Poule* he seemed quite resigned to the sudden change in his fortunes. Shrugging hugely in true Gallic fashion he told Patton "I regret m'sieu that the whole incident has been a mistake. I mistook that other ship," and he waved towards the oncoming *Berwick*, "for a merchantman and was on the point of boarding her when she opened her ports and I saw that I had taken on one of your ships of the line. Even so, my ship could easily have got clean away but, helas, I did not expect to meet another French ship," and he shrugged again, his face twisted into a wry grin.

Hoping that Leith would become his home port, Bligh wrote to Elizabeth, telling her to come across from the Isle of Man, for he had found rooms in the town. Harly had she arrived and settled in, however, than the *Belle Poule* weighed again, leaving a lonely Mrs Bligh waving disconsolately on the quay to a ship which was destined never to return there.

The frigate sailed in company with other ships of the Channel fleet and Bligh now experienced all the boredom and frustration of blockade – short rations and bad food, with ships being sighted and chased only to materialize as British or neutral. Disappointment followed disappointment until, in mid-July, she joined the main fleet off the Norwegian coast where the Baltic convoy of over a hundred merchantmen was assembling for the passage to England. It was to be escorted by Hyde Parker's flagship, the *Fortitude*, 74, *Princess Amelia*, 80, *Berwick*, 74, *Bienfaisant*, 64; *Buffalo*, 60, *Preston*, 50, and *Dolphin*, 44, together with six frigates and six smaller vessels. The line-of-battleships placed themselves at the head and stern of the large and unwieldly convoy and with the frigates and other ships scouting far out on either flank, the whole miscellaneous collection of ships headed south-westwards for Britain.

On the first day of August, when it was ploughing past Jutland, the *Busy*, cutter, came racing back with news that the Dutch fleet was out. Hyde Parker, anxious for a fight, signalled to his ships to close up and keep on course until daybreak of the

5th when the morning light revealed the topsails of Dutch men-of-war, also escorting a convoy, lifting over the horizon to the south-west. As the two fleets drew nearer it became apparent that they were of similar strength, the Dutch having the *Admiral de Ruyter*, 68, flying the flag of Admiral John Zoutman, a seventy-four and a sixty-four, two fifty-fours, a fifty and a forty-four, together with six frigates and two cutters. Soon after sighting, a string of flags went fluttering to the *Fortitude*'s yard-arms, ordering the merchantmen to break away and make for England and as the plunging line of ships began to draw apart, another signal ordered the British fleet to form line of battle.

Once again Bligh heard the pulse-quickening rattle of the marine's drum as the *Belle Poule*, on one wing of the fleet, cleared for action like the rest. The morning was fine and clear, with a smooth sea and a fair wind from the north-east which sent the English ships scudding before it, straight for the enemy fleet. Zoutman was also obviously ready to fight for he stationed his frigates and the seventy merchantmen under his lee and kept his warships under easy sail, moving steadily across the bows of the advancing British. In his eagerness to get at the enemy, Parker had placed his own fleet at a disadvantage, for before his broadside could bear, his ships would have to undertake the complicated business of going about within range of the enemy's guns. The signal for the manoeuvre was hoisted and, for several minutes, whilst the English crews were busy with tacks and sheets, and whilst the yards were swinging round to allow the vessels to steady on the new course, each English ship was helplessly open to Dutch broadsides. The seamen sweated desperately as they worked, some looking nervously across at the ominous open ports of the enemy ships and muttering the old blasphemy, "For what we are about to receive. ... "

But for some strange reason — a sense of chivalry perhaps — Zoutman held his fire and the English ships were allowed to tack in complete safety. The manoeuvre brought the two battle squadrons within pistol shot, Parker sent up the red flag as a signal for the action to begin, and the first broadsides belched thunder and flame at almost point-blank range.

The battle developed into a hard, tough and bloody slogging match. The opposing ships sailed past each other, reeling from the hammerblows of broadsides and of their own recoils, their crews loading, firing and loading again and again in a hell of crashing shot, splintering timber and swirling choking smoke, with the shrill screams of injured men puntuating the demoniac cacophony of incessant, deafening thunder. As was usual, only the line-of-battleships took any active part in the action and Bligh, with little to do, peered through the fog-like smoke which hung about the battling monsters and saw for the first time the tremendous damage caused by well-directed broadsides. The *Berwick* had led in the British squadron and broken through the enemy line but, in doing so, found herself so far down to leeward that she had to make a long tack in order to get back into her station. The *Buffalo*, an old and very unwieldly ship, was badly cut up and had to haul out of the line in order to repair the damage.

After nearly four hours of continuous firing, Parker hauled down his battle flag and took his ships out of the line, to repair and reform. Boats criss-crossed between the ships with orders and instructions, the *Belle Poule*'s cutter returning with the news that there had been a great deal of slaughter during the action. 104 men had been killed, including Captain Macartney of the *Princess Amelia* and amongst the 339 wounded, Captain Graeme of the *Preston* had lost an arm, whilst most of the ships of the line had been reduced to little more than floating wrecks. As their crews worked frantically to bring their ships into some sort of shape for the next encounter, they suddenly realized that the enemy had had enough, for the Dutch ships hoisted what sail they could and, turning their sterns to the British, made for the shelter of the Texel. Parker was forced to let them go. He had, in any case, saved his own convoy and forced the enemy to withdraw and leave him ostensibly the victor.

The next morning, whilst sailing in the wake of the retreating Dutch to see that they really meant to return to harbour, the *Belle Poule*'s lookout sighted a flag flying forlornly above the water. She sent a boat away to investigate and found it belonged to the *Hollandia*, 64, which, unable to make the land, had sunk in shallow water and in an upright position with her three mastheads above the surface.

Parker took his battered ships back to the Nore where a few days later the King came down to review them. It was not a happy occasion for Parker had already been criticized for his handling of the battle and was personally well aware that only the inexplicable chivalry of Zoutman had allowed him to close without his ships suffering crippling broadsides that might well have knocked some of them out of the fight before they even got into it. To King George's congratulations he replied, bitterly, "I wish your Majesty better ships and younger officers. For myself, I am now too old for the service."

Not long afterwards he was appointed commander-in-chief of the East Indies station and sailed from England in the *Cato*. Neither he nor his ship were ever seen again.

Belle Poule put into Sheerness early in September and on the 5th of that month Bligh's long awaited, long desired promotion came through. He was appointed fifth lieutenant of the *Berwick*. He was a commissioned officer at last!

[5]

The Rock under Siege

BLIGH FOUND THE next two years boring and frustrating. For the first few months the *Berwick* lay in the Downs, waiting for the Dutch to emerge from the Texel, but apparently the enemy preferred the safety of its own harbours. During this time, his captain, John Fergusson, allowed him compassionate leave to return to Leith and to be with Elizabeth during the final stages of her pregnancy. The baby, a girl, was born on 15th November and christened Harriet Maria.

On New Year's Day, 1782, he was transferred to the *Princess Amelia*, 80, then, with almost the whole of that ship's company, was moved into the *Cambridge*, 80, Captain John Holloway, as sixth lieutenant and had to wait with mounting impatience whilst the forty-year-old ship went into Portsmouth Dock for a complete overhaul. This impatience at the dilatory methods of the shipwrights turned to fury when he learned that Vice-Admiral Barrington's squadron, to which the *Cambridge* was attached, had captured thirteen out of nineteen well-laden merchantmen in an India-bound French convoy and estimated that he had lost at least two hundred pounds in prize money — which would have been a welcome nest egg for his new baby.

Up to this time, Admiral Lord Howe had been in semi-retirement, for he disagreed with Lord North's foreign policy and also refused to serve under Lord Sandwich whom he distrusted. A change of Ministry in March 1782, however, brought the old sea-dog back as Commander-in-Chief of the Channel fleet and everyone knew that 'Black Dick' would soon shake things up. He took command of the *Victory*, 104, on 20th April, and led his fleet to sea. Three weeks later, the dockyard people having been 'gingered up', the *Cambridge* followed and was put under his flag, to spend the summer blockading the Dutch coast, examining neutrals and chasing every suspicious sail. It was dull, routine work and although an essential part of the war, Bligh became very bored with it.

July, however, brought some excitement. Howe's ships had

gone to the mouth of the English Channel to guard a homeward bound Jamaica convoy, for there had been news of a large allied French and Spanish fleet under the command of Admiral Cordoba in the vicinity. Daylight of the 12th revealed the enemy fleet strung out to the south west and almost twice the size of the British. Howe ordered his ships to clear for action then decided not to give battle but to slip away and wait for more favourable odds. His ships sailed at night between the Scillies and Land's End where the enemy did not dare follow, a manoeuvre that also enabled him to avoid being separated from the Jamaica convoy and left the enemy staring at an empty expanse of water.

At the end of the summer, the Channel fleet returned to Spithead to prepare for an exciting venture. This was to escort a fleet of transports carrying troops and supplies into Gibraltar, which had been under siege for two years. Although the great bastion still stood, its garrison was suffering terribly from hunger and scurvy and the Governor, Lieutenant General George Eliott, continually despatched messages to England asking for help in order to combat an all-out attack on the fortress that was being built up on the mainland.

On the morning of 28th August, Bligh came on deck and looked around the anchorage at Spithead. Capacious though it was, it seemed hardly large enough to take all the ships that were assembling, for using the protection of Howe's warships, the Admiralty were also despatching two more large convoys, bound for America and India. Every day was bringing more ships to the assembly point and on this sunny morning, wherever Bligh looked, he could see tall masts rising as thick as trees in a wood, whilst the ships to which they belonged took in stores and completed last minute repairs. One, anchored near the *Cambridge*, was the second largest ship in the navy, the 108-gun *Royal George*, flying the blue flag of Rear-Admiral Richard Kempenfelt at her mast-head. With sailing time approaching there was an immense crowd on board for in addition to her full complement, there were a number of wives and sweethearts who were making the most of the few days left to them. There were also 'slop-dealers' and bum-boat women, and a number of children with the run of the 'tween decks and who added to the general confusion.

As Bligh stared at the huge vessel he noticed that she had a considerable list and judged that this had been done by running out the guns on the port side as far as possible whilst heaving in the starboard batteries and securing them amidships. Obviously something was being done to her below the water-line for he could see the figures of some men working on her hull. It was a perfect summer's morning, without a breath of wind and with the ships mirrored in the still water, and Bligh was about to go below to leave his jacket in his cabin when he heard a startled, unbelieving cry: "My God ... she's going!"

He spun around and stared across the stretch of sparkling water between his ship and the *Royal George*. It was true. A slight breeze had begun to stir the surface, slapping tiny wavelets through the flagship's open ports and as he watched, his eyes wide in horror, he saw the list increase and then across the water there came the dull rumble of gun carriages and the high sickening shriek of men and women in terror. The tilt of the ship had caused the weight of the ponderous thirty-two and twenty-four-pounders to snap their restraining tackles and, in twos and threes, the giant monsters careered across the sloping decks to burst through the lee side, sweeping everything before them as they went.

The next moment the ship had fallen right over and almost immediately disappeared although, strangely, her mast-heads suddenly reappeared above the surface. As she had gone down she had taken a lighter with her that had been moored alongside and this kept her upright on the sea bed. Bligh looked about him. Realizing that he was the senior officer on deck he bawled to the boatswain, "All hands! Call all hands! Away all boats!" and, still shouting, leapt down to the waist and began to tear at the lashings securing the ship's boats. He was joined by others and within minutes the boats were dropped into the water and pulled across to the three tragic mast-heads that marked the scene of the disaster. His cutter was one of the first to arrive and his crew began to drag several gasping, floundering people into it, men and women. Some of them looked like negroes, for an open barrel of tar which had stood on the flagship's deck had released its contents on the surface of the water, and many people emerged in the middle of this dark, viscous pool.

The ship's captain was saved, although he could not swim, but he was one of the few lucky ones. Nearly every officer was drowned, including Admiral Kempenfelt who had been trapped in his cabin by a jammed door, together with 900 others — ratings and civilians. For days after this disaster, bodies were floating to

Captain William Bligh by J. Smart

Captain Cook by
George Dance

The *Resolution* and
Adventure at Tahiti by
William Hodges

the surface, sometimes as many as thirty and forty at a time, and the local watermen were kept busy stripping the pathetic dead of money, watches and other valuables before towing them ashore.

After delays caused by contrary winds, the great armada of ships finally weighed on 11th September. It consisted of 183 sail, including thirty-four ships-of-the-line and a dozen smaller naval craft.

Bad weather met them in the Bay of Biscay and the ships were scattered, but they were all together again when the time came for the two convoys to stand away and make for America and India. As their topsails dipped over the horizon, the *Latona*, frigate, was detached and sent ahead of the battle fleet to find out what was happening at Gibraltar. She returned with good news – the fortress still held.

It had been a very close thing, however, for two days after the fleet had left Spithead, the French and Spanish had mounted a massive attack which was to end, once and for all, the resistance of Eliott and his stubborn garrison. Admiral Cordoba's fleet had arrived from the English Channel and with the ships already blockading Gibraltar, formed an allied fleet of ninety warships including forty-four ships-of-the-line together with three hundred transports. The main prong of the attack, however, was to be ten floating batteries which had been specially built for the task. They were unique. Their bottoms were of thick timber, their sides of wood and cork which had the hollow space between them filled with wet sand and also a system of ducts which circulated a flow of water. Each had a sloping roof formed of strong rope netting covered with wet skins to protect the men on deck from falling shells and their guns, which were of very large calibre, were manned by picked crews. These batteries were supported by one thousand guns in the rest of the fleet and by 12,000 French infantry who had been taken aboard as marines, whilst drawn up on the mainland were tremendous batteries backed by an army of nearly 40,000 men commanded by the famous French general, the Duc de Crillon. This great gathering was to attack the fort's garrison of only seven thousand men.

On the morning of 13th September, the floating batteries were brought into position and at 9.45 a.m., when they were anchored in position, the firing began – the greatest bombardment yet known. The sweating and cursing men defending the island found the floating batteries formidable and well-nigh indestructible. The heaviest bombs rolled harmlessly from their flexible roofs and even thirty-two pound shot failed to make any impression on the rein-forced hulls. A few fires broke out in them but were immediately quenched by teams of specially trained men. The garrison gunners, however, had a weapon which they were confident would prove effective ... red hot shot. The furnaces for heating the cannon balls had been started as soon as the enemy ships were seen to be approaching but it would be two hours before the first of the shot could be used, and another two hours before they were at maximum heat and could be fired in any quantity.

During this time the floating batteries were doing tremendous damage and at a range of about half a mile, every shot struck home. But by midday the heated shot – "roast potatoes" the men called them – were ready. They began to crash on the batteries to cause panic rather than actually sink any of the enemy ships. The crew of one battery frantically flooded the magazine so that she could no longer fire, and this panic spread along the line of anchored ships so that by the evening, only two at the far end were still in action. An hour later, at 9 p.m., they also fell silent.

Then as the British renewed their efforts, the feeling of victory spurring on their desperately tired bodies, several of the batteries began to burn. Rocket distress signals burst overhead in the night sky whilst during occasional lulls in the firing, groans and cries were plainly heard from the ships. By midnight, one of them was blazing furiously from stem to stern and the light from the flames enabled the garrison to point their guns more accurately whilst the giant Rock became brilliantly illuminated, and floating wreckage in the bay was clearly visible in the red-tinged water. White-hot globes of iron streaked across the night towards the helpless targets and by dawn, six more batteries were in flames. Their magazines began to explode and men on board were seen silhouetted against the lurid background, gesturing for help.

Daylight revealed the bay littered with bodies, wreckage and the smouldering hulks of the few batteries that were still afloat. It had been a remarkable victory.

On 10th October, as Howe was approaching the Rock, a sudden storm came shrieking from the Atlantic, forcing his ships to reduce to double-reefed topsails, but by brilliant seamanship they kept together and in some sort of formation. The enemy fleet huddled in Algeciras Bay, however, was not so fortunate.

Most of the ships were caught unprepared, cables broke, and a number were driven out to sea, two ships-of-the-line and a frigate went ashore and others were blown clean over the horizon.

Howe arrived at this scene of confusion during the following morning and brought his fleet up to the Rock in line of battle with the merchantmen ahead, their captains having had strict instructions to make straight for Gibraltar, no matter what happened. But a fast moving tide swept all but four of the merchantmen past the Mole and Howe, cursing madly, had to chase after them, beyond Europa Point.

During the next few days the ships were shepherded back to Gibraltar and their stores and infantry unloaded, whilst Howe patrolled outside, 'trailing his coat' and waiting for the enemy to attack.

They came out at last in overwhelming superiority with a fleet of six three-deckers, thirty-eight two-deckers and a whole host of frigates, zebecs and smaller vessels. Howe grouped his own fleet around the *Victory* and waited for the attack. He was still waiting on the 18th, by which time every merchantman was safely inside the Mole. Then, his work done, he saluted the Rock and stood to the west, with the enemy following cautiously in his wake. On 20th October he hove to and watched for the allied fleet to come up. Shots were exchanged at long range for several hours and when the enemy turned away at dusk, no ship on either side had been crippled or taken. The *Cambridge* had three men killed and seven wounded but apart from two guns that had been dismounted and some of her rigging shot away she was practically unscathed.

"Black Dick" watched the receding stern lanterns of the enemy fleet with great satisfaction. He had done what he had set out to do. Gibraltar had been reprovisioned and could continue the siege, he had stood up to a fleet superior in numbers and forced them to retire and, except for a brig containing stores that had gone ashore off Malaga, had not lost a single ship.

Two more months of war followed and then in January 1783 the preliminaries of peace were signed, the independence of the American colonies was recognized and the work of reducing the fleet to a peace-time footing began. Within a week, the number of seamen and marines dropped from 100,000 to 30,000. Hundreds of young, and not so young, officers were put on half pay — Bligh amongst them. He collected his share of the prize money — £22. 0s.6½d. — then returned to his wife and daughter in Douglas with the nagging thought of what he should do next ... to augment his two shillings a day.

Fortunately he had not long to wait. It was then customary for officers on half pay to seek alternative employment, preferably in the trade they knew best. The merchant service offered the greatest opportunities although, even here, with so many skilled men desperately looking for posts, there were only a limited number available. But Bligh now had a sponsor — Duncan Campbell — who was more than ready to help his niece's husband, especially as he had already proved himself to have abilities above most officers of his own age. Bligh obtained permission from the Admiralty to accept a post with Campbell's company and by September he was at sea in his first command — the *Lynx* — which, like all Campbell's ships, was engaged in the lucrative trade to the West Indies.

Bligh spent four years in Campbell's employ, including a spell ashore as the company's agent in the Port of Lucea in Jamaica. From the *Lynx* he was transferred to the *Cambrian* and then to the *Britannia*. As these ships called at London to discharge and take on cargoes, he brought his wife and family to the city, first at No4 Broad Street, St George's-in-the-East and then to their more permanent home at No3 Durham Place, Lambeth. He needed a large house for his family was growing. Mary, his second daughter was born in 1783 and two years later, another girl, Elizabeth.

At this time Bligh was quite unaware that something had taken place twelve years earlier that was to alter his whole life and to project him into history. In 1775, the Standing Committee of the West Indian Planters and Merchants had offered to reimburse anyone who successfully carried some bread-fruit plants from Tahiti to the West Indies whilst the Society of Arts and Manufacturers and Commerce promised a gold medal to anyone who conveyed six of these plants in a growing state from "the Islands in the South Sea to the Islands in the West Indies".

During Anson's stay in Tinian in 1742, no ship's bread was consumed, the officers and men all preferring to eat bread-fruit. Cook had also written on the excellencies of the fruit on his return from his first voyage.

Reading such testimonials, the planters of Jamaica and

Dominica were anxious to have the bread-fruit trees growing in
their islands for it would provide additional food for their negro
slaves at a negligible cost. They realized, however, that the task
of keeping the plants alive and healthy for the six months passage
from one group of islands to the other was going to prove
extremely difficult. The sea captains to whom they addressed
their appeal were not interested and the outbreak of war meant
that the whole project was shelved.

The return of peace, however, caused it to be revived. This
time the King himself was interested and it was decided that a
ship of the Royal Navy would be detailed to carry the cuttings
and that the expedition would be commanded by a naval officer.
A search revealed that there was not a single warship capable of
being converted into a floating greenhouse, so it was decided to
purchase a merchantman and adapt it for the purpose. Six were
offered for the purpose and that chosen was the *Bethia* which was
purchased and renamed the *Bounty*. The next step was to appoint
a commander. William Bligh, now thirty-three and homeward
bound in the *Britannia* did not know that two powerful voices
were being raised on his behalf. One was that of his uncle-in-law
Duncan Campbell who, as a prominent West Indian planter was
one of the promoters of the scheme; the other was someone who
had sailed with Cook and was now principal advisor to the King.
This was Sir Joseph Banks who was destined to play a large part
in his protégé's life.

Britannia arrived in the Downs on 31st July. A week later Bligh
was informed that he had been appointed commander of the
expedition. It was, it seemed, the opportunity of a lifetime.

[6]

Off Cape Horn

AT THE SOUND of the double bells at 6 a.m., there was a tap on Bligh's cabin door and William Musprat, his steward, entered with his breakfast. That disposed of, Bligh rose and sat at the table in his small cabin. He had not had a good night for the ship was still labouring after a succession of fiery gales which had kept her close-reefed since leaving Spithead a week earlier and which had kept him on deck for most of the time. Also, a recurrence of the migraine that he had first experienced whilst in the West Indies was making him irritable and short-tempered.

As he paced, this feeling of irritation increased as the frustrations and disappointments of the past few months began to nag at his mind once more. In the first place, there was the matter of the ship itself. Although it had been chosen by experts from the Board of Admiralty, he was convinced that she was far too small for the task of conveying her fragile cargo of living plants half way round the world. She was only 215 tons and with a length of just over ninety feet was similar in size and tonnage to a modern river barge. There was nothing he could do about the choice, however, for it had been made whilst he was still captain of Campbell's *Britannia*, and work was well under way when he first saw his new command as she lay in Deptford Dock.

She was also under-crewed, for although her complement of forty-six souls included a botanist and a gardener, there was no other commissioned officer except Bligh himself, a fact which would mean a great deal of extra responsibility.

Bligh was still furious that despite his own protestations and several letters from Sir Joseph Banks on his behalf to the Board of Admiralty, he commanded the ship as lieutenant and not as captain. There seemed no justification for this, especially as he knew that another officer, Lieutenant Moorsom, who was sailing on a far simpler expedition, had been advanced to commander.

Great annoyance, however, had been caused by the procrastination of an Admiralty that kept him at Spithead for three weeks whilst a fair wind carried other outward bound ships clear of the Channel. He knew that this delay made his proposed passage around Cape Horn that much more difficult although he at least had the satisfaction of knowing that he had asked for, and received, permission to turn about and go by way of the Cape of Good Hope if the other route proved impossible. As the days passed he grew steadily more furious at the delay, then when the sailing orders came at last, the weather had worsened and he had been forced to return to harbour several times until he was at last able to stand away down Channel on 23rd December 1787, a month after receiving the orders and seven weeks since his arrival at Spithead – a waste of valuable and vital time.

Finally, he was aware that his acceptance of this present duty had taken him from a state of comparative affluence as a merchant captain at five hundred pounds a year to a lieutenant's pay of four shillings a day – and now he had three daughters, Harriet, Mary and Elizabeth, as well as his wife to support. Nevertheless, he had known these things when he had accepted the commission and, for better or worse, he was now the lieutenant and commander of the *Bounty* or, more formally, of His Majesty's Armed Vessel *Bounty*, for she carried four four-pounder carriage guns and ten half-pounder swivels. Having accepted the command, he had not the slightest doubt that the venture, which had been made more difficult by these nagging factors, would be a triumphant success, in spite of them.

With the sounds of activity throughout the ship rising to a crescendo, Bligh strolled out of his small cabin on the starboard side near the stern and entered the 'great cabin' which, in a normal voyage, would have been his own quarters. The whole cabin – which extended about one third along the upper-deck – had been prepared for the transport of the bread-fruit plants, to the obvious sacrifice of accommodation for both officers and crew. It had two large skylights and six scuttles to provide a flow of air and the deck had been covered with a false floor into which the pots containing the young plants would be placed during the run from Tahiti to the West Indies. The deck itself was covered with lead and had a clever system of pipes and guttering to carry the surplus water into tubs for re-use.

It was now ten o'clock in the forenoon watch – the four bells had just been made – and with half an hour left, Bligh returned to his own cabin which now seemed even smaller by comparison with the one he had just left, and opened the ship's muster role to

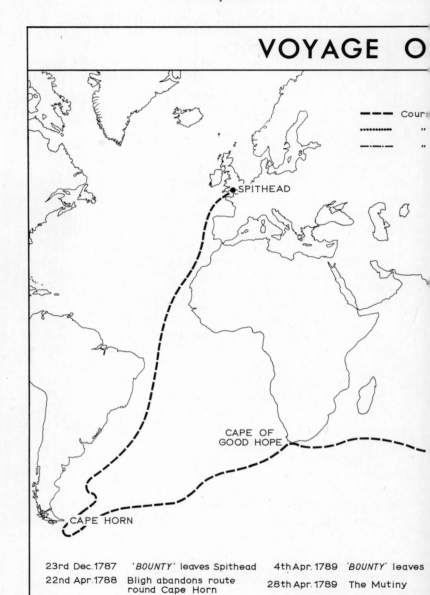

VOYAGE O

- - - Cours
∙∙∙∙∙∙∙∙∙∙∙ "
-∙-∙- "

SPITHEAD

CAPE OF
GOOD HOPE

CAPE HORN

23rd Dec. 1787	*'BOUNTY'* leaves Spithead	4th Apr. 1789	*'BOUNTY'* leaves
22nd Apr. 1788	Bligh abandons route round Cape Horn	28th Apr. 1789	The Mutiny
26th Oct. 1788	*'BOUNTY'* arrives Tahiti	14th Jun. 1789	Bligh arrives at

HE BOUNTY

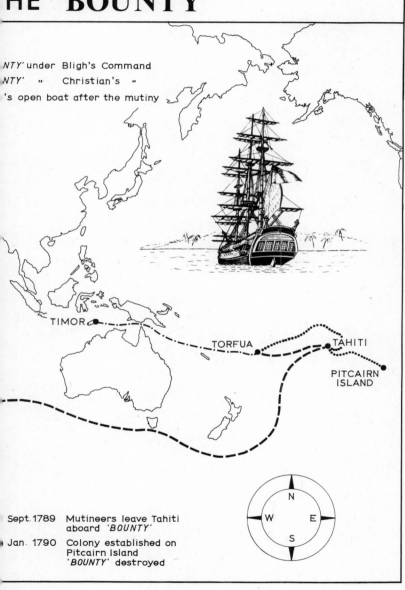

NTY' under Bligh's Command
NTY' " Christian's "
's open boat after the mutiny

TIMOR

TORFUA

TAHITI

PITCAIRN ISLAND

Sept. 1789   Mutineers leave Tahiti
aboard *'BOUNTY'*

Jan. 1790   Colony established on
Pitcairn Island
'BOUNTY' destroyed

N
W   E
S

familiarize himself with the names of his crew. Some were well known already, for he had used his 'captain's prerogative' and chosen several of the officers himself. It read:—

William Bligh	Commander
John Fryer	Master
William Cole	Boatswain
William Peckover	Gunner
William Purcell	Carpenter
Thomas Huggan	Surgeon
Thomas Ledward	Surgeon's Mate
Fletcher Christian	Master's Mate
William Elphinston	Master's Mate
John Hallet	Midshipman
Thomas Hayward	Midshipman
Peter Heywood	Midshipman
Edward Young	Midshipman
George Stewart	Midshipman
Peter Linkletter	Quartermaster
John Norton	Quartermaster
George Simpson	Quartermaster's Mate
James Morrison	Boatswain's Mate
John Mills	Gunner's Mate
Charles Norman	Carpenter's Mate
Thomas McIntosh	Carpenter's Mate
Lawrence Lebogue	Sailmaker
Joseph Coleman	Armourer
Charles Churchill	Master at Arms
Henry Hillbrant	Cooper
William Musprat	Commander's Steward
John Samuel	Clerk and Steward
Thomas Hall	Ship's Cook
John Smith	Commander's Cook
Robert Lamb	Butcher
Thomas Burkitt	Able Seaman
Matthew Quintal	Able Seaman
John Sumner	Able Seaman
John Millward	Able Seaman
William McCoy	Able Seaman
Alexander Smith	Able Seaman
John Williams	Able Seaman
Thomas Ellison	Able Seaman
Isaac Martin	Able Seaman

Richard Skinner	Able Seaman
Matthew Thompson	Able Seaman
Michael Byrne	Able Seaman
James Valentine	Able Seaman
Robert Tinkler	Boy

There were also David Nelson the botanist and William Brown, a gardener appointed as his assistant.

The *Bounty*'s complement officially should have included two midshipmen only, but there had been a flood of volunteers to sign on for a voyage which promised to be unusual and exciting. It promised more, for Cook had already described the Tahitians as "people who have not even the idea of indecency, and who gratify every appetite and passion before witnesses with no more sense of impropriety than we feel when we satisfy our hunger at a social board with our family or friends".

This was something that had to be investigated and the *Bounty* had sailed with five midshipmen together with Tinkler, the ship's boy but regarded as an embryonic midshipman.

All five midshipmen were known to him. Thomas Hayward and John Hallett were friends of the family, the latter's sister being Elizabeth's greatest confidante; George Stewart, born in St Kitts, was the son of a friend of Bligh's in the Orkneys; Edward Young was a nephew of Sir George Young whom Bligh had known during his West Indian days and was also a protégé of Sir Joseph Banks and Peter Heywood.

John Fryer, the master, was a stranger, but one of his two mates, Fletcher Christian, a young sprig of a distinguished Manx family, was certainly not. He had first met Bligh in the *Cambridge* although, as there was ten years difference in their ages, the twenty-eight year-old lieutenant had then hardly been aware of the very junior midshipman. Three years later, however, through a relation, his name was put before Bligh as the possible mate of one of Campbell's ships. Bligh already had his full complement but another letter from Christian offering to serve in any capacity in order to learn his profession persuaded him, and he engaged Christian as a supernumerary, instructing him in navigation and astronomy. He was so impressed by his young protégé that he took him with him in the *Britannia* as second mate and the appointment as Master's mate to the *Bounty* was entirely Bligh's doing.

Of the other three warrant officers he also knew William
Peckover the gunner, who had sailed on all three of Cook's
voyages; David Nelson, the botanist, who had sailed on his last
whilst Lebogue the sailmaker and Norton, one of the two
quartermasters, had both been with him in the *Britannia.*

He folded this list, took from a small pouch his Admiralty
orders, and during the final minutes before being summoned on
deck, read them through yet again. As usual, they were concise
and explicit. He was directed to proceed as quickly as possible via
Cape Horn to the Society Islands where he was to take on as
many bread-fruit plants as he thought fit. He was then to proceed
through the Endeavour Straits and call either at Prince's Island or
at some port on the northern side of Java in order to replace any
plants that had died with other suitable tropical plants.
Continuing round the Cape of Good Hope he was to sail to the
West Indies, deposit half the plants at St Vincent and the rest at
Jamaica. After refitting, he was to return to Spithead.

But this was in the far, unpredictable future, for Spithead was
as yet only some 600 miles astern.

With her sails filled with a brisk, northerly wind, the *Bounty*
headed for the Canaries where Bligh had decided to put in to
repair, refit and also take in fresh meat and vegetables and a
supply of wine to eke out the sour-tasting beer.

The *Bounty* anchored in the Santa Cruz roads on 6th January
and despite the current friction between England and Spain, the
Governor invited Bligh to dinner and helped him with his
provisioning. Unfortunately there were few supplies to be had
and when the ship sailed four days later, Bligh had only been
able to obtain a few casks of inferior quality wine, some rather
thin goats and a small supply of pumpkins. He had, however,
been able to buy some dripstones to be used in filtering the water
which, during any long voyage, had a habit of turning green and
stinking in the casks.

As it was Bligh's intention to sail direct to Tahiti without
putting in at any other port, he felt compelled to cut the daily
rations and called all hands to inform them that he was going to
put them on two-thirds allowance of bread. He also told them
that he was dividing them into three watches instead of the
customary two, which meant that they would now be able to
have more consecutive hours of sleep. This news cheered the men
and at four o'clock they entered into the usual evening dancing

session with Byrne and his fiddle with more enthusiasm than usual.

Indeed, the spirits of the men were so high that Bligh wrote a long letter to Campbell in which he said, "My men are all active good fellows, and what has given me much pleasure is that I have not been obliged to punish any one. My officers and young gentlemen are all tractable and well disposed, and we now understand each other so well that we shall remain so the whole voyage, unless I fall out with the Doctor who I have the trouble to prevent from being in bed 15 hours out of the twenty-four."

The harmony at which Bligh hinted at in this letter was not to last. For some time he had considered appointing an acting lieutenant and a second-in-command. The most senior warrant officer in the ship was the master, John Fryer, but Bligh found him slow for a man only three years older than himself and as Christian was obviously the better man for this post, promoted him over the head of someone who had been his superior, obviously not recalling his own disappointment when the same thing had happened to himself whilst service in the *Resolution*. Fryer, understandably, was furious at this slight and from that moment acted towards the captain in a cool and withdrawn manner. He also began to vent his irritation on those who could not retaliate without fear of punishment and Matthew Quintal, one of the best seamen on board, goaded beyond endurance, answered him back. Fryer stormed into Bligh's cabin and the commander, with some reluctance, was compelled to order two dozen lashes.

Relations between Bligh and his crew, however, had already begun to deteriorate, all over a matter of some cheese. Some casks had been brought up on deck and opened to give their contents an airing. One of them, when opened by the cooper, Henry Hillbrant, was found to have two of the cheeses missing and Bligh, his head throbbing from one of his attacks of migraine, began to rage against the unknown thief. Hillbrant waited for a few moments then, touching his forehead, said, "Beggin' yer pardon sir. Them two cheeses was taken out by Mr Samuel's order while we was lying in the river, and sent to y'r house."

At this Bligh's face reddened and he spun round on the cooper to scream, "Be quiet, will you! It's all lies, all lies!" and he paused, breathing heavily, whilst he glared around at the small group that had been drawn by the noise and was gathering nearby, "A lot of thieves, all of you," he went on. "The cheese ration will be stopped for all hands until this loss is made up. Stopped, d'ye hear me? As for you," he went on, swinging back on the cooper, "I'll have you flogged if you so much as mention this matter again. Now then, nail these casks up again and get them below!"

The truth of this matter was never known. Many other casks, when opened, were also found to be short of their stated contents due to the well-known "short measures" of the naval contractors of those days. Bligh's action in punishing everyone, for something that possibly had not occurred on the ship at all, caused much grumbling amongst the men and when on the following day, Samuel issued butter without cheese, many refused it, saying that their acceptance would be an acknowledgment of guilt.

Also, as the *Bounty* neared the Equator, Bligh found that the pumpkins he had bought in Tenerife were beginning to soften and spoil and he ordered Samuel to issue them in lieu of biscuit, at the rate of two pounds of pumpkin to the one of biscuit issued daily. This caused more grumbling and caused Bligh to fly into another of his sudden rages. He was very aware, if the rest were not, that the ship still had half of her outward passage to cover — more than eight thousand miles — and that every scrap of food and water had to be watched with the utmost care. The grumblings increased, however, and in another attack of fury he threatened to make the men eat grass, if necessary, before he had done with them.

After crossing the Line, the weather became steadily colder and everyone changed into warmer clothing ready for the ordeal ahead. Thanks to the procrastination in England, Bligh was forced to attempt to round the Horn at the worst possible time of the year and in conditions that, for a while at least, were to unite the crew and make it forget such petty trifles as cheese and pumpkins.

On 23rd March 1788, the grim outline of Staten Island was sighted and the ship began to buck and pitch against strong head winds. Bligh set a southwesterly course to keep clear of the barren rocks that form the coast of Tierra del Fuego, intending to hold it for more than three hundred miles before turning northwards to claw his way around the hidden and menacing mass of Cape Horn. Staten Island slipped astern on 24th and Bligh was not to sight land again for a month.

The ship staggered on, dwarfed by enormous seas that screamed and raged at her as if furious that such a fragile, useless object dared to trespass in their domain. The waves were great grey mountains on whose white crested peaks the labouring ship seemed to teeter before sliding down the slope into the deep valley beyond. Here, for a blessed spell, the incessantly shrieking winds would be silent and the men were able to breathe normally for a while until, inevitably, the ship began her long and difficult climb up the next wave and back into the full fury of the storm. Sometimes the wind lessened and for a brief spell, desperately exhausted men could look about them as if in wonder that they still existed; then the next squall would be upon them in a welter of violent wind and tortured water that crashed against the ship's side and covered her with high flung, near-solid spume.

There were heavy falls of snow too, so that when the men staggered down from aloft after a nightmare of struggling with frozen canvas and gear, it was some time before they were able to speak. Yet they responded to every order and during one of the rare spells of comparative calm, Bligh called them together and thanked them for their efforts. He, in turn, saw that they had as much comfort as he could provide. Although the *Bounty* was a new ship – not yet three years old – the continuous pounding caused her seams to open and the forward deck to leak. He ordered a large part of the crew aft, allowing them to sling their hammocks in the great cabin, whilst he kept a fire going to provide them with dry clothes and hot drinks and also gave them a daily pint of the "Decoction of Ground Malt" which had proved so efficacious with Cook.

But it was proving an unequal struggle against the massive power of wind and seas. What little progress was made on one day was lost on the next. Finally, early in April, when they had reached a position when a new course should have been set that would take them into the wide expanse of the Pacific, a particularly violent storm forced them to heave to under a mere scrap of storm staysail and for more than a week the *Bounty* was driven eastwards until, on 17th April, she was on the same parallel of longitude as she had been more than two weeks earlier. This was too much even for Bligh, who, with the entire responsibility of the ship and crew on his shoulders, snatching sleep when he could and keeping the deck during the fiercest of the storms, was now a grey-faced, suffering man. His ship was leaking badly, his men were falling ill, and the storms seemed to be increasing in strength – if that were possible. Bligh reluctantly gave orders for the ship to be put about and plotted a new course to take them to the Cape of Good Hope on the other side of the world.

Within a few hours of this decision, the wind shifted and he resumed the former course for another four days, although the *Bounty* was still being pushed slowly and inexorably to the east. On 23rd April, with a full gale thrusting her along at more than eight knots, she went plunging past Staten Island which had been sighted a month earlier and headed eastwards. Soon, in warmer latitudes, the men began to return to a life that they had almost forgotten existed although Bligh was very bitter at his failure to round the Horn. He fully realized that they were as far away from their destination – Tahiti – as when they had first sailed from England and that four months of incredible hardship and effort had been completely futile.

The *Bounty* dropped anchor in False Bay, near Cape Town after a passage in which there had been no further incidents or grumbling from the crew – the men were still returning to normal after their ordeal. A month of good weather and pleasant sailing brought the invalids back to health and Bligh proudly wrote in his journal that not one of his men had shown any symptoms of "Scurvy, Flux or Fever", and attributed this success to the diet of "Dryed Malt, Sour Krout, and Portable Soup" and to his own insistence on dry clothes, bedding and cleanliness. Indeed, this thoughtfulness had not gone unnoticed for Thomas Ledward, writing from the Cape, remarked in a letter that Bligh would "gain much credit by his resolution and perseverance and by the extreme care he took of the ship's company".

The *Bounty* left the Cape on 1st July and with his ship refitted and provisioned and with his crew in good health, Bligh squared away for Van Dieman's Land, arriving at Adventure Bay seven weeks later. This was Blight's second visit and as far as he could tell, no other ship had called in the eleven years that had passed. Here Bligh had more trouble with his crew, especially from the carpenter, William Purcell, who had not only as quick a temper as his captain, but was also something of a 'sea-lawyer'. There had been an exchange of words ashore which ended in Purcell

A contemporary water-colour of Tahitian war galleys

"Tahiti Revisited" by William Hodges

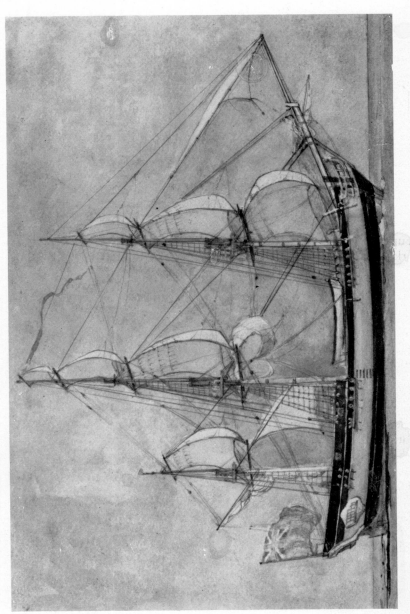

The *Bounty* by Gregory Robinson

being sent back to the ship, but the affair became more serious when Bligh returned to the *Bounty* after supervising a working party cutting wood and filling water casks. As he stepped on board, Fryer walked towards him and immediately began a tirade against Purcell who was calmly sitting on an upturned cask whilst a small party of men were busily swinging water casks into the hold. Despite the captain's orders that everyone left in the ship should be engaged in this work Purcell had refused to help in any way.

Bligh was anxious to sail for Tahiti as soon as possible and this apparent refusal of his own direct orders made him furious. He stalked forward and rasped, "What's all this about? Why are you not doing your duty?"

The other rose and in a calm voice replied, "I am ready to do my duty at any time sir, provided it *is* my duty. I am a carpenter, not a seaman, and this is seaman's work," and he indicated the group standing near the main hatch, all of whom had stopped work to watch what was going on.

Bligh's face reddened. "Damme sir. You dare to question my orders?"

The other nodded and obstinately repeated that he was a carpenter, not a seaman, and would be treated as such. At this, Bligh gave a snort, turned and walked to the quarterdeck where, with his hands clasped behind his back, he paced up and down for several minutes. For a while he was at a loss what course to take. If this had been a seaman, he would have been flogged for such disobedience, but a carpenter was different. He was of a higher rank than a boatswain or a gunner and his warrant protected him against flogging. He could be put in irons for 'mutinous behaviour' but with such a small crew Bligh did not wish to deprive himself of the services of the most skilled craftsman in the ship for what appeared to be a clash of personalities between Purcell and the master.

Then a solution came to him and walking back to the waist he called the other members of the party about him. "Did you all hear Purcell refuse the master's direct order?" he asked.

There was some shuffling at this but several of the men finally admitted that this was so. Satisfied on this point Bligh turned to Purcell who, hands on his hips, calmly awaited the outcome.

"Very well Mr Purcell," he said evenly. "For disobedience, not only to the master's orders but to my own, I am compelled to withhold your rations until you decide to work again for the good of the ship, and as I order."

Purcell's jaw dropped in surprise. This was something he had not expected and he lost all his former belligerance as Bligh went on, addressing the rest of the men and completely ignoring the carpenter, "It is my further orders that no one, d'ye hear me, *no one*, shall provide him with anything to eat or drink on pain of instant flogging. I will have discipline on my ship, by God I will!" and he turned once more and stalked below.

By the next day Purcell was back at work and turning to with the rest. For this part of the voyage, at any rate, Bligh was to have no more trouble from him.

The *Bounty* left Tasmania on 14th September, Bligh steering a course to take her south of New Zealand, and two weeks later a group of thirteen rocky islands were sighted. These were not shown on the charts and Bligh plotted their position, marked them down .and gave them the name by which they are still known — the Bounty.Islands.

This should now have been the most enjoyable part of the whole passage but Bligh was having fresh trouble, this time with the master and Huggan, the surgeon. All three had been having their meals together but Fryer, still annoyed at what he considered his demotion, now had all his meals in his own cabin whilst Huggan, whom Bligh had already referred to in his private log as "a drunken Sot", hardly ever left his cabin, but stayed there, drinking incessantly.

Bligh's break with the surgeon came during the stay in Tasmania. One of the able seamen, James Valentine had reported to him saying that he felt unwell and Huggan, not being sufficiently competent to diagnose asthma, bled him. Within a sort time, Valentine was seriously ill from a septic arm caused by the bleeding and also with congestion of the lungs. Each day Bligh solicitously asked how the invalid was progressing and each time Huggan informed him that he was steadily improving. Bligh was surprised, therefore, to be approached by one of the master's mates who told him that Valentine was seriously ill and perhaps dying. He looked at the other in disbelief then ordering him to lead the way, went forward to see for himself whether this gloomy statement was true.

As he entered the crew's cramped quarters and bent over Valentine's hammock, there was no doubt about it. The other was delirious and his breathing harsh and irregular. More furious than he had ever been in his life, Bligh stormed back to his cabin and shouted to a seaman to bring Huggan to him at once. There was a long pause whilst the surgeon was wakened and prized out of his bunk but he presented himself at last before the captain, his eyes red-rimmed and apprehensive.

He stood, swaying slightly, as the other raged at him for his neglect then managed to stammer that he had meant to tell him the night before, but as Bligh had been dining with Christian he had thought it better to leave the news until this morning.

"What news?" Bligh thundered.

The other blinked, gulped then said, "That Valentine is going to die."

This started Bligh off again and although the seaman did die the next day and Huggan fully deserved everything that had been verbally hurled at him, the surgeon considered that he had been grossly insulted and withdrew even further from the life of the ship.

Fryer was the next victim of the captain's tongue. Bligh had completed the ship's accounts for August and Semptember and as was usual, sent Samuel to Fryer's cabin in order to obtain the master's signature. He was furious when the clerk returned holding a statement which Fryer had prepared and which stated that he, as master, "had done nothing amiss during this time on board". Samuel also carried an ultimatum – that the master would not sign the monthly accounts unless this piece of paper was signed first.

"Samuel, ask Mr Fryer to be good enough to step into my cabin," Bligh replied in an icy voice and waited, fuming, until the other arrived.

"Now then Mr Fryer, what is this? You will not sign the monthly accounts. Is this so?"

The other shook his head, stubbornly. "No sir, I will not, until you sign that testimonial I have prepared," and he indicated the paper which Bligh still held.

"You dare to dictate to me, sir?" Bligh roared in reply, all the frustrations of the past few days suddenly welling up inside him. "You dare sir? Right, we'll see about that!" and stalking past the master he strode out of his cabin and mounted the ladder to the quarterdeck. Christian, who was on watch, turned a startled face, his look of surprise deepening when he was ordered to summon all hands. The pipes sounded through the ship and whilst the crew were assembling, Bligh prowled up and down the weather side of the deck, his hands locked behind his back, his face showing his rage. He stopped pacing when Christian came up and saluted, saying, "Ship's company assembled, sir."

In reply, Bligh walked to the rail and uncovering, read out the Articles of War, with emphasis on those that dealt with failure to comply with the orders of a superior officer. When he had finished he turned to the master and said, "Now sir, you will sign!" and he beckoned to Samuel who brought forward the accounts together with a pen and a flask of ink. There was a long pause then Fryer took up the pen and dashed his signature across the two pages although, as he handed back the book he muttered, "I sign in obedience to your order, but this may be cancelled at a later date."

Another clash of personalities came a few days later when the *Bounty* was sailing northwards, her weathered sails filled with the steady Trades and with the temperature rising every day. Now the flying fishes had re-appeared, effortlessly keeping pace with the ship, forging ahead of her like drifts of wind-blown spray. Men-o'-war hawks were soaring high overhead in the azure sky, whilst the now eager crew began to look out for the first signs of the islands, some, however, began to complain of aches and pains and rashes and Huggan was roused out of his cabin and ordered forward to examine them. He soon reappeared, his unshaven face even greyer than usual and lumbered heavily to the quarterdeck where Bligh awaited his report. As he drew near, Bligh wrinkled his nose in disgust. The surgeon's unwashed appearance, his untidy clothes and the heavy smell of spirits that hung about him was an offence to his scrubbed white deck and to the crisp, clean morning air.

"Well?" he rasped. "What is it?"

The other swallowed nervously before answering. "Sc ...scurvy, sir," he stuttered at last.

For a moment Bligh was too shocked to reply then, "Scurvy?" he said at last, his voice showing his incredulity. "*Scurvy?* On my ship?"

He was shattered. All his efforts, his insistence on cleanliness and diet seemed to have been for nothing. Somehow he felt that he had failed and in consequence, had let down his great mentor, Captain Cook. The fact that in any other ship, after such a long

voyage and through such bad weather, where similar cramped
conditions existed half the crew would have been ill by this time
did not matter. This was *his* ship and he had been determined to
arrive at Tahiti, as Cook had done, with all his men in good
health.

It was more than a disappointment – it was something deeper
and more personal.

He went forward and looked at the men himself. Only a few
were involved and as far as he could see, there were none of the
usual signs of scurvy – no swellings of the mouth or gums, and
none of the large, discoloured spots, that, spreading over the
body, were so typical of the disease. As far as he could determine,
the men seemed to be suffering from a rheumatic ailment, but to
be on the safe side he ordered Elphinstone to give everyone malt
extract and a dose of an "efficacious cure" – Elixir Vitriol mixed
in water. As Huggan had now firmly shut himself up in his cabin
and was dosing himself with neat rum, Bligh had cause, once
again, to be thankful that he had signed on Thomas Ledward as
surgeon's mate, for this young man went about his work calmly
and with quiet efficiency.

On the following day, however, Ledward came to Bligh and
informed him that he needed further medicines but was unable to
enter Huggan's cabin and that there was no reply to his
knocking. Four seamen were immediately sent to the cabin with
orders to break down the door if necessary. They were forced to
do so and reported that Huggan was lying in a drunken stupor
and that his cabin was a shambles. Bligh ordered the surgeon to
be carried out bodily, every drop of liquor to be removed and
locked away and for the cabin to be thoroughly cleaned, an
operation which he subsequently described in the log as being
"not only troublesome but offensive in the highest degree".

Two days later, a chastened and sober surgeon shambled on
deck and cursorily examined the crew for signs of venereal
disease. He then came aft and reported that every man in the
crew was in good health, even those suffering from 'scurvy'
having made a remarkable recovery.

The following morning the longed for cry came from the
mast-head "Land ho!" and there was a scamper to the ship's side
and into the rigging to stare ahead as the first of the Society
Islands began to rise out of an incredibly blue sea. This was the
small island of Mehetia. As the *Bounty* sailed past its rocky shore,

Bligh relaxed for the first time for five weeks. The island had appeared at the exact time he had estimated and now their next landfall should be coming into view very soon. Indeed, as soon as the ship rounded the northern end of the island there, on the western horizon, was the misty blue outline of an enormous mountain range ... Tahiti!

During the afternoon Bligh was busy in his cabin and then, whilst there was still enough light to read, he posted a notice for all to see, ordering those that could read to let those less fortunate know what it said. The men gathered round to read:

Rules to be observed by every person on board, or belonging to the *Bounty*, for the better establishing a trade for supplies of provisions, and good intercourse with the natives of the South Seas, wherever the ship may be at.

1. At the Society, or Friendly Islands, no person whatever is to intimate that Captain Cook was killed by Indians, or that he is dead.

2. No person is ever to speak, or give the least hint, that we have come on purpose to get the bread-fruit plant, until I have made my plan known to the chiefs.

3. Every person is to study to gain the goodwill and esteem of the natives; to treat them with all kindness; and not to take from them by violent means anything that they have stolen, and no one is ever to fire but in defence of his life.

4. Every person employed on service is to take care that no arms or implements of any kind under their charges are stolen; the value of such things being lost shall be charged against their wages.

5. No man is to embezzle, or offer to sale, directly or indirectly any part of the king's stores of what nature soever.

6. A proper person or persons will be appointed to regulate trade and barter with the natives, and no officer or other person belonging to the ship, is to trade for any kind of provisions or curiosities; but if such officer or seaman wishes to purchase any particular thing he is to apply to the provider to do it for him. By this means a regular market will be carried on, and all disputes which otherwise may happen with the natives will be avoided. All boats are to have everything handed out of them at sunset.

Given under my hand on board the *Bounty*
Otaheite, 25th October 1788
Wm. Bligh.

By morning light, the *Bounty* would be anchoring in Matavai Bay, Tahiti, having taken ten months and three days over a passage of 27,086 miles by the log.

[7]

Return to Tahiti

FOR A CENTURY and a half after its discovery, Tahiti was virtually forgotten. Then, in a few brief years, it became a much visited island.

It was first sighted by a white man in February 1606 when the Spaniard, De Quiros, commanding two galleons and a brigantine, stepped ashore and named it La Sagitaria.

The next to arrive was Captain Samuel Wallis in the *Dolphin* frigate, in 1767. He is regarded by many historians as the first European to discover Tahiti, De Quiros having sailed from Callao in Peru. The *Dolphin* dropped anchor in Matavai Bay and Wallis sent a well-armed party ashore – for there had previously been trouble with the natives – and the discovery was named King George's Island. The ships lay there for five weeks, taking in wood and water and stocking up with provisions.

Frank Wilkinson, a master's mate in the *Dolphin* wrote in his journal:

> The women were far from being coy. For when a man found a girl to his mind, which he might easily do among so many, there was not much ceremony on either side, and I believe that whoever comes here after, will find evident proofs that they are not the first discoverers. The men, far from having objection to an intercourse of this kind, brought down their women and recommended them to us with the greatest eagerness, which makes me imagine that they want a breed of Englishmen among them.

This "breed" must have been well on its way when in the following year the French ships *Boudeuse* and *Etoile* arrived. They were commanded by Louis de Bougainville who has been immortalized by the magnificent flowering tree which bears his name. Unaware of Wallis's visit he also took possession of the island, this time in the name of France, calling it La Nouvelle Cythere.

A year after Bougainville's departure, Cook arrived, dropping anchor on 13th April 1769. He knew of Wallis's annexation and regarded the place as King George's Island, but wishing to know

its native name received the answer "Otaheite". He wrote this
down phonetically, not realising that the prefix 'O' meant 'it is',
and that his native informant quite rightly, was replying to his
question with "It is Tahiti". This error was continued for a long
time.

Three years after Cook had departed, Captain Don Somingo
de Boenechea arrived, his country still being of the opinion that
every island in the South Pacific was theirs by Divine Right.
After spending some time on the island which he named Amat, as
a compliment to the Viceroy of Peru, he returned to Callao with
plans for colonization.

Cook returned to Tahiti in 1773 and 1774. In September of the
latter year, Boenechea also returned, had his crew build a house,
then sailed away again, leaving behind two Franciscan
missionaries together with a large wooden cross on which was
inscribed 'the indisputable right' of the King of Spain to the
island.

When Cook returned in 1777 he found that the Spaniards had
gone – the two monks having declared that there was "no hope
whatever of converting these heathen" – but their house at
Tautira, and the grave of Boenechea who had died on board his
ship, had been carefully preserved by the natives. He also realized
that the Spaniards had taken great pains to ingratiate themselves
with the Tahitians who still spoke of them with esteem and
veneration. He was taken to the cross and had a further
inscription carved upon it which stated, flatly and definitely.

> *Georgius Tertius Rex,*
> *Annis 1767*
> *1769, 1773, 1774 & 1777*

Eleven years were to pass before another ship called at the
island. During this time the natives must often have talked of the
strange white gods who had come amongst them to leave
tangible proof of their stay in the many half-castes that were now
growing into, or had already reached, adolescence. The visitor
was another English ship, the *Lady Penrhyn en route* to China to
pick up a cargo of tea. She had sailed from England with convicts
for the new settlement at Botany Bay in Australia and her
captain, William Sever, was under orders to call at Tahiti and to
report on conditions there. She arrived in Matavai Bay in July
1788 to find that Otoo was still alive and that no one on the
island knew of Cook's death. Sever ordered his crew to reply, if

asked, that the great navigator was still alive and later gave Otoo a number of gifts, saying that he had been asked to present them on Cook's behalf.

After a stay of twelve days the *Lady Penrhyn*, to the great regret of the natives, continued her passage to the Far East, sighting and naming Penrhyn Island, to the north westward of Tahiti as she went.

Eight weeks after her departure, the *Bounty* arrived. As the ship moved slowly into Matavai Bay, a fleet of canoes put off from the shore and soon she was surrounded by the bobbing outriggers, their occupants standing up to wave, shout and laugh and to offer fruit and fresh cocoa-nuts, whilst the seamen, especially those who had not visited the island before, stared almost hypnotized at the slender, tanned and half-naked girls that waved invitingly to them. As soon as the first canoe came alongside a tall young native in its bows called out, "Peretaine? Rime?", the former being the Tahitian way of pronouncing Britain, whilst the latter referred to Lima, from whence the Spaniards had come.

"Taio peretane" – English friends – came Bligh's answer and when some of the other canoes arrived, whose occupants recognised him, there were wild shouts of welcome. The *Bounty*'s deck was soon crowded with chattering and laughing natives whilst the crew could hardly tear their eyes away from the beauties that were now so close. At this time, the wind suddenly dropped and an on-shore current began to carry the ship to inevitable destruction. Using a great deal of tact, Bligh managed to clear a space in which his men could work, and to his great relief the anchor splashed down into the clear green water of the bay.

Bligh led some of his native friends aft to his cabin and was soon answering their questions and asking others. As agreed, he did not let them know that the man whom they called Toote Earee no Otaheite – Cook, chief of Tahiti – was dead, and he was very distressed when a native came into his cabin carrying a portrait of Cook which had been painted in 1777 by John Webber and which had been preserved by Otoo ever since. Indeed, the picture had been left by Cook with instructions that it should be taken out to every English ship that arrived and shown to the captain who would immediately become their friend.

At sunset Bligh ordered the male natives and the children

ashore, but allowed those women who wished, to spend the
night on board. Many did so and as he sat in the privacy of his
cabin and wrote up the day's journal, he paused several times to
listen to the laughs and snatches of song that came from the
forecastle. He smiled. His men had come through a lot — they
deserved a little relaxation. Later, when the sounds had died
away, he went on deck and stared across at the island. Bright
sparkles of light lit up the intense darkness and the distant
thudding of drums mingled with the incessant beat of the Pacific
surf as it pounded against the reef. He breathed deeply. To
someone who had spent weeks amid the smell of bilges, bad food
and the musty, tarry smell of old rope, the scents that drifted
seaward from the island were intoxicating. He sighed,
thoroughly content.

The following morning the canoes returned to cluster about
the *Bounty*, one of them bringing a message from Otoo who, it
appeared, had been away on the Taiarapu Peninsula — the island
linked to the larger Tahiti by the Isthmus of Tarava. The message
was more of a command, for Otoo demanded that a boat be sent
to bring him on board. Bligh was happy to do so, over-
estimating the importance of the 'king', a belief fostered by Cook
who had been led to believe that Otoo ruled the whole island,
whereas he was only the Chief of Pare, one of the smaller
provinces lying next to that of Haapape in which the Bay of
Matavai was situated.

The huge chief — he was well over six feet three inches tall —
duly arrived with his wife Iddeah and a large retinue, and to the
amusement of those of his crew who were on deck at the time,
Bligh rubbed noses with them in the traditional Tahitian style of
greeting. He then conducted them below and offered Otoo the
gifts of friendship — hatchets, adzes, files and similar objects and
also presented ear-rings, beads and necklaces to Iddeah. The chief
was especially eager to get his hands on any objects of metal for
what had been left eleven years ago by Cook had long worn out,
whilst Sever of the *Lady Penrhyn* had not been particularly open-
handed.

Before his guests left the ship, Bligh presided over a formal
banquet. Dusk was falling and the air had become pleasantly cool
but in the closeness of the small wardroom he sweated profusely
in his full dress uniform of heavy frock coat and knee breeches,
with ruffles at neck and wrists. He was most punctilious in this
matter of dress and when visiting chiefs and important officials

on shore, always went uniformed in this way, despite the fact that the temperature was often in the hundreds. He need not have done so, for there was none there to remonstrate with him if he had chosen to go in less formal attire, but it was typical of the man and of his sense of duty and dignity, that he scrupulously attended every official banquet, whether on board his ship or ashore, dressed as for a royal levee.

There were many times, however, when he trudged up the beach with the black volcanic lava sand dulling the polish of his silver buckled shoes, that he envied his tanned, half-naked men as they went leisurely about their work, whilst he was faced with yet another of the long and elaborate entertainments that the Tahitians enjoyed so much.

It was at one of these feasts that Bligh first broached the matter of the bread-fruit. He was Otoo's guest although he now had to address his host by another name, for it had been changed to Tynah. (Later, Otoo was to change it again to that by which he is better known in history – Pomare I). The meal was held in a large building, some fifty feet long, with a thatched roof, and open at each end to admit the cool sea breezes. The floor was of white sand spread with woven cocoa-nut leaf mats. The meal began at noon and, as usual, was extended and generous. The main course was young pigs that had been roasted on hot stones in deep pits and surrounded with bread-fruit, yams, *taro* and other vegetables. Large dishes containing fish, including the delicious red-fleshed bonito, were handed round as a kind of *hors d'oeuvres* and although the natives preferred their fish in an almost raw state, those offered to Bligh had been baked on an open fire. He was also offered lobster boiled in sea water. There were no knives, the Tahitians using shells and pieces of sharpened bamboo which served just as well.

By custom, no women attended the feast and Bligh, sitting in the place of honour next to Tynah and sweating in his thick uniform, only toyed with the tasty food. By contrast, his host who because of his exalted rank did not touch the food himself but was fed by an attendant, kept this man busy shovelling great quantities of food into his mouth long after Bligh and most of the others had finished. Bowls of fresh cocoa-nut milk and also of *ava*, the local wine were set before everyone and Bligh kept drinking deeply in an attempt to replace the perspiration that was pouring off him.

Towards the end of the meal he casually mentioned that he

would soon be leaving Tahiti to visit some of the other islands and Tynah stopped eating to turn a very concerned face towards his guest. His close association with Bligh had gained him an artificial status and he knew that once the other had gone, he would suffer from the jealousy of those chiefs who had not enjoyed such a friendship, a friendship which was also backed by the *Bounty*'s officers and crew and, if necessary, her guns.

"Why do you wish to leave us?" he asked, his voice revealing his dismay and apprehension. "Here is everything you want — you have only to ask and it will immediately be given to you. We are all friends of you and your great chief King George. Stay with us. Do not leave and go to the other islands. The people there are all great thieves and will steal everything from you."

Bligh smiled reassuringly. "You are indeed my friend, Tynah, you and your people. It is in token of the friendship that you have given to me and to my father Toote, that King George has sent me to you with those valuable gifts. Before we go, will you not send him a gift in return?"

Tynah threw his arms wide in an all-embracing and extravagant gesture. "Your king may have whatever I have," he exclaimed, and began to list the canoes, pigs and other things which might interest the king. When he arrived at bread-fruit in this catalogue Bligh put out a restraining hand.

"Bread-fruit," he repeated quietly, as if this was something that had not occurred to him before. "Bread-fruit. Yes, my great king might well be pleased with such a gift. Such plants do not grow in his kingdom of Peretane."

Delighted to be getting off so lightly, Tynah grinned broadly and assured Bligh that his whole kingdom was full of bread-fruit trees — he could have as many as he wished.

The meal ended and bowls of fresh water were brought round so that each guest could wash his hands — for the Tahitians were always most fastidious about personal cleanliness. Then, also according to custom, everyone now comfortably replete, settled himself down on his mat and slept.

Later that afternoon the feasting began again and then, in the cool of the early twilight, everyone moved outside to sit in a large semi-circle to watch the entertainment which Tynah had arranged for their pleasure. There was wrestling and boxing and then the *heivas* — the set dances. The dancers were accompanied by drummers and also by men who banged pieces of bamboo of varying lengths upon the ground to produce different notes. Still others played a kind of xylophone made from lengths of split bamboo whilst there was a choir of men and women whose sweet singing provided an effective contrast to the harsher sounds of the instruments. Bligh had seen many of these dances during his previous visit but they never failed to move him. Very much a perfectionist himself, he admired the precision and dexterity with which the men or women went through the prescribed motions of the various dances.

The last dance of all was the most exciting and unlike those that had preceded it, was performed by both men and women. It began slowly and at first was little more than the swaying of the performers' arms and torsos. Then as the music quickened and the pace increased, the dancers split into two long lines, with the women facing the men, and their advancing and retreating, the mounting frenzy of their gyrations and the abandoned, wanton gestures left no doubt what the dance was supposed to represent. It also affected the audience who clapped in time to the frenetic rhythm of the music and from time to time called out "*Hulas*" of encouragement. ...

The next day Bligh threw himself into the task for which he had come so many miles. A tent was set up on Venus Point and a party sent ashore to guard it consisted of Fletcher Christian, Peter Heywood, Nelson and Brown the botanists, and four seamen. William Peckover, the gunner, who had visited Tahiti on three separate occasions and who spoke the language better than anyone, was ordered to set up a smaller tent nearby and begin trading with the natives. By having the purchase of pigs and other commodities going through a central source, Bligh hoped to establish a controlled rate of exchange.

Within twenty-four hours there was trouble. Alexander Smith was marched in front of Bligh and accused of neglecting his duty whilst in charge of the ship's cutter. During the night someone had crept up whilst he presumably was asleep and stolen the gudgeon of her rudder. Bligh was concerned over a number of petty thefts that had already taken place and decided to make an example of the man to ensure that the rest would know that, given a duty to perform, they had to carry it out or be punished. Smith was triced up to a grating and although a number of chiefs and their wives were on board at the time and tried to persuade Bligh to stop the flogging, the prescribed dozen lashes were given.

The rest of November passed pleasantly enough. Bligh was

kept busy visiting and entertaining, the work of the men was neither long nor arduous and they soon believed that they had really come to what Bligh had already referred to as the "Paradise of the World". His officers were young and very eager to sample every pleasure that was offered, whilst his men, freed from the harsh and dull routine of life on board ship were equally anxious to sample the same pleasures. The work was easy, the conditions were perfect – with women, food and the mildly alcoholic drink of *ava* theirs for the asking ... a paradise indeed.

December, however, began with more trouble from the truculent Purcell. He had been ordered to shape a large piece of rock into a grindstone for the natives in order that they might sharpen their hatchets, but Purcell refused Bligh's command saying, "I will not cut the stone, it will spoil my chisel". He then added, viciously, "There may be a law to take away my clothes; there is none to take away my tools!"

Despite this extreme provocation, Bligh only ordered Purcell to be confined to his cabin for a few days in order that he might cool down. The next day, however, Matthew Thompson was not so fortunate. He received a dozen lashes for similar insolence and disobedience whilst Thomas Lamb, the butcher, also had a dozen for allowing his cleaver to be stolen.

On 5th of the month a sudden and violent gale came screaming in from the sea, bending the tops of the palm trees and sending white spray high into the air above the coral reefs. The normally placid water in the bay was churned into a raging cauldron by the fierce wind and Bligh hurried onto a heaving deck to make sure that the cables were holding. He was very surprised when, despite the huge waves, a canoe came bobbing alongside and he saw that it contained Tynah and his wife. They scrambled on board and embraced Bligh, crying bitterly as they did so. It appeared that they had feared for the *Bounty*'s safety and sure that the ship would be cast onto the beach and wrecked, had come to say goodbye to their friend.

He was able to reassure them on this point but kept looking anxiously towards the shore where the plants that had been collected during the previous month were protected only by a canvas tent, whilst a stream nearby was overflowing and threatening to wash away the precious tubs of shoots. Some hours later, when the storm had blown itself out, Nelson came off in a canoe and told a very relieved Bligh that the plants were safe and that the shore party had managed to divert the flooded stream by digging a ditch to carry the water away from the tent.

This near disaster, however, decided Bligh to move the ship to a safer anchorage.

During the afternoon of 9th December, a young Tahitian boy was injured and a boat hurried across to the *Bounty*, asking for Huggan's help. The surgeon had been confined to his cabin for some days and Ledward went ashore in his place. He later returned to the ship and went to see Huggan to enquire what he should do. The other was unconscious and scarcely breathing, whilst his skin was pallid and damp. Thinking Huggan would be better on deck, Ledward called for some seamen to carry the surgeon out of his cabin; but it was too late. Within an hour he was dead.

Bligh was never one to equivocate and wrote in his journal that Huggan had died "from drunkeness and indolence" and thankfully appointed Ledward surgeon in his place.

As the year 1788 came to an end, Bligh decided to shift the *Bounty* to a better anchorage on the neighbouring island of Morea, but when Tynah heard this news he became almost hysterical and begged his friend not to do so. His reasons were entirely selfish. The people of Morea were his sworn enemies, and indeed, had already attacked his kingdom. He also knew that Bligh's departure would greatly weaken his own position, for he had been boasting that the English had sworn to protect him with their guns and he had expected to have some muskets for himself. His protestations were sufficient to make Bligh alter his plans and look for a closer anchorage. He finally found one only three miles from Venus Point. It was a small bay which he named Toaroa, from an islet of coral that stood in its entrance.

774 pots of plants were taken on board and on Christmas Day the *Bounty* moved along the coast to her new anchorage, the launch going ahead with instructions to await her at the entrance to Toaroa Bay and to take the ship in tow if necessary. The men in the launch were slow in getting a line across and the *Bounty* moved past them, leaving the boat bobbing in her wake. Fryer had been sent to the masthead to look out for reefs and shallows but his warning cry came too late and the ship crunched aground on a coral bank. She had to be kedged off again with the anchors run out astern and with the crew heaving on the winches. Whilst this was going on, one of the anchors got caught on a rock, the rest of the day was spent untangling the hawsers and it was dark before the *Bounty* finally fetched up in eight-and-a-half fathoms

of water. By then Bligh was furious, but the next morning, when
he inspected the new anchorage and found it sheltered, near to a
good beach and close to a river of sweet water, his temper
subsided and he ordered the day to be spent as a Christmas
holiday, with roast sucking pig for everyone, followed by sports
and at the end of the day, a salute of guns and fireworks.

The next day saw the beginning of the leisurely task of
collecting the remainder of the bread-fruit plants. The tent party
moved ashore with Christian in command as before, Gunner
Peckover set up his trading store and with the ship in perfect
condition, the men had ample opportunities for shore leave and
more time to spend with their respective 'taios'. It seemed an
idyllic existence with discipline growing more lax, but this state
of affairs was not to last.

On 5th January, when the watch was relieved at 4 a.m.,
Thomas Hayward, the midshipman in charge, was found to be
sound asleep and the ship's small cutter had gone. Bligh was
summoned immediately and the crew mustered. It was soon
discovered that three men – Churchill the master-at-arms, and
two able seamen, William Muspratt and John Millward, were
missing. A further search revealed that although the ship's
weapons were kept in a locked chest, the deserters had also
managed to make off with eight muskets and some ammunition.

During the afternoon Bligh went ashore and learned that the
deserters had sailed for Teturoa, a small island not far from Tahiti
and sent Fryer away with a party to search for the missing cutter.
Hardly had they set off, however, than they saw the boat coming
towards them, rowed by five natives who had found it
abandoned on the beach. Bligh now followed Cook's practice
under such circumstances and seized Tynah and several of his
chiefs as hostages saying that he looked to them for help, as they
had always been his friends. He was not anxious to show any
force, however, because he feared that the natives might be
stirred to reprisals and even destroy the bread-fruit plants that
had been gathered with such care and effort. He went ashore
himself and learned that after beaching the cutter, the three men
had gone on to Teturoa by canoe. Two chiefs, Ariipaea and
Moana agreed to go in search of them.

News of the missing men came later in the month and Bligh
decided to go after them himself. After a difficult boat passage
through some reefs, he landed on the shore near the village of a
friendly chief who told him that the deserters were hiding in a

hut not far away. He walked boldly up to this hut and when they heard him coming the three men emerged, arms raised above their heads in surrender, and gave themselves up without any further trouble. Their ammunition was wet and useless but it is doubtful whether they would in any case have dared resist their formidable commander.

Bligh took possession of the muskets, gave them to the chief for safe keeping then marched the deserters back to the boat. As a passage through the reefs in the darkness was out of the question, Bligh decided to stay on shore for the night. There was a small hut near the beach and he took it in turns with two of his men to guard the deserters, whilst the remainder of the party slept in the boat, huddling together under a sail which gave some protection from the incessant rain and wind. By 8 a.m. they were all safely back on board the *Bounty*. Bligh assembled the ship's company, read the Articles of War and punished Muspratt and Millward with four dozen lashes, whilst Churchill, for some reason, received only two dozen. These were given half on that day and the remainder twelve days later.

In this matter, Bligh had again shown his leniency, for the punishment for desertion could have been at least a hundred lashes. Captain Cook would certainly have given more for it was said his own sailors got "more floggings than compliments".

Early in February it was found that the *Bounty*'s anchor hawser had been all but cut through and Bligh immediately suspected that it had been done by the natives. He questioned Tynah when he came on board but it soon became obvious that the chief had nothing to do with it, and after he had cringed for a while under the lash of Bligh's tongue, promised to do his best to find out who was responsible. The search went on for several days but the culprit was never found. All this time Bligh was sure that someone ashore had cut the hawser; it was only much later that he realized that it could well have been done by one of his own crew who hoped, by letting the ship swing free, to cause the *Bounty* to drift ashore, become a total wreck, and thus enable the crew to continue the lotus days that they had been enjoying for so long.

A month later Bligh found that there were more thefts – part of an azimuth compass, a water-cask and some of Peckover's bedding were stolen during an exceptionally dark night from the tent ashore. He blamed both Christian and Peckover for the loss but they assured him that a good look-out had been impossible because of the darkness and the heavy rain. Tynah was again called in and this time he was more successful, returning later with the culprit and most of what had been stolen. The chief strode along, holding the unhappy thief by the arm and as he approached Bligh he called out, "Here is the thief – kill him!" adding that as Bligh always punished his own crew for trifling offences, one of his own people who had also sinned should receive similar punishment. Bligh saw that the chief was determined that his subject should have a flogging and ordered a hundred lashes. After this drastic punishment, which the native bore extremely well, Bligh had him put in irons. The lax state of the discipline on board the *Bounty* became apparent when, five nights later, the prisoner managed to escape from his fetters, dive overboard and disappear ashore.

This time George Stewart was the officer of the watch and although he was not disrated, he came in for another verbal lashing from his commander who by now was anxious to get back to sea, confident that once they were away from the siren call of the island and its people, normal discipline and the sense of duty would be restored. During the past few weeks he had felt very much alone. He was at loggerheads with every officer in the ship, even Christian had proved a disappointment, for Bligh had expected that someone who was after all his protégé, would be an example to the rest. But this was not so. At this time Christian was twenty-three, a young man with a great zest for life and with a tremendous appetite for the native women who readily yielded to his charm and good looks. It was Christian's amoral activities that changed Bligh's attitude towards his young lieutenant from one of almost paternal regard to one of contempt and occasionally almost, of hate. As the months passed a sense of deprivation began to nag, especially when Christian's own amorous proclivities were constantly being drawn to his notice. On several occasions when he had gone up to the tent to inspect the progress of the plant collecting and potting, he would find that Christian was missing and the appreciative grins of the seamen who had been ordered to stay at their post made it obvious where the missing lieutenant was and what he was doing.

On one occasion, Bligh sent a seaman to fetch Christian and stalked up and down the beach until an over-casual and quite unrepentant Christian appeared. As he waited, Bligh was conscious of the muttered comments and suppressed sniggers of the shore party. They had made him feel foolish – and Bligh did not like to be put into a position of ridicule.

This attitude of mind existed, in a lesser degree, with the other officers, most of whom greedily grasped what the island had to offer without attempting to gain more than a superficial understanding of Tahitian culture and way of life, being entirely unappreciative of the warmth and natural dignity of their hosts. The only exception was Peter Heywood who although not yet seventeen, made extensive notes on the Tahitian language and later, under far less happier circumstances, was to compile a comprehensive dictionary of the various dialects of the islands.

But the stay on Tahiti was coming to an end. The bread-fruit plants, all 1,015 of them, were stowed on board with specimens of other tropical plants that had been especially asked for by Sir Joseph Banks. The *Bounty* also began to be crammed with provisions for the next stage of the journey, pigs and goats being penned in the waist, whilst the upper-deck and boats were filled with cocoa-nuts, bread-fruit, *taro* and other vegetables.

As this work went on an air of gloom descended over the whole island. There was no more singing or dancing on the beach; many of the natives were seen standing near the shore openly crying. Even the tough seamen were depressed at the thought of leaving the 'wife' or 'wives' with whom they had been living and to whom they had become deeply attached. Tynah and Iddeah moved on board the *Bounty* until sailing time and were quite inconsolable, the former even pleading with Bligh to be allowed to sail with him to England. Tynah's regrets, though genuine enough, were also intensified by fears for himself, for he was more sure than ever that his grandiose airs would have to be paid for as soon as his protectors had gone.

Bligh was well aware of his predicament and presented him with two muskets, two pistols and a thousand rounds of ammunition. That, at least, should keep him safe for a while!

Heavy and incessant rain held up sailing until the evening of 14th April. Then, with the shores lined with thousands of weeping natives, including many of the 'wives' who were now big with child and who wailed and cut themselves with knives in their misery at this parting. With the early twilight illumined by the red-yellow flare of hundreds of torches, the *Bounty* weighed and stood out to sea. Her crew lined her rails or hung in the rigging and watched as the island on which they had been treated with "the utmost affection and regard", slid slowly astern in the deep purple haze of a tropical night.

[8]

Mutiny!

THE FOLLOWING day the Island of Huaheine was sighted and the *Bounty* brought to off the northern part of Owharre harbour. No canoes were visible for the natives obviously thought that the ship was coming in to anchor, but after a while a large double canoe bearing ten men came alongside one of whom called out to Bligh, using his name. When he came on board, Bligh was delighted to find that the native had lived with Omai and was able to relate all that had happened since their last visit. This was the main reason that the *Bounty* had called at Huaheine, for the 'noble savage' had made such an impression upon London society that Bligh knew that many would be eager to learn how he had fared.

It was discovered that Omai had died some thirty months after being left by Cook and the new New Zealand boys some time earlier. All had died from natural causes. Omai had remained 'civilised' to the end for he had always ridden around the island in boots. Obviously Omai would be remembered for a long time, for several of the natives who had accompanied Bligh's informant had a man riding upon a horse tattooed on their legs.

As he stared across to the island, Bligh had a feeling of intense sadness. Omai had been left here ten years before – more than a quarter of his own lifetime – and the visit brought back a flood of memories of the earlier voyage. He gave the natives some presents then made sail on a course that would take him westward to the Friendly Islands. It was now too late in the year to run the easting down to round Cape Horn, for in May there were always mountainous seas in the latitudes south of the Cape, so he steered for the Torres Straits and Batavia, intending to round the Cape of Good Hope and then sail across the Atlantic to the West Indies.

The crew continued to go about their duties in a lazy, indifferent manner, but none were sufficiently lax to earn a flogging except John Sumner who earned himself a dozen for 'neglect of duty', thus becoming only the tenth man to be flogged during the *entire* voyage. Altogether the men thus punished were:

Matthew Quintal	2 dozen for 'insolence and contempt'
John Williams	½ dozen for neglect of duty
Alexander Smith	1 dozen for 'indolence and disobedience'
Matthew Thompson	1 dozen for 'insolence and disobedience'
Thomas Lamb	1 dozen for neglect of duty
Charles Churchill	2 dozen for attempted desertion
William Muspratt	4 dozen for attempted desertion
John Millward	4 dozen for attempted desertion
Isaac Martin	19 lashes for striking a native
John Sumner	1 dozen for neglect of duty

This total of ten floggings, totalling 217 lashes over a period of nearly seventeen months was remarkably low in comparison with many other ships of the period. By contrast, Hugh Pigot, captain of the *Hermione* frigate, and a contemporary of Bligh, was a ruthless and sadistic bully. During a period of thirty-eight *weeks* he ordered eighty-five separate floggings representing a total of 1,392 lashes. On two separate days he had twelve men flogged, six on each day, and on two others, a further ten, five on each day. Finally his crew could stand no more. They mutinied and killed their sadistic captain.

Over the same period, therefore, the number of lashes Pigot dealt out was twelve times as many as those ordered by Bligh who, unjustifiably it would seem, has gone down in history as a cruel, inhuman monster!

Bligh was very concerned over the slackness and lethargy of his men. Obviously the memories of the fleshpots of Tahiti were still very strong and few amongst them relished the long, hard haul to the West Indies. In his attempts to try and restore discipline to something approaching normality, he unfortunately became a consistent 'nagger', damning and cursing his men for the slip-shod way they went about their work. Even so, his outbursts rarely lasted for long and, as stated much later by some of the crew, "he was never angry with a man the next minute, he was not fond of flogging, and some deserved hanging who only had a dozen; and he was a father to every person in the ship".

The unsettled atmosphere was caused by the long stay ashore and although the men grumbled incessantly, there was certainly no suggestion of any mutinous conduct. Everyone suffered from

Bligh's outbursts; the one who felt it most was his own protégé, Fletcher Christian. This man, now acting as his second-in-command, had been on shore during the whole stay in Tahiti and to a great extent had been his own master. He, more than anyone, found it irksome to be back under severe discipline again and to be the main recipient of his commander's verbal lashings.

Things seemed to come to a head when the *Bounty* anchored at the island of Nomuka and he was sent ashore in command of a wood and watering party. Although Nomuka was one of the so-called Friendly Islands, Bligh knew that the natives were of a far more belligerent temperament than the peace-loving Tahitians and he was careful to warn Christian to keep his men away from them as much as possible and that their firearms should be left in the boat and only used as a last resource. The tragic memories of Cook's death were never far from his mind and he was well aware that a clumsy, trigger-happy seaman might well provoke a massacre.

As soon as the watering party reached the beach, however, a crowd of chattering and excited natives surrounded it and tried to steal everything they saw. Within the hour they had managed to get away with an axe and an adze. When the loss was reported to Bligh he was furious and went ashore himself to blame Christian for the thefts. When the other retorted that the natives had become so troublesome that he found it difficult to carry out his duties, Bligh rounded on him, "Damn you for a cowardly rascal," he yelled. "Are you afraid of a pack of naked savages whilst you had firearms?"

Stung by this, Christian shouted back, "What good are firearms to us if you order them not to be used?" then stalked away along the beach, leaving Bligh staring after him. As soon as the commander's rage subsided he realized the validity of Christian's remarks and on the following day, when another party was sent ashore, he ordered Peckover, the gunner, to stay in the boat and use a musket if necessary. This time the party was under the command of Fryer who showed his customay indecision, and almost as soon as the boat grounded it was surrounded by natives who managed to steal not only a spade, but even managed to get away with the boat's anchor!

The unfortunate Fryer had to receive the full impact of Bligh's fury at this latest theft, shifting uncomfortably from one foot to the other. Finally he said, "The loss of an anchor is not so great, surely, sir. We have plenty more in the ship."

Bligh's explosion at this caused him to retreat several paces. "Not great sir? By God, if it is not great to you, it is great to me!" He then waited until several of the chiefs were on board the *Bounty* and made sail, threatening them that they would not be freed until the missing anchor was restored. At the same time he ordered the ship's company to stand at arms, but the way they handled the muskets – something they had not done for nearly six months – caused him to shout, "Damn your eyes for a parcel of lubberly rascals. By God, if I had four more reliable men with me I could disarm the whole lot of you with sticks!"

He glared down at them from the quarterdeck then suddenly gave a further bellow of rage and dashed down amongst the men for he had seen that an able seaman, William McCoy, was not listening to him but was staring over the side, towards the island. Bligh dragged a pistol from his belt and pointing at the suddenly very attentive seaman, threatened to shoot him if he did not listen whilst his commander was talking. He then turned abruptly and stalked to his cabin. He was still there when a canoe put off from the shore with the news that the thieves had come from another island and had already returned there with what they had stolen. Bligh at once went to the weeping hostages, apologised for what he had done, and gave them a quantity of presents before seeing them over the side of the ship into their canoes.

As this was to be the final port of call before making the Endeavour Straits, the last of the barter goods were exchanged for cocoa-nuts, bread-fruit, yams and other vegetables and more live pigs were taken on board, whilst many of the officers and men collected a number of native souvenirs which they knew would always bring a good price in London. Then, dispensing with the customary salute because he feared that the discharge of the guns might damage the precious plants, the men gave three cheers, and the *Bounty* stood away to the northward.

On noon on the following day, 27th April, the ship was barely moving, for a fitful breeze was barely enough to stir her sails. Sea and sky were of an intense blue, far away on the horizon there were purple smudges, the islands of Tofoa and Agoodoo in the Tongas. It was a gentle kind of day and for the first time in several weeks Bligh felt at peace with the world. He came on deck during the afternoon watch and began to stroll leisurely up and down the quarterdeck. After several turns he glanced at a heap of cocoa-nuts piled between the guns of the half-deck and realized that they seemed far less than on the previous night when he had given implicit instructions to the officer of the watch to make sure that none were taken, for he had decided to issue them some days later in order to conserve the precious water.

He ordered his officers to assemble and began to question them about the missing nuts. When he came to Christian the other replied, quietly, "I don't know sir, but I hope you don't think me so mean as to be guilty of stealing yours?"

Something about the other's manner caused Bligh to lose his temper and he shouted in reply, "Yes, you damned hound, I do! You must have stolen them from me or you could give a better account of them!"

Christian's face paled and he stared in disbelief at the other before replying, "I was dry. I thought it didn't matter if I took one of them. But I only took one, and I am sure that nobody touched any of the others."

But Bligh had worked himself into an almost uncontrollable fury. All the frustrations and anxieties of the past months suddenly seemed to crowd in upon him. This set of so-called officers, men who should have taken so much of the burden of command off his shoulders now seemed to be conspiring against him. He stepped forward until his chest nearly touched that of the other and yelled, "You lie you scoundrel. You have stolen half of them!"

Christian swayed back, his dark eyes staring deep into the pale blue eyes of the other and asked, "Why do you treat me like this, Captain Bligh?" but the other only snarled in reply then rounded on the others. "God damn you, you scoundrels. You're all thieves and combine with the men to rob me. I suppose you'll steal my yams next, but I'll make you sweat for it, you rascals. I'll ... I'll make half of you want to jump overboard before we get through Endeavour Straits!"

He stopped at this, breathing heavily, glaring along the line of officers then calling to his clerk, added, "Mr Samuel, stop these villains' grog and give them only half a pound of yams tomorrow. If they steal any more I'll reduce them to a quarter."

He then dismissed the chastened officers and stood at the rail watching some furtively grinning seamen carry the remaining cocoa-nuts aft and store them near his cabin. He then went below and as was customary after one of these outbursts, was soon cheerful again. He summoned Samuel and asked him to convey his compliments to Mr Christian and invite him to be his guest at dinner. The clerk soon returned with the answer that Mr Christian sent his apologies but he did not feel well enough to attend and asked to be excused.

At eight o'clock the watch changed and Bligh came on deck for his customary check to see that all was well. He spoke briefly to Fryer, who had the first watch, confirmed that Peckover and Christian, who had respectively the middle and the morning watches had been alerted, wrote down the course to be steered during the night – west-nor'-west to pass the Island of Tofua – then went below. He poured himself a drink, put on his nightclothes, then sat down to write up the day's log. He completely omitted the trouble over the missing cocoa-nuts and ended with the words: "Thus far the voyage has advanced in a course of uninterrupted prosperity, and has been attended with many circumstances equally pleasing and satisfactory."

He sanded the page, rose and stretched himself, then climbed into his cot, leaving the door open to admit the cool night air into his cabin. All was well. His ship was refitted and fully provisioned, his men were in excellent health, and every one of the precious bread-fruit trees was flourishing admirably. The mission had been a complete success. ...

He awoke as he felt a tug on his arm and like most seamen, passed rapidly from deep sleep into complete wakefulness. He looked up and was able to make out in the dim light of his cabin, for it was not yet dawn, that Christian was standing over him. His first thought was for the safety of his ship but as he sat upright, his nightcap askew on his balding head, he realized that the cabin seemed filled with people. Blinking in surprise he saw that Christian was holding a cutlass and that three men behind him, whom he recognised as Churchill the master-at-arms, able seaman Burkitt and Mills, the gunner's mate, were also armed with muskets, with bayonets fixed.

At a loss to know what was happening he put one leg out of the cot and began, "Mr Christian, what is going on? Is anything ... ?" but before he could say anything else the other stepped forward and put the point of the cutlass near his chest and hissed, "Hold your tongue, sir! Another word and you're a dead man!"

For a moment Bligh stared at Christian, his mouth open in disbelief. It was all a dream, surely. This sort of thing could not happen on *his* ship. He slid the other leg onto the deck and as the other threatened him again began to shout, "Mutiny! Mutiny! Come to your captain's aid!" then as the enormity of the offence struck him and his anger began to rise he went on, "Come and help me put down these mutinous dogs!"

Christian snarled something in reply and advanced the cutlass until the point was touching Bligh's throat. There was a moment of sudden quiet as the two men stared at each other then the point wavered and fell. Bligh immediately began to shout for help again despite Christian yelling at him to be quiet, then the other men began to move forward, handling their muskets in a threatening manner. Bligh stopped at last, not because of the implied threat but because his mouth had become dry and he realized that in any case, no one was coming. He had hoped that Fryer, who had the cabin next to his, and also Peckover, Ledward, Nelson and Samuel who slept immediately below would by now have come rushing to his rescue, but Christian had already sent Smith, Sumner and Quintal to guard their respective cabins and to stop them from aiding their commander. Bligh was forced out of his cot and standing in his nightshirt and his bare feet, had his hands tied together behind his back with a length of thin log-line. Indeed, the cord was pulled so tight that it cut into his flesh and he began to suffer agonies from the stoppage of the circulation. He was then taken from the cabin, Christian and Churchill going in front, Mills and Burkitt following, their muskets cocked. When they reached the deck they all went aft and Bligh was tied to the mizzen mast whilst the mutineers went about the ship securing those men whom they believed would remain loyal.

Bligh kept shouting for someone to come to his assistance but although it was becoming obvious that the mutiny had not been planned – for several of the men stood irresolutely as if they did not know what to do next – his would-be supporters were now confined below; and the fore hatchway was also guarded by sentinels. Realizing this, Bligh now began to call out to the mutineers to realease him saying, "Come on my lads – it's all been a great mistake. Let me go and you'll not suffer, I promise you."

Some of the men edged nearer, the expression on their faces

revealing their indecision, and he went on, "Yes, do that and we'll all be friends again, eh? But let me warn you; if you persist in this mutiny you'll be writing your own death warrants. Sooner or later you'll have the navy in these waters and every man jack of you will be strung up to the yardarm. You have my word on it."

But Christian, whose distraught and hysterical manner revealed the terrible strain he was under, walked up to Bligh and again threatened him with the cutlass.

"*Mamu*, sir!" he said, using the Tahitian word for silence. "*Mamu*! Not a word. Not another word or death is your portion!"

Bligh stopped at this, for the other's eyes had the look of a desperate cornered animal, then stared miserably along the length of the ship that was no longer his. Small knots of men were gathering on the deck and he realized, with a feeling of despair, that had there been a handful of loyal men with some initiative, the *Bounty* could well have been retaken. He also realized, with annoyance, that many of those whom he swore would have supported him appeared to be siding with the mutineers. One of these came nearer and smirked, his plump face split in a near-toothless grin. This was Edward Young, a midshipman who had been most highly recommended and who was, also the nephew of Sir George Young. He sidled up to Bligh who turned his head to warn the other of the consequences of his action, but Young's grin became more evil as he replied, "Aye, it is a serious matter; and it is a serious matter to be starved, too. I hope to get a belly full later on," and he ambled away again. Obviously the collective punishment that Bligh had meted out over the unfortunate cocoa-nut incident still rankled.

Cole the boatswain and Purcell the carpenter were now allowed to come on deck, and the former was ordered to hoist out the jolly-boat. He gathered some of the mutineers to help him clear the boat of its accumulation of bread-fruit and other vegetaeles, watched by Purcell who sat on one of the spare booms with a smug expression on his face. Knowing the ill-feeling that existed between them, Bligh expected that the carpenter would be taking an active part in the mutiny but to his surprise the other appeared to be content with a more passive role.

At this moment one of the seamen came up from below and

told Christian that Fryer, who was still confined to his cabin, had asked to be allowed to come up. Christian shook his head at this but after Fryer had sent twice more, finally allowed the master to come on deck. Fryer arrived on the quarterdeck to find that most of the men were helping to get the jolly-boat over the side and that Bligh was virtually alone except for Isaac Martin who was standing guard. The seaman held a musket in one hand and an orange-like fruit called a shaddock in the other with which he was feeding Bligh, whose mouth was still dry from so much shouting. Fryer looked around then called across the deck to Christian, asking "Will you let me remain in the ship?"

This drew a positive "No!" at which Fryer paused for a moment then, edging closer to Bligh asked, "Have *you* any objections, Captain Bligh?" but as he spoke he made some furtive signs as if asking what he should do next.

Bligh took a quick look around then nodded towards Christian and hissed, "Knock him down and cut me loose!"

"What about him?" Fryer replied, indicating Martin.

"He is with us: Christian is the villain!"

But Fryer hesitated too long. He turned to speak to Martin but Christian, realizing that something was being planned, ran to the quarterdeck rail and called out to Mills, Burkitt and others to come up and take over the custody of Bligh. He then sent the reluctant mutineer forward to help with the boat. Fryer was also ordered to return to his cabin and after looking helplessly at Bligh, he turned and disappeared from sight.

Two other midshipmen, Hayward and Hallet, were brought up from below and ordered into the boat, but they saw at once that it was rotten and taking in water fast. They made their way aft again and begged Christian to replace it with the launch. The leader of the mutiny was still vacillating, for it was obvious that events had moved much faster than he had anticipated, and he looked towards some of the men as if asking their advice.

"Dump 'em over anyway," Churchill growled. "The jolly-boat's too good for 'em!"

Mills and Burkitt also moved forward and the former, pointing at Bligh snarled, "Shoot him now! That'll be the best way out in the end. Shoot him and all his friends and have done with it, then let's get back to the island."

Christian hesitated, then shook his head. He would not have the deliberate murder of the others on his conscience, neither would he be responsible for their deaths by sending them away in a leaking boat. Curiously it was Purcell who, sauntering aft, pointed out that the jolly-boat was far too small to take all the men they wished to get rid of and that to overload it was also equivalent to an act of murder. This settled the matter and to the obvious disgust of some of the men, Christian ordered that the launch should also be cleared of its yams and other vegetables and put over the side in place of the other. Once again the tackles were manned and the launch put into the water. Young Heywood and Stewart helped in this work, and from the way they were jumping about and appearing to enjoy the situation. No doubt to both of them – Heywood was only seventeen – the whole thing was something of a 'lark' and they had not stopped to appreciate the full significance of what was happening.

Bligh now began to shout at the mutineers again and Christian walked across to him, changed the cutlass that he had been holding for a bayonet, yelled at him to be quiet, and threatened that he would kill him on the spot. At the same time, Mills and Burkitt edged nearer, with their muskets cocked, ready to fire at a word. Despite this threat, Bligh continued to shout and even dared the two seamen to fire and be damned. At this, the men actually uncocked their pieces and drew back. Meanwhile the launch was being stocked with provisions and water but there was a great deal of confusion amongst the crew for Christian had announced that he did not wish to keep anyone on board against his will – whoever wanted to go in the boat was free to do so. At this there was a great deal of arguing, as those that had been confined in their cabins were now allowed on deck and asked where their sympathies lay, although it soon became apparent that almost all the petty officers wished to leave, whilst the majority of the seamen were in favour of sailing with Christian. Whilst this was going on, Bligh again tried to dissuade the other from this irrevocable step.

"Mr Christian – Fletcher – you still have time to change your mind and let us continue as before. I'll … I'll pawn my honour; I'll give you my bond never to refer to this unhappy incident again if you will desist."

Seeing that the other's face relaxed slightly at this he went on, "Think of our friendship. By your action you are committing me and more than a dozen of your shipmates to certain death. Think again. Remember Elizabeth and also my children who have such a high regard for you. Think again, I beg of you."

But it was too late. Indeed, as some of the mutineers came aft to see for themselves what was going on, Christian suddenly flew into a hysterical frenzy and shouted, "No, Captain Bligh. If you had any honour, things would not have come to this; and if you had any regard for your wife and family, you should have thought about them before, and not behaved so much like a villain!" and he turned away to stand at the quarterdeck rail, staring moodily ahead.

Cole came to stand below him and looking up, also tried to persuade him to change his mind, but received the answer, "It's too late. I have been in hell this fortnight past and am determined to bear it no longer, and you know Mr Cole, that I have been used like a dog all the voyage."

By now, those that were going had run below and grabbed their personal belongings. Samuel was the most far seeing of them all for he went straight to Bligh's cabin and brought out the ship's journals and other important papers, together with some uniforms. He also tried to hand into the boat a portfolio of Bligh's maps and drawings, some of which were his original surveys of the west coast of America and the Sandwich and Friendly Islands – the accumulated work of fifteen years – but it was snatched from his hand by one of the seamen who hustled him down into the boat with "Damn your eyes, you're well off to get what you have," whilst another, remembering Bligh's skill as a navigator added, "I'll be damned if he don't find his way home, if he gets anything else".

An altercation broke out between Christian and Bligh's *bête noir*, Purcell the carpenter. The latter was anxious to stay in the ship but Christian, remembering what an inveterate trouble-maker he was, ordered him to go, but kept his mates, McIntosh and Norman against their will. At this, a surly Purcell climbed into the boat, taking his large tool chest with him, but Quintal called out, "Don't let him take that for, damn my eyes, he'll have a new ship built in a month!"

Purcell, however, was adamant and he stood up in the boat, shouting back at Quintal and retained the important chest.

Fryer also repeated his plea to be allowed to stay in the ship hoping, as he said later, to find some means of regaining command, but Christian was adamant and he, too, joined the rest in a launch which was sinking ominously with the number of men already packed into her. Bligh, with his hands still tied behind him, was taken into the waist, a laughing and jeering band of mutineers surrounding him as he went. Christian was waiting for him and said, "Come along Captain Bligh, all your officers and men are in the boat and you must go with them. Any attempt to make the least resistance and you will instantly be put to death."

"Can I not have some firearms then?" Bligh asked, but his request met with a roar of laughter.

"You don't have to worry about firearms," Churchill jeered. "You'll be among your pals in the Friendly Islands – they'll look after you!"

Bligh now realized that there was nothing more that he could say that could help the situation, but he said to Christian, with an air of bitter finality, "Is this treatment a proper return for the many kindnesses I have shown you," to which the other answered, with some emotion, "That Captain Bligh, that is the thing. I am in Hell ... I am in Hell."

At this, Bligh climbed stiffly down into the boat and stood whilst his bonds were cut, staring up at the jeering men who crowded the rails and who walked slowly aft as the boat dropped astern then fetched up on the end of a rope so that the *Bounty* was towing her. A few pieces of pork were tossed into the boat, together with four cutlasses, and realizing that they might be cut adrift any moment, Bligh shouted up for his commission and sextant. The former was thrown into the boat whilst Christian took his own sextant and a book of nautical tables and handed them out of the stern window, saying, "This is sufficient for every purpose, and you know the sextant to be a good one."

His head disappeared and was replaced by those of Norman and McIntosh who shouted out to Bligh, asking him to remember that with Coleman the armourer and Byrne the fiddler, they had been kept on board against their will.

"Never fear my lads, you can't all go with me, but I'll do you justice if ever I reach England," Bligh shouted back.

The suggestion that he might, after all, return to England and bring retribution on them for what they had done, sparked off another outburst of jeering and abuse from the mutineers with cries of, "Shoot the bastard!" and "Let the bugger see if he can live on three-quarters of a pound of yams!" A moment later there came a sharp crack and a musket bullet whistled over the heads of those in the boat. It was probably fired in a spirit of devilry but Bligh was not taking any chances. He ordered the tow line to be cut and the oars got out, for there was not even a hint of the morning breeze. This proved difficult to do for some of the oars were buried under piles of cordage and canvas, but even when they were freed the crowded state of the boat made it extremely difficult for them to be swung out and settled in the thole pins. But it was managed at last and the boat began to pull slowly away from the *Bounty*'s stern.

Bligh stared at his ship, his eyes misted with tears. To any captain the loss of his ship is a personal, unforgettable thing. That this – his first naval command – should be wrenched away from him by a gang of mutineers was the greatest blow that fate could deal. The loss of a ship in battle, in a storm or even by an accident, was bad enough. But this – this was humiliating … overwhelming.

Suddenly, white with fury, he stood up in the stern sheets of the boat and shook his fist at the ship and screamed in a voice that was high-pitched with emotion and fury. "You villains – you God-damned villains. I'll be revenged on the whole pack of you. I'll have every man jack swinging at the yardarm before I've done – God damn me if I don't."

As if in answer to this outburst, there came the sound of cheering across the sparkling stretch of water that separated ship from boat. "Hurrah; Hurrah for Otaheite!"

Bligh being cast adrift by the mutineers by R. Dodd

The route of the *Bounty*'s launch

Bligh and the crew of the *Bounty*'s launch being welcomed by the
Governor of Timor

[9]

The Incredible Journey

WITH THE *Bounty* moving slowly to the west-nor'-west, the launch was turned and began to head towards the Island of Tofoa, some thirty miles away. As it crept through the water, pulled by the six heavy oars, Bligh had ample time to take stock of his position. He had been cast adrift in a boat that was only twenty-three feet long and six feet nine inches wide and which was loaded to within seven inches of the gunwale with nineteen men. In addition to Bligh they were:

John Fryer	Master
Thomas Ledward	Assistant Surgeon
David Nelson	Botanist
William Peckover	Gunner
William Cole	Boatswain
William Purcell	Carpenter
William Elphinston	Master's Mate
Thomas Hayward	Midshipman
John Hallet	Midshipman
John Norton	Quartermaster
Peter Linkletter	Quartermaster
Lawrence Lebogue	Sailmaker
John Smith	AB and Bligh's Servant
Thomas Hall	Ship's Cook
George Simpson	Quartermaster's Mate
Robert Tinkler	Acting Midshipman
Robert Lamb	Butcher
John Samuel	Clerk

The remainder of the crew had gone in the *Bounty* and with fourteen able seamen amongst its twenty-five, represented the most capable men in the ship's company.

An inventory was made of what had been put into the launch and in addition to canvas, lines, sails and cordage, there were found 150 pounds of ship's biscuits; sixteen pieces of pork, each weighing two pounds; six quarts of rum; six bottles of wine; twenty-eight gallons of water and four empty barricoes.

As they moved slowly towards the island, Bligh slumped miserably in the launch's stern, one hand on the tiller, trying to find logical reasons for the mutiny. There was no doubt in his mind that the principal reason was the eagerness of the men to return to Tahiti and resume relations with the women they had so recently left behind. He also remembered having overheard some of the chiefs promising his men tracts of land and servants if they would settle amongst them, offering them the additional lure of a life of dissipation and ease.

The suddeness and well-kept secrecy of the mutiny were what puzzled him most — for he was unable to accept, as was later proved — that it had been virtually spontaneous. The whole affair had been carefully planned, he was sure of that, but could not understand why no hint had leaked out. Thirteen of the men with him in the boat had berthed forward with the mutineers, whilst those warrant officers who had been messmates with Christian and the three defaulting midshipmen, had not seen or heard anything suspicious. He regretted, once again, that no marines had been provided, for a marine sentry at his door would surely have prevented him from being seized whilst asleep. The mutiny had been a success mainly because by some ill chance, the most desperate characters in the ship happened to be in Christian's watch — Quintal, Smith, Williams, Muspratt and Millward — six of the men he had flogged and who, presumably, still bore him a grudge. These men, supporting Christian and having the arms in their possession, must have found it a simple matter to persuade the rest of their shipmates to join them. This superiority of numbers, coupled with the lack of initiative on the part of the officers, put them in control of the situation from the outset. Otherwise, he felt sure, the mutiny would not only have failed, it would probably never even have been attempted.

As the boat drew nearer to Tofoa, he became conscious that the rest were looking at him, waiting for him to speak and to tell them what was going to happen for they all appeared to realize that their chances of survival depended on what he decided to do. They were adrift in an over-loaded boat in waters which hardly ever saw a European vessel. There was, therefore, little point in landing on an island and waiting there in the hope of being picked up by some ship that one day *might* come along. In any case, although these were the Friendly Islands, the very name was a misnomer, for Bligh was well aware that when the natives realized that they were without the all-powerful fire-arms, their reception would be far from 'friendly'.

The alternative was to try and reach the nearest trading post in the East Indies where there would be a reasonable chance of finding a ship. This would mean a journey of more than 3,500 miles, without charts and with only a compass, sextant and some navigational tables to take them through practically unknown waters. There was a third alternative – to try and reach Australia – for Bligh knew that a settlement was to be established at Botany Bay. He did not know whether this had yet been done, however, and in any case this would only cut the voyage by about five hundred miles.

He looked up at last and faced his crew, firmly resolved. They would make for the East Indies – probably the Dutch trading post on the island of Timor – and hope that a European ship would be available to take them home. Of one thing he was certain. Somehow he was going to get back to England to start the processes that would bring Mr Christian and his mutineers to justice.

But first it was vital that the four empty barricoes must be filled with water and fresh vegetables and fruit collected as soon as possible. For this they had to call at Tofua which was steadily coming closer and which was easily recognisable by the column of smoke which clung about its high, volcanic peak.

The boat had been set adrift at 8 a.m. but the flat calm forced them to row throughout the day. This, to men who had not been accustomed to much manual labour for six months, was hard work indeed, but late in the afternoon a breeze sprang up and a lug sail was set on one of the two stumpy masts. Even so, the island was not reached until dark, and as the coast was both steep and rocky, Bligh was forced to lay to under the lee of the island for the night.

Cramped and miserable, the men tried to get what sleep they could, only slightly cheered by an issue of half a pint of grog to each man. At dawn they began to row slowly along the coast looking for a landing-place and at ten o'clock they came across a cove where the anchor was dropped and Samuel ordered ashore with a small party of forage for food and water. As they waited Bligh was delighted to see that the remainder were in surprisingly good spirits for they had the comfort of being near solid ground and with every prospect of a good meal immediately the others returned. At midday, however, the others re-appeared with disheartening news. They had only been able to get a little water, which they had scooped from some holes, and had not been able to find any cocoa-nuts or vegetables. They climbed back into the boat and as a strong wind made it dangerous for them to put out to sea, Bligh continued to make his way along the coast, looking for signs of food, for he was determined to preserve their own stock as long as possible.

Some palm-trees were sighted but they were growing at the summit of a high cliff which rose precipitously from a shore which had a nasty surf breaking upon it. Despite this, the boat was run near the beach and some of the younger men waded through the shallows, then scaled the cliff. They returned with about twenty nuts which were taken aboard and then, with this pitiful collection, the boat moved back to its former anchorage, and after each man had been given a cocoa-nut, they spent another miserable night huddled together in the boat.

The next morning the wind was still blowing as strongly as before and after everyone had been given a spoonful of rum, Bligh, Nelson and Samuel and some of the others went ashore and hauled themselves up the side of a cliff with long vines that had obviously been slung there for that purpose by the natives. After they had scrambled to the top they saw a few deserted huts and a neglected plantation from which they were able to pick three small bunches of bananas. Exploring further they came to a deep gully which led upwards to the crater from which smoke was drifting in heavy, choking clouds. They began to search for water but managed to find only a few gallons and at last, desperately tired, they trudged back over a carpet of lava, until they reached the top of the cliff and the trailing vines. As Bligh bent down to pick up one of them he had a sudden and violent attack of vertigo, and it was only the prompt action of Nelson and some of the others that enabled him to get back to the beach.

They regained the boat at noon and Bligh doled out an ounce of pork and two bananas to each man, together with half a glass of wine. Those men that had stayed with the boat had been ordered to hunt for fish, but had been unsuccessful.

During the later afternoon a cave was discovered near the beach and some of the crew spent the night inside it to allow more room in the launch for the others. On the following day they made their first contact with the natives of the island: two men, a woman and a child who were sent away to search for bread-fruit, plantains and more water. They returned later with limited supplies and also with other natives, all of whom appeared very friendly, and by noon about thirty were hunting for water and vegetables. What they brought back, however, made Bligh realize that Tofua had very little to offer and he decided to make for the island of Tongataboo as soon as possible.

The next day he sent some of his men amongst the gullies in the mountains with empty shells to collect what water they could and whilst they were away, more natives appeared including an elderly chief named Macca-ackavow, who had met Bligh at Annamooka. He had already heard that the *Bounty* had been sunk and that Bligh and his eighteen men were the only survivors, and wanted to know further details of the sinking. During the day, as the numbers of natives increased, the earlier friendly mood began to change. On one occasion some of the natives even attempted to haul the boat ashore, but Bligh hurried towards them, waving his cutlass, and they dropped the hawser and ran off. By the time the party had trooped back from their excursion inland with some three gallons of water, Bligh was busy trading buttons and beads for what little bread-fruit was offered to him. He also bought some spears, for they only had the four cutlasses for protection, and two of those were in the boat.

He had good reason to be uneasy, for the beach began to fill with natives who now began to knock stones together, the customary sign of an attack. With this monotonous banging as a sinister accompaniment he gave orders for everything to be carried into the boat — a difficult enough business because of the high surf — under the watching eyes of the natives. It was getting dusk and some of the Tofoans began to pile up mounds of driftwood on the beach as if they intended to spend the night there, and perhaps attack the seamen as they slept.

As the light began to fade, Bligh gave the word and everyone who was on shore picked up what was left and made for the boat. As they went, one of the chiefs stopped Bligh and asked him whether he would stay with them for the night and received the reply, "No. I never sleep out of my boat; but in the morning we will trade with you again and I shall remain until the weather is better."

At this, Macca-ackavow, who had heard what was said remarked casually and deliberately, "You will not sleep on shore? Then *mattee*!" using the native phrase for "We will kill you."

He then strolled away to join the main group of natives which had now increased to more than two hundred and the sound of the banging stones rose to a crescendo. Bligh paused for a moment then deciding to use the hostage method once more, grabbed the chief's arm and began to drag him down to the beach and to the water's edge. All the time he was conscious of the natives massing behind them and as they both neared the waiting launch the chief suddenly wrenched his arm away from Bligh's grip and ran screaming back up the beach, towards the rest. At this, Bligh gave a yell himself and waist deep in water, struggled towards the boat whilst a barrage of stones whistled about him. He was still being dragged over the gunwale when John Norton, one of the quartermasters, noticed that some natives had grabbed at the hawser and obviously intended to pull the boat back towards the beach. Without saying a word, he slipped over the side of the boat and waded back to the shore, calling out to them to release the hawser. He was met by a fusillade of stones, was knocked down as he set foot on the beach and battered to death. The line was still held by some natives and Bligh hastily whipped out a knife to saw through the rope. As he did so he glanced shorewords and saw with horror that five of them were fighting over Norton's trousers, whilst another two were still beating at his head with large stones.

Others were tumbling into canoes and their brown backs were beginning to rise and fall in unison as they plied their paddles. There came another heart-catching moment when the boat's grapnel caught on the sea bed and only broke free when one of its prongs snapped off. The men began to row desperately for the open sea, with stones still falling about them and frequently striking them as they rowed or crouched behind the deceptive shelter of the gunwale. Those that were not rowing picked up the stones that fell into the boat and hurled them back, but their aim was erratic and they did little damage. Soon the first of the war canoes was almost alongside, the paddles flashing with a fast rhythm, whilst a number of warriors, armed with spears, stood poised on the prow waiting to leap into the launch.

It was a desperate moment. Then, thinking quickly, Bligh shouted to his men to throw some of the spare clothing over the side and as the garments began to float on the surface of the water, the pursuing canoes slowed, whilst everyone in them began to grab at the garments which, when recovered, often led to fights within the canoes as one native contested possession with another. The launch pulled ahead, the sails were set and as the darkness was falling and the wind was still very strong, the canoes stopped the pursuit, turned and headed back towards the island.

After such an escape, in which nearly every man had received injuries from the stones, Bligh was convinced that it would be useless and even foolhardy to land on Tongataboo as planned, for without firearms their lives would be in danger. Even if these were spared, they would certainly lose everything else, including the precious compass and sextant without which he could not hope to reach Timor. As the boat scudded along the western side of Tofoa, they discussed what should be done and it was obvious that the decision would by general consent once again be left to Bligh. He wanted to be sure that everyone knew what lay ahead, and pointed out that they were 3,500 miles from Timor and that should they succeed in reaching this port, it would be the longest boat journey ever recorded. He also reminded them that they had very little food and that it would be necessary for them to survive on an ounce of biscuit and a quarter of a pint of water a day. But the rest fatalistically accepted all this and after the boat had been emptied of stones and made ship-shape, its crew, which was now reduced to eighteen men, thanked God for their escape and began the journey which was to carry them into history.

Daybreak brought a fiery red sunrise, forecasting wind, and by eight o'clock they were rolling and pitching in a sea that was so high that the boat was becalmed between the waves but shuddered to the full force of the wind as it teetered on their crests. Bligh stared up at the taut canvas, worried that it would be ripped away. From time to time, a following sea curled over the launch's stern to drench him as he sat at the tiller and half filling the boat so that the men were forced to keep bailing. With so much water swirling around inside the boat, Bligh began to be concerned about their stores, particularly the biscuit, some 150 pounds of which still remained, for he knew that if this was spoiled their chances of survival would be almost negligible. Fortunately Purcell's much argued about tool chest was a good stout one and the bags of biscuit were stored within it and were kept moderately dry.

For dinner on that first day, everyone was issued with a teaspoonful of rum – for the wind was bitterly cold – together with some bread-fruit which was only just edible, for it had been trampled on during the recent struggle. Bligh worked out his position at noon and laid a course to the west-nor'-west, hoping that he might sight some islands that had been spoken of by the natives on Tofoa and which they called the "Fidgees".

The launch battled on, plunging and butting through steep waves, rolling and shaking as the wind caught her, shipping water as she went, while the numb and hungry men bailed and bailed until it seemed as if their whole lives had been spent in this exhausting and monotonous exercise. The nights were cold as shivering in their sodden clothes the men huddled together for warmth whilst Bligh, as tired and cold as the rest and with the heavy responsibility of command upon him, went amongst them to force a teaspoonful of life-giving rum between their chattering teeth. By the morning of 4th May, some six days after the mutiny, the first of the Fijian Islands loomed up to the westward, half obscured by mist and driving rain. Soon more came into view, slipped past and vanished astern, small and lonely many of them for even today, out of the 322 islands in the archipelago, little more than 100 are inhabited.

During the afternoon the gale lost a great deal of its fury and conditions became a little easier. Bligh had attempted to ease the discomfort by putting the men on watch and watch, so that nine always sat up whilst the others lay down and tried to sleep, although as the nights continued cold and there was nothing with which to cover themselves except some spare canvas, they found that after a few hours fitful rest they could barely move their cold and cramped limbs. Yet, despite these appalling conditions, Bligh managed to work out the position of the islands through which they were passing and, balanced precariously on a thwart in the crowded, plunging boat, he actually made sketches of some of them. It was typical of his fanatical devotion to duty and to his own love of navigation that he even considered doing so for as his log-book states, "Being constantly wet, it is with the utmost difficulty I can open a Book to write, & I am sensible that I can do no more than point out where these Lands are to be found & give an Idea of their extent ... ".

By the morning of 8th they were in open water again. Bligh was thus the first European to pass through the Fiji Archipelago, having sailed right through from east to west. As a tribute to this achievement for years afterwards the 'Fidgees' were known as 'Bligh's Islands'.

The problem of drinking water was eased for a while for a heavy rain squall enabled some to be collected in a spread sail and for their stock to be brought up to thirty-four gallons. Bligh also made a pair of scales from two half cocoa-nut shells and having found some pistol-balls in the boat, adopted one of them as the standard weight of the biscuit ration.

The squall passed away but was replaced by another and yet another until the men lay shivering in soaked clothes and, having "no dry things to shift or Cover us, we experienced Cold and Shiverings scarce to be conceived".

Every morning Bligh would dole out the spoonful of rum per man and the usual allowance of biscuit and water for breakfast, for dinner and for supper. It was monotonous fare and by the end of the week the men were begging him to let them have a piece of the salt pork. He relented at last, giving each an ounce, preferring to issue it in small quantities than let it all be eaten in fewer and larger helpings – something that the rest would doubtless have done had he not been there to curb their unthinking appetites. He also drew a map of their approximate position together with that of New Guinea and New Holland, and gave them a talk in which he related everything he knew about these places. He did this in order to keep up their spirits and also in the belief that should anything happen to him, "those who survived might have some Idea of what they were about, and arrive safe at Timor, which at present they knew nothing of, more than the Name".

His men certainly needed cheering for the weather showed no signs of improvement and Bligh held the tiller with cold and chapped hands, constantly on the alert for any rogue waves, for the least error would have been disastrous. When he handed the tiller to another for a spell he would try and snatch a little rest or write in his log something of the ghastly conditions under which they were all suffering.

From 11th May, for nearly two weeks, the log told of strong gales and high seas, of waves breaking over the stern so that the men were constantly bailing, day and night. There was no shelter in the boat and the men sat crouched and miserable, soaked and cold, their bodies wracked with pains and cramp.

Continual entries in his log told of

our limbs being so crampt as scarce to feel the use of them.

The day showed to me a poor Miserable set of Beings full of
Wants but nothing to relieve them. Some complained of great pains
in their Bowels and all of having but little use of their Limbs.

As I saw no prospect of our getting our Cloaths dryed, I
recommended it to every one to strip and wring them through the
Salt Water, by which means they received a Warmth that while
wet with Rain they could not have, and be more exempt from
Catching Cold and violent Rheumatic complaints.

So he went on, day after day, suffering as much as the rest but
managing to keep up their morale whilst writing his log. It was
more than a day-to-day diary for he entered regular observations
and notes and, most surprising of all, managed to stand upwright
in the storm-tossed launch to sketch and chart the islands they
passed for the benefit of future seamen sailing in those parts.

By the 15th he was writing in a manner that revealed his
amazing optimism.

We are now but little better than starving with plenty in View,
yet the risk was so great to get that relief that prolonging of life even
in the midst of misery is preferable while we have hope of
surmounting all our hardships, but for my own part I consider the
general run of Cloudy and Wet Weather to be a providential
blessing to us. Hot Weather would have caused us to have died
raving Mad with thirst, yet now altho we sleep covered with Rain
and Sea, we suffer not that dreadful calamity.

Day followed day, bringing rain and violent squalls so that by
the 20th he was forced to write: "our appearances were horrible,
and I could look no way but I caught the Eye of some one.
Extreme hunger is now evident, but thirst no one suffers or we
have an Inclination to drink, that desire being satisfied through
our skin. What little Sleep we get is in the midst of Water, and we
wake with Severe Cramps and Pains in the Bones. ... "

By the 22nd he was writing: "I presume to say our present
situation would make the boldest Seaman tremble that ever lived.
Watching with the utmost care, as the least Error in the Helm
would in a Moment be our destruction."

The following day he found everyone so distressed that he
began to fear that another such night "would produce the End of
several who were no longer able to bear it".

The morning of the 24th broke fine and clear. For the first time for fifteen days the sun had some warmth in it and its effect on the wretched men was amazing. On the following day they managed to catch a sea-bird called a noddy, which had settled on the gunwale. It was very small, being only the size of a young pigeon, but Bligh managed to divide it into eighteen portions which he allotted by the method known as "Who shall have this?" in which one person who turns his back to the man holding the shares is asked the question as each piece is indicated, a system that gave everybody the opportunity of having the best share. That evening a booby – a duck-like bird – was also caught and eagerly devoured, bones, entrails and all, "with salt water for sauce", although its blood was given to Nelson, Ledward and Lebogue who were plainly suffering more than the others.

These birds, together with another caught the next day, helped their diet considerably and also raised their spirits, whilst Bligh had time to report that to make his allowance of biscuit a little more savoury, some of the men dipped it in salt water, but that he preferred to break his portion into small pieces and eat it with a spoon from a cocoa-nut shell, chewing each fragment as long as possible "so that I was as long at dinner as if it had been a much more plentiful meal".

During the morning of the 27th branches of trees and driftwood were seen in the water and these, together with the increased flocks of birds wheeling overhead, told him that they were nearing New Holland. At one o'clock in the morning of the following day the helmsman shouted out in sudden warning and as Bligh struggled upright he was able to make out the white of the surf breaking on reefs not more than a quarter of a mile away. He immediately hauled off for the night and some hours later part of the Great Barrier Reef was sighted. But now there was another danger. The wind had backed and as they were on a lee shore they were unable to use their sails, otherwise the boat might well have been smashed to pieces on the vicious reefs. The weary, starving men had to strain at the oars again although they were now so weak that they could hardly move them.

The launch continued to drift along the line of the reefs until a gap of a quarter of a mile wide was sighted and shortly afterwards the boat passed through it and lay on what seemed miraculously placid water. The mainland of Australia was next seen and they continued to sail on the calm water lying within the Great Barrier Reef until, sighting a convenient sandy point, Bligh ran the boat aground on an island and went ashore. He was followed by the rest of the men, some supporting the others, for they had been in cramped conditions for so long without using their legs, and were all so weak from lack of nourishment, that they staggered like drunken men. Bligh scouted round and finding no signs of life, decided that they would be safe from attack. They then began to look for something to eat and soon found that the rocks near the shore were covered with mussels and oysters. There was also plenty of fresh water. Darkness put an end to their foraging and they settled down for the night, half of them on shore, the remainder on the boat.

The next morning, by the aid of a small magnifying glass, Bligh managed to light a fire and with a copper pot which had been brought away by one of the crew, cooked an appetising stew of oysters and other shell fish mixed with pork and biscuit, giving every man a full pint. During this meal, the first they had enjoyed for a month, Bligh remembered that the date was 29th May, the anniversary of the restoration of King Charles II and thereupon named the place Restoration Island.

But this feeling of well being was soon to change, for now that the immediate dangers and miseries seemed past, Fryer, Purcell and one or two others began to grumble and complain, the former even moaning that there should have been more water in the stew to increase the quantity! At this, Bligh decided to continue their journey although they were still weak, and after a supply of shellfish had been prised off the rocks, they began to embark. As they did so there came the sound of shouting. Looking towards the shore, Bligh saw about twenty natives had arrived there and were making signs for them to return. He also saw that they were armed with spears and lances and that more were running down to the water's edge to join them. Their black bodies were quite naked, all had short bushy hair, and their ferocious appearance caused Bligh to hoist the sails to get away as quickly as possible.

The launch passed other islands, sometimes going close enough to see groups of natives standing on the shore, some of whom waved green branches in an inviting manner. But they sailed on until the evening of 31st May, when they landed on an island which because of the day he subsequently named Sunday Island. Here there was more trouble from some of the crew led, as usual, by Fryer and Purcell. This time the carpenter was the ringleader and during a heated argument with Bligh he shouted, "Damme sir; I'm as good a man as you, any day!"

The other stared at him for a moment then, determined to preserve his authority, seized a cutlass and shouted, "Arm yourself sir! We will see who is the better man – here and now!"

As Purcell hesitated, Fryer stepped forward and in a half-jesting, half-serious manner called on Cole to seize Bligh and put him under arrest. This was the last straw. Bligh rounded on the master and shouted, "If you dare interfere with me, sir, I'll run you through – and that'll be the end of it!"

That was quite enough for Fryer who hastily retreated, protesting his loyalty. Bligh then turned back to Purcell and half-crouching, and with his legs apart, stood waving the point of his cutlass, daring the other to come at him.

His resolute bearing and the ingrained habit of obedience were enough, especially as Cole and Nelson moved forward to support their captain. Purcell muttered some excuses – "making concessions" as Bligh put it later – and the affair was over; but from that moment, Bligh continued to have a cutlass always at hand should another similar situation occur. The rest of the crew were completely loyal and supported Bligh as best they could, but undoubtedly it was his resolution and stubborn determination that kept them going at all.

By 3rd June the launch had rounded the northern-most part of the mainland and was once again rising and falling to the surge of the open sea. They had now reached the half-way mark of their voyage and a fair wind was blowing them to Timor. This wind, however, which would have sent a ship bowling along at a fair speed, was too much for the small and overloaded boat and the men once again were desperately bailing incessantly to keep it afloat. They were cold, soaked and miserable and, Bligh concluded, were suffering more than at any time during their voyage. Lebogue, especially, was sinking fast but all that Bligh could do to relieve him was to give him occasional sips of wine. A small dolphin was caught but when divided amongst the eighteen men yielded little more than a few mouthfuls each. With the steady wind pushing them on at a hundred miles a day, the men lay weak and exhausted wherever they could. Movement was difficult for they were all suffering from swollen legs and they stared ahead, from salt-stung weary eyes, as if willing their landfall to show up that much sooner.

At last, at three o'clock in the morning of 12th June, the island of Timor was dimly seen through the morning mist — a triumph of navigation. Everyone shouted aloud at the blessed sight, even Lebogue stirring to peer over the gunwale at the mountainous ridge which promised so much.

At daylight, Bligh bore away along the shore, passing pleasant prospects of woods and lawns which gave the area the appearance of being laid out by landscape gardeners. A high surf, however, made a landing impossible and they kept on until the following day when they anchored at last in a small bay. After some argument, Fryer and Purcell were allowed ashore but finding very little in the way of supplies, they continued along the coast until another anchorage was found. This time Peckover and Cole went ashore to return with some Malay villagers from whom Bligh learned that they were to the south-west of Coupang where the Governor of the island lived, and one of the natives agreed to go with them to show the way.

By dusk the wind had died away, but stimulated by the prospect of food and rest, the men got out the oars and rowed for a while. Then Bligh issued double rations to everyone and the men settled down to the best night's sleep they had had since the journey had begun.

Dawn found them at the entrance to a channel and passing through this Bligh blinked in surprised relief as he saw two square-rigged ships and a cutter anchored in a small harbour. The grapnel was dropped and the boat swung to it opposite a small huddle of buildings which was the Dutch settlement of Coupang. Even at this stage Bligh was punctilious and in accordance with naval etiquette hoisted a raddle of signal flags to the masthead as a signal of distress "for I did not think it proper to land without leave".

A soldier strolled onto the quay and on seeing the launch, called across the narrow stretch of water, asking them to land. The grapnel was pulled in again and the boat touched the quay to allow Bligh to heave himself ashore, to arrive in the middle of a group of locals amongst whom, to his surprise, was an English seaman from one of the anchored ships. Seeing his distressed condition, the seaman took him straight to his Captain Spikeman, an English officer in the Dutch service, who received him with a great show of sympathy and when told what had happened, sent orders that the rest of the crew should be brought ashore to receive proper treatment.

Some clambered painfully onto the quay, others had to be lifted ashore. All were like scarecrows, gaunt and haggard, covered with open sores and with their tattered clothes bleached by wind and salt water. They were soon in the care of the local surgeon, Mr Max, who dressed their sores, bathed them and ensured that each man had a change of clothing.

The governor of the settlement, Willem Adrian van Este, received Bligh very warmly and assured him that a large house would be provided for him and that his men would be accommodated on Captain Spikerman's ship. Bligh would not have this, however. He insisted that as they had come this far together they should not be separated but that his men should share the house with him. He took one room for himself; Fryer, Ledward, Nelson and Cole had another; the loft was allocated to the other officers and the men settled on a large and comfortable piazza.

After seeing his men well looked after, Bligh then sat down at a table where good food and wine were thrust upon him. To his surprise, however, he found that he was neither hungry nor thirsty. Rest was what he needed most and he retired to his room. He lay down upon the bed but he was restless and could not adapt himself to a comfortable, stable bed after the cramped conditions and continual motion of the small launch. He finally rose and taking up his salt-stained log-book wrote a description of their arrival in Coupang that had ended a nightmare journey that had lasted from Tuesday 28th April to Sunday 14th June, 1789, covering 3,618 miles through mainly uncharted waters. It concluded with the words, "thus happily ended through the assistance of Divine Providence without accident, a voyage of the most extraordinary nature that ever happened in the world, let it be taken in its extent, duration and so much want of the necessities of life. ... "

This may almost be regarded as an understatement.

[10]

Court Martial

BLIGH RETURNED to England in the spring of 1790, having travelled from Batavia in a Dutch ship, the *Vlydte*, bound for Middleburg, coming ashore at Portsmouth from an Isle of Wight boat on 14th March after an absence of two years and six months. At Timor he had realized that very few English-bound ships called there and he had bought a small schooner, which he named the *Resource*, to take him and his companions to Batavia where the chances of obtaining a passage home were far more likely.

During his stay in Batavia he was seriously ill with fever and was advised to leave the treacherous climate as quickly as possible. As the ships in the harbour were already overcrowded, he took the first available berth for himself, John Samuel and John Smith, his servant, leaving the remainder under the command of Fryer, to follow as quickly as possible.

By this time their number had been reduced to sixteen. David Nelson, the botanist, had died in Coupang of an 'inflammatory fever' and Thomas Hall died of a similar fever in Batavia only a few days before Bligh sailed for England. When the *Vlydte* called at Table Bay, Bligh wrote a long account of what had happened to the man who had proposed him for the command, Sir Joseph Banks. This, with other letters he had written to Elizabeth and to the Admiralty arrived in England before him.

His first days at home passed in a flurry of excitement and activity. His family had grown in his absence for twins — Frances and Jane — had been born on 11th May 1788. Their sisters, Harriet, Mary and Elizabeth were now nine, seven and five respectively and Bligh had the pleasure of breaking down the reserve of these three who at first were naturally shy when so suddenly confronted with a father whom they had to get to know all over again. Bligh also had a constant stream of callers, all anxious to hear about a voyage that had gained so much publicity; there was a visit to the Admiralty to place his official report before the Secretary of the Navy and a further visit to Sir

A portrait of Bligh by George Dance drawn in 1794 after the *Bounty* court-martial

Sir Joseph Banks by Thomas Lawrence

Joseph Banks to add to what he had already written from Coupang and Table Bay. He was delighted to find the other most sympathetic — for a sense of failure had nagged at his mind for months — and to listen to him suggesting another mission to the South Seas. Encouraged by this reception, he had invited the great man to dinner and entertained his patron and his lady, a charming girl some sixteen years younger than her husband, together with other Fellows of the Royal Society, all of whom were eager to hear at first hand those details of the mutiny and the epic boat voyage that so far had not appeared in the newspapers.

At this meeting Sir Joseph again referred to the possibilities of a second voyage to Tahiti to carry out the original plan and promised that when the time was opportune, he would mention the matter to the king.

The next day, following a suggestion of Sir Joseph's, Bligh began to sift through his material and to draft the outline of a book concerning his adventures. As he sat in the small room which he had turned into a study for this purpose, and wrote page after page in his elegant, flowing hand, memories became so bitter that he often found himself compelled to stop work and go for long, solitary walks until he had regained a sense of proportion, for he was determined that the book should be as unbiased and as well balanced as possible.

At this time London was a noisy, bustling and exciting city. The streets around St James's were crowded with carriages, the pavements with sedan chairs and with elegant chattering strollers. Here were the houses of the great, mansions thronged with society in its silks and laces, its jewellery and powdered wigs; here too were the fashionable coffee houses and clubs where fortunes changed hands nightly.

When refreshed by the sights and sounds of the metropolis he would return home and in the peace of his study, begin again.

He now had a dead-line to keep. His friend, as promised, had interested a publisher and an announcement in the *London Chronicle* on 1st April stated that, by permission of the Lords Commissioners of the Admiralty, George Nicol would be publishing the account of Bligh's "wonderful escape at sea, in an open boat, for 49 days".

He had become quite a celebrity and the number of callers increased, especially after an article that had appeared in the newspaper giving details of the mutiny and which ended with the words,

> This officer only holds the rank of lieutenant in our navy. His merit pointed him out to the Admiralty as highly qualified for this expedition and the distress he had undergone entitle him to every reward. In navigating his little skiff through so dangerous a sea, his seamanship appears as matchless as the undertaking seems beyond the verge of probability.
>
> We felicitate those who were companions in this hazardous voyage, that in the present Admiralty Board exists a disposition to foster and protect suffering merit, and our dock-yards, it is hoped, will prove an asylum to most of them to the end of their lives.

There was even a stage play about it. The programme read:

Eighteen Men in a Boat

ROYALTY THEATRE

Well Street, near Goodman's Fields

This present THURSDAY, May 6, 1790.

will be presented

A FACT, TOLD IN ACTION, CALLED

T H E   P I R A T E S!

or

The Calamities of Capt. BLIGH

Exhibiting a full account of his Voyage from his taking leave at the Admiralty.

AND SHEWING

The BOUNTY sailing down the River THAMES.

The Captain's reception at Otaheite and exchanging the British Manufactures for the BREADfruit trees. with an OTAHEITEAN DANCE.

The Attachment of the OTAHEITEAN WOMEN to, and their Distress at parting from, the BRITISH SAILORS.

An exact Representation of
The Seisure of Capt. BLIGH in the cabin of the BOUNTY, by the pirates.

With the affecting Scene of forcing the Captain and his faithful
Followers into the boat.

Their Distress at Sea, and Repulse by the Natives of One of the
Friendly Islands.

Their miraculous Arrival at the Cape of Good Hope, and their
friendly Reception by the Governor.

DANCES AND CEREMONIES of the HOTTENTOTS

On their Departure. And their happy Arrival in England.

Rehearsed under the immediate Instruction of a Person who was on-
board the Bounty, Store-Ship.

Bligh was unable to find out whether it was Samuel or John
Smith who was the "person" who had been on board the *Bounty*
and who had 'supervised' the production. It could only have
been on of these two — for the others had not yet returned from
Batavia. Thinking of this, Bligh was reminded that he would,
inevitably, have to face a court-martial for the loss of his ship.
This, however, could not be held until the remainder of his
boat's crew returned to England.

A few days later he learned that it was also planned to bring
back the rest of the *Bounty*'s crew, for an announcement in the
London Register stated:

It is said that by the express command of His Majesty two new
sloops of war (one of them the *Hound*, now on the stocks at
Deptford) are to be instantly fitted to go in pursuit of the pirates
who have taken possession of the *Bounty*. An experienced officer
will be appointed to superintend the little command, and the sloops
will steer a direct course to Otaheite where, it is conjectured, the
mutinous crew have established their rendezvous.

The project had to be postponed, however, for during May,
Pitt announced that England and Spain were on the point of war.
When Bligh learned the reason, he became intensely interested,
for the main reason stemmed from his voyage with Cook in 1778.
The high prices obtained by the crews of the *Resolution* and
Discovery at Canton for the half-worn furs brought from the
north-west coast of America had attracted the attention of the
East India Company and a settlement was formed in Nootka
Sound. Trading had already begun with Canton when two
Spanish warships, the *Princessa* and the *San Carlos*, arrived to take

possession of what they considered their country's property. Four small British vessels were seized at anchor and the Spanish commander then settled himself in the new colony and made claim to all coasts and islands in the vicinity and the Pacific as far as China.

Bligh was furious when he learned of this, for he knew that much of what was known of the Pacific had been due, in large measure, to Cook and himself. He watched as the matter was thrashed out in Parliament and applauded Pitt who was determined to force the Spanish to climb down or make them realize the alternative was war. In the event of it being the latter, Lord Howe took a powerful fleet into the Channel and headed for the Spanish coast.

At first the Spaniards were belligerent, counting as in the past, on the support of France. That country, however, was still in the throes of its Revolution and on reflection, Spain hesitated about introducing French revolutionaries amongst her own loyal sailors. She finally changed her tone to a conciliatory one, agreed to surrender Nootka Sound, make full compensation for any damage caused and also to allow British subjects to make settlements on any coasts not already occupied.

Before the end of the summer, the rest of Bligh's boat companions returned to England in a Dutch East Indiaman. The final reckoning was twelve out of the original nineteen. In addition to Bligh, Samuel and Smith, they were Fryer, Peckover, Purcell, Hayward, Hallet, Lebogue, Cole, Simpson and young Tinkler. Norton had been killed on Tofua, Nelson had died at Coupang and Hall, Elphinston and Linkletter at Batavia. Ledward took passage on a Dutch ship, the *Welfare*, which foundered on the way home; Robert Lamb died a natural death whilst homeward bound on another ship.

Although Bligh told himself over and over again that he had nothing to fear, he was naturally disturbed by the arrival of the official order which "requested and directed" him to report on board H.M.S. *Royal William* for a court-martial "to inquire into the cause and circumstances of the seizure of His Majesty's armed vessel, the *Bounty* and also to try the officers and seamen for their share in the affair". For the next few days he became withdrawn and morose and was grateful for the escape afforded by his writing. As his quill scratched across page after page, thoughts about the coming trial were submerged and would only surface again at night when, his mind would run free and he found himself imagining every king of unpleasant consequence.

The time came for the court-martial at last and he posted down to Plymouth where he stayed the night at an inn, to be up early on the morning of 22nd October 1790. He dressed himself in his best uniform — a long-tailed blue coat with white cuffs and lapels and gold anchor buttons, with stockings and breeches of white silk. He hired a boat and as it ran alongside the towering mass of the *Royal William*, a single gun cracked out from above. It was the signal for all those attending the court-martial to assemble on board. He stepped in through the entry port to be civilly saluted by the officer of the watch whilst other officers standing nearby eyed him with interest, for he had become a national celebrity.

The escorting officer led him aft and invited him to step into a small cabin. After taking his sword from him he wished him good luck before he left, closing the door behind him. The next half hour dragged interminably. Bligh could not remain still but with hands clasped behind his back prowled up and down the narrow length of the cabin, pausing occasionally to stare out of the port at the huddle of shipping that was packed into the Spithead Anchorage. From time to time he heard the twittering of pipes overhead as high-ranking officers arrived on board to take their places as both judges and jury at his trial.

The door opened at last and a young captain flanked by two marine sentries entered to say, "If you will come this way please, Mr Bligh. ... "

He straightened his uniform, put his hat firmly beneath his arm and followed the other into the great cabin, a huge room which ran from the poop to the stern gallery and which also extended across the entire width of the ship. He heard his name called, then stepped into the cabin where, outlined against the mullioned stern windows sat the officers appointed to sit in judgement. In the centre of a long table was the president of the court, Admiral the Hon. Samuel Barrington, in full dress uniform. He was flanked by three vice-admirals, six rear-admirals and three captains and the flash and glitter of the gold lace and decorations was almost overwhelming. He was invited to stand to one side and then the others on trial with him, led by Mr Fryer, filed into the cabin. This was the first time he had seen most of them for a year almost to the day and he eyed them with interest as the judge-advocate, the only lawyer present, read out the report he had sent from Coupang which gave details of the mutiny and what had followed. There was a long pause when the judge-advocate finished reading and Bligh shifted uncomfortably as he realized that most of the eyes of those in the cabin were fixed on him.

The president then asked, "Before we begin the Court-Martial proper, have you anything to say against any of these men concerning the mutiny?"

"I have not sir, except those charges against William Purcell, carpenter, as contained in my report to the Admiralty of the seventh of this month in respect of disrespect and misconduct during both the voyage and afterwards."

He stared stolidly ahead whilst Barrington shuffled some papers which lay on the green baize-covered table before him and read through one of them. Barrington then had a quick conference with the vice-admirals seated on either side of him and finally looked up and said, "We will take this indictment first. Mr Bligh and Mr Purcell will remain. Captain, you will lead out the rest."

Bligh moved across to the starboard side of the cabin to watch as Purcell marched up to face the court. The report having been passed along the table, the judge-advocate cleared his throat and read out six charges against Purcell, which included the matter of the wood-cutting, his refusal to cut the grindstone for the natives, and the incident of the cutlass when he had dared, for a brief moment, to face up to his commander. He was questioned on these matters and showed up badly, then he and Bligh were asked to withdraw whilst the court came to decision.

After another interminable wait, the twelve men of the *Bounty* were ordered to return to hear the verdict of the court which was, "That the charges had been in part proved against the said William Purcell, and did adjudge him to be reprimanded".

That matter over, the full court-martial began. Bligh was again asked whether he had any complaints to make against any of the officers or men present with the exception of Purcell, as already stated, and he replied firmly, "No sir".

As he spoke he was conscious of an indrawn sigh of relief from Fryer, who stood at his side. He could, as it happened, have brought almost as many charges against the master as he had against the carpenter, but he had had enough. He was prepared to let the matter rest there.

The others were then asked if they had any "objection or complaint" against Lieutenant Bligh and all swore that they had none. After this they were led to one side of the cabin and told to seat themselves on a bench until called upon to give evidence. When Fryer was called he was asked, "After the mutiny broke out, did Captain Bligh and the rest of you use your best endeavours to recover the ship?"

"Everything in our power," he replied.

The midshipmen, Hallet and Hayward were then called and both corroborated the master's statement, their evidence closely following that contained in Bligh's report. When this evidence had been given and Bligh had posed a few questions, the president and his neighbours again put their heads together. After a few moments, to Bligh's surprise, Barrington said, "That concludes the questions. The accused will retire."

As he filed out at the head of the rest, Bligh was staggered at the brevity of the proceedings. No one had bothered to enquire deeply into the reasons for the mutiny, no one had probed into the brief evidence of Fryer and the two midshipmen when they had stated that "everything in their power" had been done to retake the *Bounty*, for he knew that the master had proved uncertain and dilatory, Hallet, the midshipman of the watch had done little but stand aside and cry, and Hayward, as usual, had been asleep instead of on watch when the mutiny began.

After a short wait the twelve men were ushered back into the great cabin where, to his great relief, Bligh saw that his sword had been placed in front of the president with its hilt pointing towards him. He had been adjudged not guilty, and he listened in a state of exhilaration as the president read out the finding of the court — that "the said armed vessel the *Bounty* was violently and forcibly taken from the said Lieutenant William Bligh and such of the Officers and Ship's Company as were returned to England and then present, to be honourably acquitted".

Later that day, Bligh and the rest of his men were formally paid off from the *Bounty*. He was then placed on half-pay for three weeks until appointed commander of the *Falcon* on 14th November. This ship, a small sloop, was still fitting out for sea and Bligh was able to spend most of his time in London.

Now that he had been completely exonerated by the court-martial, he found even more invitations pressed upon him. The most memorable of all took place in mid-November, a few days after the *Pandora*, a twenty-four gun frigate, commanded by Captain Edward Edwards, and with his former midshipman Thomas Hayward promoted to third lieutenant, sailed for the South Seas to search for the mutineers. Sir Joseph Banks had called upon the Blighs during the previous day and warned them to prepare for a special outing, but smilingly refused to divulge where they were going and whom they were to meet, only suggesting that they looked their best.

At this, Elizabeth demurred, protesting that she had no new clothes and as she was already six months pregnant, did not feel that a new dress was warranted and, in consequence, could not go. But Sir Joseph's cajolery prevailed and the three of them set out during the early twilight of a November day to arrive in the courtyard of the pleasant red-brick building known as Buckingham House which the king had bought for his queen twenty-eight years earlier.

At the sudden realization of whom they were going to meet Elizabeth began to tremble and clutched at Bligh's arm, but Sir Joseph was ready to reassure her and they passed into the palace to wait with others in an ante-chamber until a flunkey, resplendent in crimson and gold, came forward and ushered them into the levee room. Here, at the far end, was a group of people who continued to chatter animatedly until those who were to be presented had been formed into a line extending down one side of the large room which blazed with clusters of candles, the light from which winked and sparkled from gold lace and jewels and illuminated rich hangings and damask covered gilt furniture.

The Blighs and Sir Joseph were placed near the head of this line and soon the latter was introducing them to His Britannic Majesty, King George III. Bligh looked with great interest at the monarch and saw a ruddy-faced man with white eyebrows and a fleshy, pendulous chin who despite elegant satin clothes and lace collar and cuffs seemed short, plump and quite ordinary. He gave a nod to Bligh's low bow and said in a thick voice, "So you're the Bligh everyone's talking about. Lost one of my ships and made yourself famous in the doing of it, eh?"

Bligh could think of no suitable reply to this, so he bowed again and as he straightened himself the other continued "Damned lot of scoundrels — deserve hanging, the lot of 'em, damme if they don't."

Then, as his eyes focussed briefly on the other's face he went on, "You look well enough after your misadventures, damme if you don't. But that scar on your cheek now. Did the ruffians cause that, eh?"

Bligh blushed slightly. "No sire. This scar," and he touched it lightly with a forefinger, "has nothing to do with my recent voyage."

"Then what ... ? Tell me," King George went on, with a strange persistence. "Tell me about it, sir," and waited whilst Bligh had to explain that the scar was a legacy from an accident in his youth.

When he had finished the other nodded his head and said seriously, "Very interesting, very interesting indeed."

Bligh bowed again and the king passed on, nodding with a "Your servant ma'm", to a very flustered Elizabeth, then moving further along the line. Members of his court followed, lords and ladies resplendent in uniforms or magnificent gowns. Finally the king paused at the door, turned to give a vague wave of farewell, then disappeared into his private apartments.

Less than three weeks after his presentation, Bligh was commissioned captain of the *Medea*, sloop, a command which had been given him solely for the purpose of giving him 'post', to place him on that important rung of the naval ladder which, in time, would take him to flag rank. This promotion, also, proved that he had been utterly vindicated in the eyes of the Lords Commissioners of the Admiralty.

Christmas came and went. It proved a happy time for the family for an unexpected windfall of £500 arrived, which had been voted to Bligh by the House of Assembly in Jamaica for his efforts on their behalf to bring bread-fruit to the island. With it came the hope that he would be more successful on the next mission.

The next mission — this was what was now occupying all his thoughts. His book had been published and become a 'best seller'. Now, he felt, it was time to return to duty. Sir Joseph Banks was very active on his behalf and in March 1791, Bligh received the orders for which he had been waiting — to begin the search for one or more ships which could be adapted for another bread-fruit voyage. Soon afterwards a suitable vessel was found and purchased — a newly launched West Indiaman — which was named *Providence*. A small brig, to be used as a tender and consort, was also acquired and named *Assistant*. Bligh was formally appointed captain of the former and by the middle of May both ships were fitting out for the long voyage ahead.

This time Bligh had known what to look for and undoubtedly the *Providence* was a far more suitable ship for such a venture than the *Bounty* and he noted down a comparison between the three ships, finding it most interesting.

	Bounty	*Providence*	*Assistant*
Tonnage	215	420	110
Length	90 ft	98 ft 11 in	51 ft
Beam	24 ft	29 ft	20 ft
Complement	46	100	27

Assistant was to be commended by Lieutenant Nathaniel Portlock, a friend of Bligh's and himself a very capable navigator, having served as master's mate both in the *Discovery* and *Resolution* during Cook's last voyage which had allowed both men to know and respect each other. The *Providence*'s first lieutenant, Francis Bond, was related to Bligh through his sister and George Tobin, the third lieutenant, was related to another captain, Horatio Nelson who, at this time, was eating his heart out ashore, having been on the beach without a ship since July 1787, and with no prospect of service in view.

Amongst the midshipmen in the *Providence* was a youngster of seventeen who was destined to become one of the world's greatest maritime explorers — Matthew Flinders.

When Bligh scanned the ships' station bills he was delighted to see that both Lebogue and John Smith had signed on to sail with him. Obviously they regarded him as a man under whom they were pleased to serve and not as the cruel and sadistic monster that others were to make him out to be.

On 22nd June 1791, both ships dropped down to Galleons Reach and took their powder and guns on board — twelve carriage guns and fourteen swivels for the *Providence*, four four-pounders and eight swivels for the brig — and then, fully provisioned and with large stores of articles of 'trade', they sailed from Spithead on 3rd August.

And this time Bligh was determined to succeed.

[11]

A Sad Return to the Islands

AS SOON AS THE ships had cleared the Channel, Bligh put both companies onto three watches as before, instead of the customary watch and watch, keeping the masters of both ships always available. He was delighted with the sailing qualities of both sloop and brig and also with the quality of the men. In contrast to the former voyage he now had three commissioned lieutenants, eight midshipmen and a strong marine detachment under the command of a lieutenant with a sergeant, two corporals, a drummer and fifteen privates – a sure guard against any possible trouble from the crew.

Less than three weeks after sailing they arrived at Tenerife, putting into Santa Cruz for provisions. The weather was close and sultry and the malaria which had nearly cost Bligh his life in Batavia flared up again forcing him to take to his cot. When the fever was at its height the shivering made him unable to hold a pen, and his surgeon, Edward Harwood, wrote his reports and letters for him. In one of these, written to Elizabeth, he explained the reasons for the strange handwriting and begged her not to be alarmed, ending the letter with typically affectionate phrases, "I am confident it is ordained for us once more to meet, you may therefore cherish your dear little girls in that happy hope" and ended with "God bless you, my dear love and my little angels".

Unable to shake off the fever and the persistent migraine which accompanied it, he was forced to hand over command of the *Providence* to Lieutenant Portlock, replacing him in the *Assistant* with Lieutenant Bond, for he was anxious not to lose any more time. For a while he was desperately ill and as the ships ploughed southwards towards the Cape, his headaches became so severe that the men were ordered to go about their duties with as little noise as possible.

After crossing the Line, however, he began to improve and early in October was able to resume his normal duties.

From the day of sailing, there had been perfect discipline in both ships but on 30th October he had to order the first punishment. John Letby, a quartermaster, was found guilty of extreme insubordination, having refused to obey orders and when rebuked had knocked down the boatswain's mate. Letby was triced up and given thirty lashes — one of the few instances of punishment during the whole voyage.

The ships stayed at the Cape for nearly two months for Bligh decided that a spell ashore in the "pretty village" of Stellenbosch would help him fully regain his health. During this stay, he with Lieutenant Tobin, a careful observer and an accomplished artist, and also Lieutenant Bond and Matthew Flinders, who wrote detailed descriptions of the places, the people and the customs of Cape Town and the surrounding country.

Continuing their passage the ships reached Adventure Bay without incident on 2nd February 1792. Bligh knew exactly where to anchor and where to send parties ashore for wood and water for this was familiar territory. During their stay, he explored a great deal of the coastline but, as before, still believed that Van Diemen's Lane (it was not to become Tasmania for another sixty years) was part of the Australian mainland. Bligh was the first white man to see a great deal of the region and he explored much more of the coastline than he has since been given credit for, even by Tasmanian historians.

Less than two weeks after leaving Adventure Bay, the island of Maitea thrust its high peak over the horizon, the signpost to Tahiti. Once again Bligh called his crew together and issued orders similar to those that he had posted on the *Bounty*. No one was to mention that they had come to collect more bread-fruit, to reveal that Cook had been killed, or that the *Bounty* had been lost. He also impressed upon everyone the importance of discipline and kindness and ordered that no one should carry arms on shore without his express permission. Anyone who disobeyed these orders would be liable to severe punishment.

The ships sailed into Matavai Bay soon after sunrise on the morning of 9th April and Bligh stood on the *Providence*'s quarterdeck pointing out the magnificent scenery of the bay to his officers, none of whom had been to the South Seas before, when he was surprised to see a whaler putting off from the shore and heading towards his ship. For a moment he caught his breath for at this distance one of the men pulling at an oar looked remarkably like one of the *Bounty* mutineers, but as the boat drew alongside he realized that its occupants were all strangers.

The men came aboard to tell him that they were survivors of the whaler *Matilda*, which had been wrecked nearby and whose captain had already sailed for assistance in a small schooner. Others of their number had gone to Oparre. He was delighted to see them – to any naval captain trained seamen were manna from heaven – and he gladly welcomed them on board.

Once again the same crowd of jostling canoes began to cluster around the ships but this time, Bligh realized, something was missing. The warm and vociferous welcome that had greeted him in the past was no longer there and only those with whom he had been friendly during his previous visits showed any genuine emotion at his return. He greeted a number of old acquaintances and asked after Tynah, to be told that the chief was away but that the great news that 'Bry' had returned would go to him by their fastest canoe. He led his guests down to his cabin and offered them wine. To his surprise, they asked for rum, something that they had never done before, calling it *Avah Tyo*, or 'friendly draught'.

He then enquired what had happened during the three years that had passed since he had been away and was disturbed to learn that the mutineers had returned to the island in the *Bounty* and said that Toote (Cook) had decided to live on Aiutaki and that Bligh had returned to England with the bread-fruit. They went on to say that Christian had told them that Cook had ordered him to return to Tahiti to collect the bull and cow that had been left on the island, together with as many pigs as they cared to let him have to take to Cook on Aiutaki.

Bligh listened to this story with growing astonishment and finally asked, "How long did Christian stay here?"

There was a brief discussion between his guests then one held up both hands, fingers extended. "Eight, ten days, maybe. He then sailed away to join Toote with some of our people."

"Is that the last you saw of him?"

"No Bry. He came back again and left fifteen or sixteen of his men here with us, then sailed off again. We have not seen him since."

Some days later Tynah appeared, to be greeted with a salute of ten guns. He brought his wife Iddeah and also the portrait of Cook, on the back of which Bligh saw that two new names had been added – Edwards in the *Pandora*, and Vancouver in the *Discovery*. The dates written alongside the name of each ship told him that the former had arrived in Tahiti on 23rd March 1791 and the latter some four months later. Tynah greeted him effusively but later, in the privacy of Bligh's cabin, he was disturbed when he realized that Bligh already knew much of what had happened and drew back, his eyes rolling in alarm, when the other asked him with an edge to his voice, why he had been so friendly with Christian.

"Only the first time, Bry. Only the first time. I believed him then when he said he had come from Toote. The next time he came I knew that something was wrong and told my people not to be friends with him any more. He quickly sailed away again, as soon as he had put the other men ashore here. In fact, he was in such a hurry to go that he left an anchor which I gave to Captain Edwards before *he* left."

This settled any suspicions that might have existed. Completely satisfied, Bligh was able to treat his friend more warmly, and they were soon exchanging gifts.

Bligh was now anxious to get on with the collection of the bread-fruit and he put up some tents ashore, fencing off a large plot of ground near the beach. Within two weeks nearly two hundred pots had been filled and as the work was going well under the supervision of the botanists, Wiles and Smith, he had an opportunity to explore the island more thoroughly than before and to write down in detail some of the strange customs of the Tahitians. As he went amongst them, however, the sense of change that was so evident on his arrival became even more pronounced and he remembered Cook's misgivings about the effect that the impact of Europeans would have upon these happy, care-free children of nature. Whaling ships had been calling regularly at the island and the natives had quickly assimilated the grosser habits of the tough and brutal seamen. Many were no longer bothering to keep themselves clean but were content to lounge about, dirty and dishevelled, wearing the filthy shirts, waistcoats and trousers that the sailors had given them, obviously proud of their 'civilized' appearance.

A great number of English words had also crept into their vocabularly including, inevitably, a quantity of foul oaths and lewd expressions. The native craftsmanship was also declining. No one bothered to make cloth, axes or other implements when such things could easily be purchased from the ships in exchange for a few pigs or vegetables. The other 'benefits' of civilization had also taken hold of large numbers of the islanders — the craving for spirits, especially Cape Brandy — firearms, which were now making inter-tribal warfare that much more deadly, and the curse of venereal disease, which, with other European ailments against which their bodies had no built-in resistance, were later to decimate the island. It was a sad state of affairs and Bligh who genuinely loved the island and its people, was profoundly distressed by what he saw and heard.

4th June was the birthday of King George and Bligh decided to give everyone a great show in honour of His Majesty. Most of the crews from both ships were ferried ashore and at noon Lieutenant Pearce of the marines drew up his men and ordered them to fire three volleys. As the sound of the fusillade rumbled and echoed amongst the high mountain ranges, Bligh raised his hat and led his men and the thousands of assembled natives in three cheers. The ships then fired a salute of twenty-one guns, everyone was issued with wine or spirits and the rest of the day was spent in sports and a general relaxation of normal discipline.

When darkness fell, a dozen rockets shot into the night sky, bursting into balls of red and white, to the great delight of the Tahitians. Lieutenant George Tobin had also managed to make two small balloons which were successfully released, floated up into the air and drifted away with many "oohs" and "ahs" into the darkness of the night. To end the day, everyone toasted His Majesty, Tynah leading them all with cries of "Mahannah no Erree Bretannee, King George" or, "The King of England's birthday! King George!"

During the three months the ships were at Tahiti, Bligh was rarely free from his nagging migraine yet despite this, his relationship with his crew was excellent and there were no floggings, no incidents, and not the slightest suggestion of desertion although, when sailing time drew near, five of the men from the wrecked *Matilda* took to the hills. With a shrug Bligh let them go, they were really no concern of his. As it was, he had added the whaler's chief mate, surgeon, boatswain and carpenter, nine more seamen and two boys to his strength. He was more than satisfied with that.

The ships were ready for sea on 16th July, with 2,126 bread-fruit and five hundred other plants stowed on the quarterdeck and galleries where they could get the maximum amount of air. Once again, when Tynah realized that his friend was leaving, he became hysterical, pleading to be allowed to sail to England with him. Bligh again had to refuse, although he finally consented to take one of the natives, a man named Mydiddee in his place. Then, to the sounds of sobbing and wailing, the ships weighed and moved out of the bay, slowly at first, then with increasing speed as more and more canvas was sheeted home. Whilst they were still within sight of land a stowaway was found, a youngster named Bobbo who had worked with Wiles and Smith and who, apparently, could not bear to see them go. Bligh was half-tempted to throw him overboard to swim back to the island, but the youth looked so pitiful and as both botanists said that he could be useful, he allowed him to stay.

With the *Providence* leading, the ships sailed westward until they reached Aiutaki, the northernmost island of the Cook Group which Bligh had discovered only two weeks before the mutiny and which he believed might have become the home of Christian and those men who had gone with him. The ships anchored on the west side and a party went ashore to question the natives. It learned that the *Pandora* had also called at the island but that there had been no sign of the *Bounty* and that no one had any knowledge of where the ship might be.

From Aiutaki Bligh set a course for the Tongas and then the Fiji Islands which he had last seen under terrible conditions from the stern-sheets of the *Bounty*'s launch. Then he had only made rough charts that would assist future navigators. This time he was determined to take far more accurate observations. Soon the first of the numerous islands of the great archipelago were raising themselves above the horizon and Bligh and his officers were busy with sextants and charts, putting each of the islands in its correct position. The majority of them had never been seen by white men before, for Bligh was following a course more to the north than previously, and each island had to be charted and named.

As the first came abeam, an island now called Mothe, Tobin and Bond looked towards Bligh for a name, for it was the captain's prerogative to christen new places. Bligh stood deep in thought, hands clasped behind his back, searching for something suitable. Had he been one of the earlier explorers, a Columbus perhaps, or a Magellan, he would have had a whole catalogue of saints from which to draw inspiration. But Bligh was neither a Catholic nor one for flights of fancy.

He turned at last and said to his surprised lieutenants, "The devil take it; there are scores of these islands, all as yet without names. We'll take the easy road. We'll name them alphabetically. Put this one down as 'A'!"

There was a moment of stunned silence at this then Bond enquired, with an answering grin, "But there are only twenty-six letters in the alphabet sir. We'll soon use them up if there are as many islands as you say."

Bligh shrugged, turned away and stared over the weather bulwark as the newly christened island slid past then said, flatly, "Then we'll start on numbers ... we won't run out of *them*!"

By 9th August, Island 'Z' (now Viti Levu) was marked down on the charts although Bligh added the name of "The Cockscomb" to its mountain peak, nearly 4,000 feet from the sea level. Then, when the next island was sighted (that of Mbengha) he ordered it to be marked as Island No. 1.

It was pleasant sailing weather. Both ships were heeling to a steady breeze under an incredibly blue sky and the islands that they passed were extremely beautiful with their tall palms and encircling spray dashed coral. Sometimes the ships sailed close enough to see the natives on the beaches and fishing in the lagoons, whilst occasionally canoes would put off and follow them for a while. Sometimes the natives would wave white cloths in welcome and as an invitation to anchor, but Bligh kept on. He knew of the ferocity of the Fijians and in any case, was anxious to get his precious cargo to the West Indies as soon as possible, and there were still the treacherous reefs and shoals of the Torres Strait ahead.

The entrance to the Strait was reached on the last day of August and Bligh signalled to the *Assistant* to go ahead, for she drew less water than her larger consort. With the brig picking her way slowly and deliberately through a tortuous maze of half-submerged islets and vicious coral reefs − any one of which could have ripped open the ships' bottoms − and with the *Providence* following carefully in her wake, they moved slowly westwards. The passage took nineteen days, every hour of which was filled with perils and narrow escapes from danger. Bligh not only had the natural dangers to contend with, he was also troubled by natives. On one occasion Tobin, who was sounding ahead in a boat, was attacked by several canoes filled with natives, but drove off his assailants with musket fire.

On another, the brig herself was attacked by a fleet of war canoes, some of which were fifty feet long and Bligh, realizing that the *Assistant* was liable to run onto a reef under her lee, sent his own ship hurrying to her aid. He opened fire with two grape-loaded quarterdeck guns, the shots from which smashed into some of the canoes and sent their occupants, and those of the other canoes, diving overboard to swim frantically for the shore. Some of the brig's crew were wounded in this encounter, William Terry, the quartermaster dying later of gangrene caused by an arrow wound.

Portlock had good reason to be grateful for Bligh's prompt dash to rescue him from the Fijians for, as he later wrote in his log, "Their weapons are extremely dangerous and they are good marksmen, therefore any vessel that comes should be well prepared ... ".

Every day brought new dangers, the most terrible of all occuring just before the ships cleared the Strait. The weather was now bad, a strong wind making navigation difficult and the *Assistant*, as usual, was groping her way ahead until upon a labyrinth of reefs, she came to anchor. The *Providence* was swept past her on a four-knot tide and with hideous dangers all about him, Bligh shouted for the sails to be taken in and the anchor to be dropped, walking to the forecastle to see that it ran true. To his horror, when it was halfway out, it was prevented from running further by a rope stopper which had been left on it, and only his prompt action in cutting the stopper and yelling for the other anchor to be dropped prevented the ship from running onto a reef.

That the stopper had been left on was sheer carelessness and a younger Bligh would have ranted furiously and probably ordered a flogging for 'neglect of duty'. As it was, he swore heartily at the world in general then stumped aft. No more was said about the affair and he wrote in his log, "The men who had done this were no more faulty than the officer who was in the Tier to command them, therefore I did not punish them".

Both ships were in an extremely dangerous situation, ringed by rocks and with a fast tide making their cables bar taut. By midnight it was blowing a full gale with a fierce wind that almost drowned the crash of waves on the surrounding reefs. There was no sleep for anyone that night for had the cables parted, nothing could have prevented the ships from being smashed to pieces. Dawn brought calmer weather, however, and with the boats once more sounding ahead, the ships continued to claw their way along a narrow and winding route where the rocky bottom of the sea was often only a few feet beneath the *Providence*'s keel.

But they were through at last and into the joyous relief of open water. Looking back at the dangerous and tortuous passage through which they had sailed, their commander ironically named it Bligh's Farewell. This name, together with Bligh's Entrance and Bligh's Channel, Portlock's Reef and Tobin's Islet, and also Providence Shoal which commemorates Bligh's ship, still mark a passage through what, even today, is considered one of the most dangerous stretches of water in the world.

Twelve days later, after a comparatively easy run, the ships anchored off Coupang and Bligh was rowed ashore. As his boat moved towards the quayside he could not help contrasting his two arrivals. Now, in the full dress uniform of a captain, with cocked hat, gold buttons and dress sword, he sat in the sternsheets of a boat which was pulling away from the two smart ships under his command. On the previous occasion he had staggered ashore, starving and ill, his clothes hanging in tatters about his thin body – a captain without a ship.

He asked for the Governor who had helped him so much during the former visit but was told that he had since died. His successor, however, was also well known to Bligh and he made all the arrangements for the reception of the ships' companies. One of the first pieces of news that he told Bligh was that Captain Edwards had also arrived, hungry and shipless, more than a year previously. The *Pandora* had gone down after striking a reef, and although Bligh learned that some of the mutineers were in one of the four boats that had struggled to Timor, he could learn little else.

Edwards, it seemed, had been very tight-mouthed about the whole affair and was obviously saving his comments for the court-martial.

The bread-fruit stowed on board the *Providence* had suffered during the voyage, for the distilling plant had been out of order for some days and nearly a hundred had died despite Bligh's efforts – and those of the botanists – to keep them alive. Indeed, he had been forced to cut the crew's ration of water although the midshipmen managed to assuage their thirst by licking the drops of water that fell from the water cans. Several of the crew got to hear of this and one of them deliberately watered the plants with sea water. When Bligh was informed he flew into a justifiable rage for this stupid and malicious action could well have nullified the whole purpose of the voyage. The culprit, however, was never caught.

The losses were made up with local plants, including more bread-fruit, and after a week the ships resumed their homeward passage. Bligh was thankful to be at sea again, for the oven that was Timor had brought on his headaches again and he also had another but milder attack of malaria. Others of his crew also suffered terribly and one, a marine, died soon afterwards from the effects of the heat. Only the two Tahitians who had eagerly explored the town were sad at leaving.

The ships called at St Helena where ten pots of bread-fruit were taken ashore. Before they sailed again the Governor and Council presented Bligh with a letter in which they thanked him for the plants. The ships then set a course for the West Indies, reaching Kingston Bay, St Vincent on 22nd January 1793. Here the Assembly showed more practical appreciation. On receiving over five hundred pots it presented Bligh with a piece of plate worth one hundred guineas, as well as inviting him and his officers to a banquet, whilst two prime bullocks were sent to the ships for the men.

Before leaving St Vincent Bligh took on board a collection of tropical plants for Kew Gardens, then set sail for Jamaica. It was early in February when the two ships were still at last with their sails in a neat harbour stow, they lay so perfectly reflected that it was impossible to distinguish their water-lines. Even when the glassy water was disturbed by the casual emptying of a bucket overboard, the shattered fragments soon reunited to form the double picture again.

Bligh again donned his full dress uniform and was rowed ashore to pay his respects to Commodore Ford, the Senior Naval Officer. He trudged through the hot dusty streets of the official quarter, where leisurely palm trees and English-type gardens relieved the orderliness of the houses of the naval and army officers, and entered the refreshing coolness of Fort Charles, to be warmly greeted by Ford and his staff.

The next day he was busy organizing the transference of the plants to the mainland and whilst this was going on he was waited on by a Committee which told him that the Jamaican Assembly had voted him £1,000 for his efforts in bringing the breat-fruit to the island and that Portlock, his second-in-command, was to receive five hundred pounds.

Landing the plants was completed in just over two weeks and the provisioning for the final stages of their voyage began. Just as the last stores were being swung inboard, however, the *Cumberland* packet arrived with tremendous news. France had declared war upon England and Commodore Ford was ordered to seize every French ship in the vicinity. As the *Providence* and *Assistant* were the only naval ships of any size in the harbour, he took command of them both, hoisting his broad pendant in the former. A few prizes were taken but found to contain little of value and when a squadron of men-of-war arrived at Port Royal, Bligh was permitted to depart. He left with orders to rendezvous off Cuba and convoy home ships of the Honduras fleet but only four ships were waiting at the rendezvous, and as he was worried about the safety of the plants he had on board, he sailed without waiting for the rest.

His two ships, which had hardly been separated during the whole voyage finally sailed up the Thames together, reaching Deptford on 7th August. On the way, Mydiddee, the Tahitian who had been ill for some time, became terrified at some corpses he saw swinging in gibbets near the water's edge and took to his bunk, dying soon afterwards. He was buried in Deptford Churchyard.

The plants were taken ashore and carted westwards to Kew. The second bread-fruit voyage was over – a complete success in every way. The ships were paid off on 6th September 1793 and on this occasion Bligh had to undergo what was, for him, an ordeal. Reporting it the *Kentish Register* stated,

It was a scene highly gratifying to observe the cordial unanimity which prevailed amongst the officers; and decency of conduct and the healthy and respectable appearance of the seamen, after so long and perilous a voyage, not one of whom but envinced that good order and discipline had been invariably observed. The high estimation in which Captain Bligh was deservedly held by the whole crew, was conspicuous to all present. He was cheered on quitting the ship to attend the Commissioner; and at the dock-gates the men drew up and repeated the parting acclamation.

This was altogether a disturbing experience for Bligh who was quite unaccustomed to such spontaneous outbursts of loyalty and affection from his crew.

[12]

Mutiny at Spithead

THE EIGHTEEN MONTHS ashore had been miserable ones. Indeed, as Bligh reviewed the events of that time he could remember few really happy moments. There was his family, of course. He could never fully express his gratitude for their love and support. Even the blow that had fallen upon it – the death of his twin sons – had only served to draw them closer together. The two babies had only lived a day, barely long enough for them to be named William and Henry, before their tiny hearts ceased to beat. Their death was naturally a great shock to Elizabeth, coming so soon upon her joy when, after having given Bligh six daughters, she could at last proudly offer him the sons for which he had so earnestly longed, only to have them snatched away again.

Then there was his small circle of friends who had been very loyal indeed. There was also the brief gratifying moment when the Royal Society for Promoting Arts and Commerce awarded him the Gold Medal when they learned that he had accomplished the feat of being the first man to convey bread-fruit trees "from the islands in the South Sea to the islands in the West Indies".

But they were the happy entries in his personal ledger. On the debit side there were a great many disappointments and depressing experiences that had, at times, driven him to the brink of utter despair.

When the excitement of his return had receded and allowed him to appraise the altered world to which he had returned, he soon realized that he was no longer a popular hero – all that had changed. Fickle public opinion had turned against him and he now found himself often snubbed or ridiculed, whilst the callers at his home had been reduced to a comparative few. Much of this change of atmosphere was due to the publicity given to the court-martial of the mutineers.

Whilst he had been away, Edwards had returned with the survivors of the wreck of the *Pandora*, together with ten of the mutineers. These were all that remained of the sixteen men left at

Tahiti before Christian had sailed with the rest to an "unknown" island. This, of course, was later found to be Pitcairn Island where all but two of the nine Europeans met with violent deaths. Captain Edwards proved himself to be a sadistic and heartless person for when he had taken on board the fourteen mutineers from Tahiti, he had constructed on his quarterdeck a "round-house" measuring eleven feet by eighteen, in which to confine his prisoners. The men were shackled within this enclosure where they were exposed to the sun during the day, to rain day or night and to suffer hunger and thirst, vermin and disease and the stink of their own ordure. With grim humour, the prisoners named their prison "Pandora's Box". Even when the ship struck the reef and was obviously about to break up, Edwards refused to let the men be released from their shackles until the very last moment. As it was, five went down with the heavy irons still clamped to their wrists and only one of them was saved. The others, who were not so fortunate were midshipman George Stewart, Richard Skinner, Henry Hillbrant and John Sumner, able seamen.

Even so, this was a higher proportion of survivors than amongst the *Pandora*'s crew, for Edwards had only eighty-nine men left of his original 160. After a series of adventures the survivors reached Timor from where the mutineers, who had been terribly treated during the boat voyage, were taken in a Dutch ship to Cape Town and returned to England in the *Gorgon*, arriving on 18th June 1792.

Their court-martial was delayed for a considerable time for with Bligh absent, the Admiralty were undecided what course to take. At last they realized the inhumanity of keeping the men in captivity for an indefinite period and the trial began at last on board H.MS. *Duke* at Portsmouth on 12th September 1792. The President was Vice-Admiral Lord Hood, attended by eleven captains. Those that faced this imposing court were Peter Heywood, James Morrison, Charles Norman, Joseph Coleman, Thomas Ellison, Thomas McIntosh, Thomas Burkitt, John Millward, William Muspratt and Michael Byrne, the nearly blind fiddler. They were collectively charged with "mutinously running away with the said armed Vessel the *Bounty* and deserting from His Majesty's Service ... ".

Bligh's letter from Coupang and an extract from his journal were read to the court, together with a letter from Captain

Edwards. The trial ended on 18th September, and although a great deal of evidence was heard, none of the court seemed interested in the reasons for the mutiny. That there had been one was enough — their task was to separate the sheep from the goats — and determine who had been actively implicated, stayed with the ship from choice, or had been detained in her against his will. Norman, McIntosh, Coleman and Byrne were discharged. Heywood, Morrison and Muspratt were condemned to death but subsequently acquitted. Burkitt, Ellison and Millward were not so fortunate. They were hanged on 29th October.

That should have been the end of the matter but for Bligh, a fresh ordeal was just beginning. The trial had been followed with intense interest by Edward Christian, Fletcher's brother. He was a man of considerable erudition. a Downing Professor of Law, a fellow of St John's, Cambridge and also a skilful writer, being the editor of *Blackstone's Commentaries.* Determined to clear his brother's name — and that of his family — he interviewed eleven survivors from the *Bounty* in the presence of several worthy clerics and a provincial editor, then published the results as an appendix to the minutes of the court-martial which had been taken by Muspratt's counsel, Stephen Barney. He named the men who had given him the material, but did not specifically state who had actually said what, excusing this by stating that this cloak of semi-anonymity would save them from possible reprisals.

The appendix made the most of Bligh's principal weakness — his ability to control his temper and his tongue — and quite overlooked the fact that Bligh's outbursts seldom lasted for very long and that when his temper had cooled he expected to resume the same relationship as before. Even after the altercation over the cocoa-nuts, Bligh had sent an invitation to Christian, who had received most of the verbal lashing, and invited him to dine with him. Whatever Fletcher Christian's feelings — and he was obviously a sensitive man — there was no justification for what had followed for he should have remembered the first rule of the service — accept what was dealt out by his superior officer and on his return home, request the Lords of the Admiralty for a court-martial. Instead, he fostered and led a mutiny — the unforgiveable crime in the navy.

This was something that Edward Christian, no seaman himself, chose to ignore. This whitewashing of his brother and the tarnishing of Bligh's name caused a sensation when it was published and although nine months after his return Bligh countered with his "Answer to Certain Assertions", backed by statements from some of his former crew, the damage had been done. That it resulted in a certain amount of ill-feeling Bligh hardly minded at all. What did upset him, however, was that Edward Christian's accusations were accepted by some of those in authority where it mattered most — the Admiralty. This became apparent when Lieutenant Portlock was graciously received by Lord Chatham, the First Lord, but Bligh was refused an interview. This ill-feeling was undoubtedly the cause of his enforced idleness, for although Britain and France had been at war since the beginning of 1793, Bligh remained on half-pay, a captain without a ship.

He envied his luckier fellow officers their moments of glory. He also envied them their prize money for he was endeavouring to run his home on a captain's half-pay of £120 a year, and with six rapidly growing daughters, his own and Elizabeth's needs, and the contribution towards a daily cleaning woman, this was not easy.

It was a worrying and frustrating time without even the escape previously afforded by writing, for although he was anxious to bring out another book to cover his second voyage, he was informed by the Admiralty that they were not prepared to contribute towards the cost of engraving the charts and drawings with which it was to be illustrated. In any case, he was bluntly told, there was a glut of such books at the moment. They were not interested.

Finally, Chatham, or one of his subordinates, relented and allowed Bligh to return to active service. On 30th April 1795 he was appointed captain of the *Calcutta*, a newly launched armed transport of twenty-four guns, with orders to report for duty under Admiral Adam Duncan, commander-in-chief of the North Sea fleet. It was a time of crisis for Britain, for the war on land was going badly. When it had begun Britain was allied to Spain, Holland, Austria and Prussia, but this unnatural coalition soon began to disintegrate.

One of the biggest setbacks was the invasion of Holland. Detachments of the British army were serving in this country, commanded by the Duke of York. He returned home in December 1794, leaving the chief command to General

Walmoden, a Hanoverian. Walmoden had gone into winter quarters on the Island of Bommel, quite forgetting that the thickness of the ice left him exposed on all sides. The French arrived in overwhelming numbers and after some severe fighting, the British were forced to retire, suffering terrible miseries from lack of food, tents and proper clothes although they repeatedly turned to engage the enemy before withdrawing from the country.

Holland then proclaimed herself a free Republic and Britain immediately began to seize the ships and colonies of her former ally. Some British fleets were constantly kept at sea to watch the French fleets which were lurking in the harbours of Brest and Toulon, others to intercept the homeward bound Dutch Indiamen.

Duncan's task was to blockade the Dutch ships anchored in the Texel, watching and waiting for an enemy that apparently preferred the comfort of his home base. The monotony was relieved at one time by the arrival of twelve ships-of-the-line and seven frigates flying a flag new to Bligh – that of Russia, now Britain's ally. These ships, however, were more of a hindrance than a help, being 'ill-found' and remarkably casual when it came to signals and normal fleet discipline. Duncan was glad to see them finally go.

The North Sea fleet was based at Yarmouth and from time to time, individual ships slipped back into this harbour to refit and reprovision. The weather was terrible, a continual series of gales that sent Duncan's ships pitching and tossing under scraps of canvas, driving them so far down to leeward that it was often several days before they painfully beat back to their stations. But the blockade went on with dour stubbornness and only once, during the two and a half years that Duncan kept his grip on the Dutch coast, did the enemy put to sea.

Early in January 1796, the *Calcutta* was ordered back to harbour and taken out of commission. Bligh, to his great joy, was given his first important command, the *Director*, a third-rate of sixty-four guns and with a complement of nearly 500 men. Happy with his new command although she was twelve years old, Bligh went back to the familiar ground off the Texel, back to the foul weather and long, monotonous days of blackade.

During the summer a French squadron had plundered the Newfoundland coast, gathered up a considerable number of

British merchantmen and managed to slip back to France, unobserved, through a thick fog. Some months later an invasion fleet from Brest managed to slip out and sail for Ireland with seventeen sail-of-the-line, four frigates, corvettes and brigs and six transports carrying 25,000 men. The fleet was met by a vicious storm and only seven ships-of-the-line and ten other vessels managed to reach the rendezvous, Bantry Bay. The storm continued to batter them and as there was no sign of the rest of the fleet, they returned to Brest. Hardly had they gone than more French ships arrived, also giving up the struggle against the elements to return to France. Not all returned, however. Of the forty-three sail, only thirty-nine managed to make port and thousands of the soldiers were drowned in the foundering transports.

Sir Edward Pellew, in the *Indefatigable*, 44, and Captain Reynolds in the *Amazon*, 36, fell in with the *Droits de l'Homme*, a seventy-four, and after a fierce fight south of Ushant, left her a grounded wreck. Out of her crew of 1,800 men, barely 300 were saved.

In October of 1796, Spain opted out of the coalition and declared war on Britain. With her armies defecting or being over-run it was apparent that Britain would soon be fighting the war on her own, a disturbing prospect, for her armies were continually being bested by those of France. In compensation, however, a great naval victory was won in February 1797 when Admiral John Jervis, with a fleet of fifteen ships-of-the-line smashed a fleet of twenty-six Spanish ships giving Jervis a new title, that of Earl St Vincent. It was remarkable for a particular piece of bravery. One of his younger officers used a captured Spanish ship as a gangway across to another — a technique which was dubbed, with much justification, "Nelson's Patent Bridge".

At the end of April, Duncan took advantage of an easterly wind that he knew would keep the Dutch from coming out and led his fleet back to the shelter of the Yarmouth Roads. As the ships dropped anchor, Bligh learned of a situation which had already spread alarm and consternation throughout the country; a situation with which he was already painfully familiar — mutiny!

An atmosphere of insubordination was spreading throughout the fleet. Bligh noticed it amongst his own crew, and was compelled to order eleven floggings in two weeks, an unusual

occurrence for the *Director* which hitherto had been considered a
'happy ship'. Bligh, naturally sensitive on this subject, was
disturbed by this unrest but was unable to understand why men,
who up to this time had appeared conscientious and loyal, should
suddenly behave in a manner that was little short of mutinous.

What was happening on his ship, however, was indicative of
the restless spirit that was growing throughout the whole Navy.
It owed a great deal to the heady doctrine of equality and
fraternity that had sprung from the recent Revolutions in
America and France, encouraged by an avalanche of books and
pamphlets which helped spread the gospel. A wind of change
was blowing through the crowded, stinking lower-decks of the
men-of-war, fanned by men who, willy-nilly, were being
pitched into a service for which they had little aptitude and less
respect.

In time of peace, Britain's ships were manned by professional
seamen — the true volunteers — doing what they had elected to do
and obeying the orders of their superiors without question. Now,
with the war already in its fourth year, these men had become
outnumbered by reluctant conscripts whose continual
grumblings about the bad food and conditions and indeed, about
everything, began to affect the rest. Many of these newcomers
had been the victims of the 'press', that pernicious system
whereby anyone who did not possess 'protection' was caught up
in the vast, man-hungry net that was cast upon waterfronts from
Cornwall to Caithness. Most of these were simple enough
persons, uneducated for the most part and who, in time,
generally accepted their lot and frequently were turned into
excellent seamen.

In 1795, however, Pitt steered through a law which was to
bring in others. This was the Quota Act which obliged every
county and borough to produce a certain number of men for the
navy which because of the war, needed every man it could get,
for its strength had quadrupled since 1793. This Act encouraged
magistrates to hand over "rogues, vagabonds, smugglers,
embezzlers of naval stores and other able-bodied, idle and
disorderly persons" to the service. Amongst these 'quota men'
were large numbers of petty criminals — and worse — who
brought disease, crime and vice to the ships to which they were
drafted. Many brought something that was to prove even more
dangerous. These were the educated men — bankrupts,

embezzlers, lawyers, tradesmen and ruined sprigs of the nobility, men who were not prepared to accept conditions that others took for granted but were ready to use their knowledge and education to try and alter them. Many had Thomas Paine's work, *Rights of Man* with them when they were tossed into their various ships and they lost no time in passing on its inflammatory gospel to the hitherto generally complaisant Jacks.

One question that they kept raising was the vexed one of pay. For more than a century the wages of able seamen had remained at twenty-five shillings a month. That of the Merchant Navy, on the other hand, had steadily increased until at this time it had reached four pounds a month, whilst men manning the coal-ships in the North Sea were earning twice that amount for a single run. The merchant seaman, also, was sure of his money at the end of the voyage, whereas the naval seaman never knew when he would get paid. This particularly was true of pressed and quota men who received no advance of pay and did not get any wages at all unless they happened to be in a naval dockyard. Also – and this was a great source of contention – they did not receive their money in hard cash but in 'pay-tickets' which had to be encashed at the Pay Office.

This led to all manner of abuses. Sometimes a crew would be paid off from one ship but before it could present its tickets was turned over *en masse* to another ship for a cruise that might last several years. Men were compelled to send their tickets to their wives, and these unfortunate women often had to travel for miles to reach the Pay Office and then, being unable to understand the forms, they were often refused payment, and had to return home, frequently to hungry children, with nothing to show for their trouble but the piece of paper they had started with. The alternative was to sell the tickets elsewhere, at scandalously low rates of discount, to one of the legion of professional 'ticket-buyers' who shared their profits with others including, it was said, the Pay Office clerks themselves.

By the end of 1796 it was estimated that the arrears of pay owed to seamen amounted to nearly $1\frac{1}{2}$ million pounds, and this at a time when the country was pouring millions overseas to support her foreign allies.

The first major rumblings of discontent began during the winter of 1796-7 when Bligh was with Duncan and the North Sea fleet, blockading the Dutch who were lying in the Texel.

Lord Howe, who had commanded the more important Channel Fleet, had been forced through illness to resign his command and hand it over to Lord Bridport. Soon after his retirement to Bath, a number of seamen began to send Howe anonymous letters and Round Robins, relying on his well-known affection for his men. They wrote direct to him because they knew that any letter to the Admiralty would be referred back to their own officers and that should any of the writers be identified, they would undoubtedly be noted as trouble-makers.

Lord Howe, or "Black Dick" as the men called him, realized that the remonstrances he was receiving were couched in similar phraseology and dismissing them as the work of a few cranks, passed them on to the Admiralty for attention. As other letters arrived, however, he was compelled to take the correspondence more seriously, realizing that the unrest expressed by them could assume dangerous proportions. He consulted the Admiralty on the matter but was told that the whole affair was the work of a few mischievous persons who wished to bring scandal upon the government, and that much of it, in fact, was a political ruse by the Opposition who were encouraging a few malcontents for its own ends. Howe continued to be concerned, but did nothing more.

Realizing that the one man whom they hoped would have championed their cause had failed them, the seamen decided to take matters into their own hands and to act in unison when a suitable opportunity arose. This opportunity came on Saturday, 15th April 1797 when Lord Bridport, Vice-Admiral of England, made the signal for the Channel Fleet to weigh and drop down to St Helen's Anchorage. The hoist fluttered up to the yard-arms of his flagship, the massive first-rater *Queen Charlotte*, and revealed an order that should have spurred the thirteen hundred or so men under his command to a flurry of intense activity. Instead, it was the signal for them to man the flagship's fore shrouds and to give three cheers. Almost before these ended, answering cheers came rolling across the water from the other ships of the fleet. Whilst the officers looked at each other in disbelief, the men scampered below to work out the next move. The Mutiny of Spithead had begun.

The next day was Easter Sunday and a deputation of four seamen from each ship assembled on board the *Queen Charlotte* and conferred in the great cabin. Routine went on as usual, although during divine service, parties of seamen and marines rowed in procession through the anchored ships of the fleet. During the morning, the *Romney* began to weigh, preparatory to sailing as convoy to a fleet outward-bound for Newfoundland, but a deputation boarded her and her anchor stayed down.

After a while the committee emerged from Howe's old cabin in the *Queen Charlotte* and presented Lord Bridport, Sir Alan Gardner the Port-Admiral, and other senior officers with a courteous and well phrased petition. It set forth their simple and justifiable demands: that the pay of able-seamen be raised to a shilling a day, to bring them into line with soldiers; that their grievances regarding pensions and rations should be investigated; that reasonable leave should be given after a long voyage at sea in order that men might see their families and friends; that seamen wounded in action should remain on pay until they were recovered or were discharged and that everyone concerned with the mutiny should receive a full and free pardon from the King.

Until these requests were granted the fleet would remain at anchor.

When this petition was passed to London and was laid before the Lords Commissioners of the Admiralty, they were panicked into hurrying down to Portsmouth to treat with the delegates in person. This news broke in the newspapers and the mutiny became the main talking point in every public place, street corner and fireside, for the untarnished loyalty of the navy, supported by centuries of brilliant victories, had always been the theme dearest to an Englishman's heart. To a generation raised on songs and ballads about Jolly Jack Tars and of Britain Ruling the Waves, the suggestion that the great British Navy could no longer be depended upon, made the whole country feel suddenly naked and insecure, with its shores no longer safe from invasion and its hearths vulnerable to attack.

Despite the arrival of the First Lord himself and his imposing group of Lords Commissioners, the seamen at Spithead were determined not to relax their demands, whilst carefully abstaining from any act of violence or rudeness towards their officers who were, however, forbidden to go ashore. Any breach of discipline amongst their fellows, especially drunkenness, was severely punished, every ship in the fleet had a rope with a hangman's noose dangling from its fore-yard as a constant reminder to anyone who might be tempted to step out of line. At eight o'clock every morning, each ship gave three cheers and when the men of the *Royal William* omitted to do so, they were warned that if they refused to conform on the following morning they would get a broadside from the ships lying on either side of her.

The negotiations dragged on, the Lords of the Admiralty meeting daily with Lord Bridport, Sir Peter Parker and Admirals Gardner, Colpoys and Pole. These gentlemen, however, found it difficult to appreciate the implications of the situation, having had no experience of treating with men who they essentially regarded as automatons, ready to obey any command without question and to die without argument or complaint in the line of duty.

This attitude was typified by Admiral Gardner who stalked angrily to the forecastle of the *Royal George* to shout abuse at the seamen, accusing them of being "skulking fellows" who knew the French were ready for sea but were afraid to meet them, declaring that the reasons they gave for their disobediance were sheer hypocrisy and that the real reason was cowardice. Within moments the crew exploded into violence and in the ensuing scuffle the Admiral, suddenly regretting his own forthrightness, was nearly bundled overboard. He managed to struggle into the ship's hammock-nettings and placing his neck inside the noose of the rope-yard cried out to the men advancing towards him. "If you return to your duties, you may hang me at the yard-arm!"

This unexpected gesture appealed to the seamen who lustily cheered him and then escorted him off the ship.

Whilst the negotiations dragged on, the *Romney* was again ordered to put to sea, having received a signal that the convoy was under sail. Her crew wished to stay and see the results of the mutiny but was told by the delegates that "the country requires your services; you must, therefore, weigh anchor immediately and drop down to St Helen's". These orders were obeyed and the *Romney* duly sailed.

A form of agreement was reached at last but the delegates were naturally adamant on one point – a royal and general pardon for every man who had taken part in this very well conducted and almost 'gentlemanly' mutiny.

At 6.30 on the morning of Sunday, 23rd April, a tired courier arrived at Portsmouth with despatches from Windsor, having ridden the distance in seven hours. The Lords Commissioners

Lord "Black Dick" Howe by H. Singleton

Richard Parker, leader of the mutiny at the Nore, by W. Chamberlain

Deptford 1824 by W. Anderson

The Battle of Camperdown by de Loutherbourg

were informed and at 11 a.m. Lord Bridport stepped on board the *Royal George*, hoisted his flag and informed the ship's company that he had brought with him a redress for all their grievances and a full pardon from the King. Captains of other ships were then summoned to the *Royal George* to receive copies of the proclamation which they were directed, in turn, to read to their own crews. By 2 p.m. the whole fleet had learned the news and cheering spread across the anchorage.

Only the *Queen Charlotte* kept the red flag of mutiny flying because her two delegates were ashore and the remainder of the men would not act without them. They were fetched by boat, discussed the proclamation and advised the fleet to return to duty without delay. By 6 p.m. every red flag and yard-arm rope was hauled down and normal discipline was resumed.

But the 'Breeze at Spithead', as it became known, had not died away completely for as nothing seemed to happen, the red flags and yard-ropes were soon hoisted again. In the *London*, ninety-eight guns, Vice-Admiral Colpoys drew up his marines and prevented the delegates, who had arrived alongside in a boat, from coming on board. His own men then unlashed a gun and trundled it around so that its muzzle pointed at the quarterdeck. At this threat, Peter Bover, one of the *London*'s lieutenants, went forward, drew his pistol and ordered the men to stop what they were doing. When they jeered at him, daring him to fire, he did so, others followed and several of the seamen rolled onto the deck, three being mortally wounded. There was a rush for the quarterdeck, the marines threw down their muskets, and Bover soon had his neck inside the noose of the yard-rope, but Colpoys bravely stepped forward and shouted that the firing had been done by his orders. This started an argument, but there was no more bloodshed.

This incident was the only serious one in the whole mutiny which now needed the presence of the old and gouty Lord Howe to resolve it.

He came jolting down from London to be rowed from ship to ship to talk to the men, and after a great deal of discussion it was agreed that the crews would return to duty provided that certain officers were removed from their ships. Howe had to agree to this stipulation and a considerable number of naval and marine officers were sent ashore and replaced by others. The King's Pardon arrived on 9th May; and this time the 'breeze' had definitely blown itself out.

The following morning "Black Dick" was rowed through the fleet in one of a procession of boats, some of which carried bands and blared out "God Save the King" and "Rule Britannia" alternately. At the end of a long and hard day, he landed to receive the cheers of the largest gathering of people ever assembled at Portsmouth. The gallant old admiral smiled wearily in reply, stumbled forward to his carriage in which he slumped down, utterly exhausted. He was to die soon afterwards.

By this time, however, another mutiny was under way by comparison with which that at Spithead was a 'breeze' indeed. Bligh, innocently moving the *Director* round from Yarmouth to the Nore, was to find himself in the middle of it!

[13]

Mutiny at the Nore

BLIGH PICKED UP his cocked hat and cast a final look at himself in a small mirror placed near his cot. He was in full dress uniform, with the new fangled epaulettes heavy on his shoulders (they had been introduced two years earlier) and with gold stripes on his cuffs marking him as a captain with more than three years seniority. He settled his sword, then moved from his cabin onto the *Director*'s deck. As he appeared there came the shrilling of pipes and all came to attention until he had heaved himself down into the small boat that rose and fell with the gentle motion of the morning tide. He settled himself by the side of Mr Midshipman Purdue in the sternsheets and nodded briefly.

The youngster cleared his throat, looked along the length of the boat where four stolid seamen, two a side, sat with the blades of their oars pointing towards the sky, whilst a coxswain, boat-hook in hand, crouched in the bows and looked back for orders.

"Larboard oars!" Purdue said, and two blades smacked the water. "Shove off cox'n," and the bows of the boat slid away from the dark, weather-stained timbers of the ship. "Starboard oars!" then, "Give way together!"

Bligh stared upwards, his eye running over details which could only be seen from outside the ship – the condition of the hull, paintwork and her trim, then he looked higher, studying the rake of the masts, the precision of the yards with their white threads of canvas set in a neat harbour stow. The *Director* was a typical sixty-four of some 1400 tons, with twenty-six twenty-four-pounders on her lower-deck, twenty-six eighteen-pounders on her upper deck, ten nine-pounders on the quarterdeck and two more nine-pounders on her forecastle. Her class, which had superseded the old seventies was also disappearing and within a few years was to become almost extinct. Yet to Bligh, at this moment, she was beautiful, as well as being a compact fighting machine. And she was his to command.

Yet, even as he looked at her, he was uneasy. There was this spirit of unrest which was so disturbing. The previous day he had received a deputation from the crew requesting – no, ordering – that two of his lieutenants, Ireland and Church, together with Mr Birch the master, should be dismissed from duty for ill-treatment. He had temporized, saying that the matter would be looked into, and he was aware that later in the day it was something that would have to be faced. But at the moment he had other duties on his mind. He had been ordered by Vice-Admiral Charles Buckner, commanding the Medway and the Nore, to attend a court-martial on a Captain Savage, to be held on board the *Inflexible*, another sixty-four, that was anchored nearby. Other captains were to come from the *Montagu*, 74, and another six sixty-fours, *Monmouth, Repulse, Nassau, Lion, Standard* and *Belliqueux* and also the *Isis*, fifty guns. Buckner, as President of the Court, was coming from his flagship, the *Sandwich*.

This had been originally a ninety-gun ship but had been converted into a receiving ship. All but her upper-deck guns had been removed and now her middle and lower decks were crowded with some 500 pressed and quota men awaiting allocation to ships of the North Sea fleet. Because of the dangers of desertion, none of them was allowed to go ashore and they had little to do but sit around, complain and ... plot.

Amongst the quota men was a man who had been sent down from Scotland where he had been arrested for debt. His name, Richard Parker, was soon to become well-known throughout the country. Parker had served in the navy before, having been a midshipman in the *Culloden* and *Leander*, from both of which he had been discharged for immoral behaviour. He was subsequently disrated, sent before the mast and then invalided into hospital. Managing to get away from this hospital he turned up again, some years later, as a school-teacher in Scotland. By then he was thirty years old, a fully trained sailor, well educated and a fluent and persuasive speaker.

He soon established himself as a leader amongst the other unfortunates in the *Sandwich* and when the news of the first mutiny arrived, he had no difficulty in persuading them to join him in another similar to that staged by their brothers at Spithead. The date was to be Friday, 12th May; the time, 9.30 a.m.

Not a word of his plans leaked out, even though messages were passed in and out of the *Sandwich*'s lower ports and smuggled aboard ships at the anchorage. As it happened, Parker could not have picked a better date or time, for Buckner had chosen the same day for the court-martial, to begin at 8.30 a.m. This meant that all captains were absent from their ships at this crucial moment.

Having been rowed round his ship, Bligh looked at his watch and saw that it was just on the hour. Indeed, as he was returning the watch to his pocket, the double strokes of eight bells sounded through the anchorage.

As the boat moved steadily along, Bligh stared around at the crowded anchorage, the busiest stretch of water in Britain. In addition to the naval ships that anchored here – ships from every fleet currently on station – others passed through to enter the victualling base at Sheerness or negotiated the bends and twists of the Medway to arrive at Chatham dockyard. There was also a constant flow of merchantmen from London, either entering or clearing the Thames, together with hundreds of small coastal vessels which carried nearly all the country's merchandise, for it was to be more than a quarter of a century before the railways began operation.

Soon the dark bulk of the *Inflexible* loomed up ahead and as the gig drew near there came a shout from overhead, "Boat ahoy!"

The coxswain looked back at Bligh, received an affirmative nod then bawled back, "*Director!*" the one word being sufficient to tell the officer of the watch that a captain was about to come on board. A few minutes later Bligh was stepping onto the deck of the sixty-four to the twittering of pipes, his hand held rigidly to his hat in salute until the officer of the watch stepped forward to usher him aft. He was shown into the cabin of Captain Ferris, the *Inflexible*'s commander who rose hurriedly as the other entered and the two captains chatted, breaking off from time to time as other captains arrived and were introduced. Just before one bell there came louder twitterings and the boom of a gun to announce Buckner's arrival.

The members of the court took their seats in the great cabin, Captain Savage was brought in, and the trial began. It was proceeding at a leisurely pace when there came a loud and quite unexpected burst of cheering from the direction of the *Sandwich*, followed by cheers from other ships and even from the very ship in which they were sitting. Buckner paused, looked around the cabin in consternation then rose hastily, spilling a pile of papers as he did so and pausing only a moment to shout, "Court adjourned," made hurriedly for the door. The rest of the captains were close behind him and they arrived at the entry-port, jostling each other as they called for their boats, conscious that they were looking ridiculous in front of the now silent men who thronged the *Inflexible*'s forecastle and foreshrouds.

Bligh's boat was soon bumping alongside the *Director* and he stepped onto the deck, looking round to see what was happening. As far as he could determine, only two things had changed. A red flag was now flying at the masthead and an ominous noose was swaying from the fore yard-arm in the gentle May breeze. Otherwise nothing appeared to have altered. He was still received by the boatswain's pipes and a detachment of marines presented arms, but he knew that during his brief absence the ship was no longer under his command.

He forced himself to remain calm and placid and with his face quite expressionless, clasped his hands behind his back and strolled slowly to the quarterdeck and then to the poop. When there he turned and looked forward along the 150-odd feet of white deck that stretched away to the bows, and waited. Now knowing what had happened, he was prepared to let the next move come from the men. Very slowly they began to sidle aft, doing their best to appear nonchalant and unconcerned, looking everywhere but at the upright, lonely figure that waited for them at the quarterdeck rail. Soon the entire ship's company seemed to be below him, looking up, waiting for someone to take the lead.

That someone came at last, pushing through the press of men to mount the ladder to the poop. He was closely followed by another. Both men knew Bligh well and his eyebrows lifted in surprise, for he would have been prepared to wager that neither of them had mutinous tendencies. The men, John Hulme and James MacLaurin, stood before him, twisting their hats – which they had automatically removed – in their hands. There was a long silence, broken only by the shuffling of some of the men below and by an occasional cough. Bligh waited, feeling very alone, for he could see none of his other officers. He was soon to know why. Two of his best officers and his master had gone, put off whilst he was still at the court-martial. The men had worked very quickly indeed.

He was told that his men had nothing against him, personally, and that they would continue to obey orders except that they would not take the ship to sea until their requests had been agreed. When Bligh asked what these requests were MacLaurin thrust a sheaf of paper into his hand. He glanced down at them.

The writing was good and had obviously been done by a scholar. Promising to read them over in his cabin, Bligh raised his hat to the crew, received a cheer in reply, then walked aft. He was relieved to see that the bunch of keys which contained those belonging to the small-arms chest were still there and the memory of that other mutiny, eight years earlier, flashed into his mind. Then, the possession of the small-arms had played a vital part in the success of that mutiny and he was surprised that during his absence someone had not gone straight to his cabin and secured the keys. He looked around for a suitable hiding place, found one, then began to read the papers. They were obviously the draft of a manifesto to be issued later and gave the list of items which the mutineers insisted should be put right before returning to normal duty. As he read them, Bligh found himself agreeing that many seemed long overdue for revision.

When he had finished he stood up and changed back into normal uniform. That done, he stood irresolute, not sure what he should do next, for he was in a most unusual position — the captain of a ship in which there appeared to be perfect discipline, yet knowing that he was only in command by sufferance. He moved across to the stern windows and peered out. There appeared to be a great deal of activity; boats were criss-crossing between the various ships from one of which, the *Swan*, sloop of sixteen guns, there came the sound of confused shouting. As he watched, a boat moved away from this sloop and headed straight for the *Director*.

It moved out of the line of vision and he turned and stared along the black, shiny barrel of one of the two eighteen-pounders that seemed to dominate his cabin and waited until the boat once more came into view as it ran alongside. A burly looking seaman, cutlass in hand and with a pair of pistols stuck pirate fashion in his belt, stood up in the sternsheets then clambered on board the *Director*. There seemed to be a long argument between him and the two ship's delegates then after a while Hulme came aft and asked Bligh for permission to have some arms and also to use one of the ship's boats.

Bligh shook his head firmly. "No." he replied. "No boat, and definitely no arms."

Hulme took this reply back to the newcomer who, Bligh learned later, was Thomas McCann, a delegate from the *Sandwich* and sent by Parker, now undisputed leader of the mutineers.

There was a great deal of abuse and Bligh, wishing to hear what was said, moved out of his cabin and stood at the break of the poop.

"If I was one of you," McCann was shouting, "I'd know how to deal with that Bounty bastard!"

"That Bounty bastard!" That was the first time that Bligh had heard himself called that, although he realized from the familiar way in which the expression came out that this must have been his nickname around the fleet for some time. The shouting went on, McCann appearing to be as much enraged with the crew of the *Director* as he was with Bligh. At last, after a few final epithets, the delegate turned and still grasping his cutlass, climbed awkwardly back into the boat. Alone and unarmed, Bligh watched him go and grinned. The delegate had not been so brave after all.

The following day the *San Fiorenzo*, frigate, arrived at the Nore and the mutineers, believing that she had come to join them, cheered her vociferously as she anchored. As it happened she was a loyal ship and her captain Sir Harry Neale, realizing from the display of red flags what was going on, ordered his men not to return the cheers. This was a direct challenge to Parker, now calling himself President of the Floating Republic, and he ordered the *Flexible* to range up alongside and fire a warning shot. One was enough. The men of the *San Fiorenzo* obediently returned the cheers and rove a yard-rope noose, although this was only a pretence of solidarity for they, like the men of the *Clyde*, a thirty-eight-gun frigate, were still loyal.

On 19th May Bligh received the order he had been expecting for nearly a week. During the morning a number of delegates arrived and told him that he must leave his ship and to hand over the command to his first lieutenant, John McTaggart. He was rowed ashore, with three of his young midshipmen, and for some days was in Sheerness, awaiting further orders. They came on the 25th, in a letter marked Secret and Private, and were from Evan Nepean, Secretary of the Admiralty. He was ordered to go to Yarmouth, make contact with Admiral Duncan and hand him the despatches which had accompanied his orders. There was also a letter to Duncan which read:

We send you Captain Bligh on a very delicate business on which the Government is extremely anxious to have your opinion. The welfare and almost the existence of the country may depend upon what is the event of this very important crisis. But till we know what we can look to from your squadron it will be very difficult for us to know how to act.

EVAN NEPEAN

At the same time, Earl Spencer, the First Lord of the Admiralty was penning a note to the King, telling him that Bligh was off on a most important mission which could, he hoped, bring the mutiny to an end.

Bligh set off at once but arrived too late. Duncan had returned to his blockading station and Bligh arrived in time to see the ships which had sailed with him return to Yarmouth Roads with their crews cheering and bands playing as if they had won a victory instead of deserting their admiral. For that was what they had done, turning back when only a few miles from harbour, leaving Duncan in his flagship, the *Venerable* with *Adamant*, the only other ship-of-the-line which had remained loyal. Bligh had himself rowed around the fleet but had little success. Many of the men lounging at the entry ports recognized him and he was told, "Fend off. We don't want you Bounty Bastard on board our ship. Off with you. Ship's boats only."

Only in one ship, the *Glatton*, was he received with anything like courtesy and realizing that he could do no more, he returned to London to report in person. He was then sent back to Sheerness under orders to join an anti-mutiny command, for the Admiralty considered that with his past experience in the *Bounty*, he could contribute quite a lot. He was subsequently thanked by the Admiralty for the work he did amongst the malcontents, convincing many of them of the advantages of returning to duty.

In this he had much success for, by now, the mutineers were becoming desperate. They tried other measures. The Thames was blockaded and more than a hundred and fifty colliers were detained, whilst the few small vessels that got through the cordon only did so when armed with a passport signed, Richard Parker, President. But they were also running short of provisions and were forced to add piracy to mutiny. In addition to unloading the cargoes of any ships carrying foodstuffs up-river, they also landed on the Islands of Sheppey and Grain and carried away the cattle and sheep. This act, coupled with the defection of most of Duncan's squadron which had left Britain open to an invasion from Holland, forced the Government to take most drastic measures. From that moment their plans to deal with the mutiny took on all the characteristics of civil war.

Loyal ships-of-the-line were readied for an attack on those at the Nore; troops and volunteers began to march into Sheerness; the officers of the East India Company, the Waterman's Company and members of Trinity House also sent down hundreds of volunteers whilst large sums were subscribed, and rewards offered, for all who would help end the mutiny. Batteries were erected on both sides of the Thames and Medway and the buoys, beacons and even lightships were removed, making it impossible to navigate the intricate channels.

On 6th June came the blow that was to speed the end — an Act of Parliament that made all communication with the mutineers an indictable offence.

That day, however, saw fresh activity at the Nore. The *San Fiorenzo* and the *Clyde* had managed to escape a week earlier and encouraged by this, the *Serapis*, forty-four guns, and a sloop of war, the *Discovery*, also made a dash for freedom under the guns of the whole fleet, and although damaged, successfully got away. Unfortunately, at this critical time, when these new desertions might have dissolved the mutinous confederacy, the *Agamemnon, Ardent, Leopard* and *Isis*, four ships-of-the-line, sailed in from Yarmouth. Their arrival was a great fillip to the morale of Parker and his delegates and that night effigies of 'Billy Pitt' and Henry Dundas, Secretary of War swung from their yard-arms.

A day or so later, the *Leopard* managed to get away, the loyal men amongst her crew fighting with the mutineers, even whilst setting sails and handling the ship. The *Repulse*, 64, followed but immediately ran onto a sandback and lay exposed to the fire of the whole fleet for an hour and twenty minutes. Those ships whose guns could not bear, got springs onto their cables and the *Director, Monmouth* and *Isis* were particularly active in firing at the helpless vessel. The men of the *Agamemnon* begged that they too might be allowed to fire to prove that they were still with Parker, but deliberately pointed their guns so that every shot went wide of its mark.

The men in the *Repulse* did not return the fire but were busy lightening the ship, and she finally floated off with the tide to reach the safety of Sheerness.

The *Ardent*, 64, cut her cables and taking advantage of the confusion, set her fore-topsails and moved past the fleet, coming under fire from the *Sandwich, Inflexible* and other ships, but also got away, after ripping a broadside into a ship that tried to come across her bows.

These defections had a dampening effect on the spirits of the crews in those ships that remained. Soon only half of the twenty ships at the Nore were flying the red flag, whilst their crews of the others passed a vote of no confidence in Parker and his committee in the *Sandwich*. On the still-mutinous ships, orders and counter-orders followed rapidly, and as each prevailed the red flag and the union colours were alternately hoisted and lowered. Arguments were continually breaking out in nearly every ship, even the delegates cursing and swearing at each other and occasionally coming to blows. Parker was desperately trying to keep the men in one mind and accompanied by the principal members of his committee, visited every ship in turn. Whilst on one of them, someone brought up the rumour that he had lined his pockets with money that had been entrusted to him by the seamen.

"That is entirely false," he exclaimed, vehemently. "The fact is, I owe my washer-woman eighteen pence, and don't even have the money to pay her."

At this confession, one of the assembled men echoed the thoughts of the rest when he shouted back, "Why then, you're a precious admiral indeed!"

Flags of truce began to pass between the mutinous ships and the shore, the chief activity being on the part of the Admiralty which, with a strong fleet standing by to attack, was naturally concerned about the safety of numbers of loyal officers who were still held prisoner in some of the rebel ships. The firm attitude shown by the Government, the silence of the King to any petitions sent to him, the gathering of armed forces on land and of ships at sea made the mutineers realize at last that only a miracle could save them. Some of the hot-heads began to speak of taking the fleet to France, to Ireland, to America or to a country where they could sell the ships and live on the proceeds. This needed leadership, however, and Parker's days as 'President' were nearly over and no one else seemed anxious to take over the responsibility for what had patently become a lost cause.

On Friday 9th June, Parker made the order for the ships to weigh. The fore-topsail of the *Sandwich* was loosed, a gun was fired and the signal was answered by all the ships. For the first time for some days, the wind was favourable – a fresh breeze from the south-east. But the signal was not obeyed. The capstans were not manned, no one went aloft to shake out the sails; the fleet stayed where it was.

Early on the morning of the 13th, *Agamemnon, Standard* and *Vestal* slipped their cables and stood away up the Thames, followed soon afterwards by the *Nassau* and *Isis* and before nightfall, by the *Lion*, not a gun being fired to deter them. By the next day only one red flag was seen to be flying in the few ships that were left – in Parker's 'flagship', the *Sandwich*. Thinking that he might escape after all, a reward of five hundred pounds was offered for his capture and his description was circulated.

Richard Parker is about thirty years of age; wears his own hair, which is black, untied, though not cropt; about five feet nine or ten inches high, has a rather prominent nose, dark eyes and complexion, and thin visage; is generally slovenly dressed in a plain blue half-worn coat, and a whitish or light-coloured waistcoat, and half-boots.

But there was no need for this. At three o'clock in the afternoon of the 14th the *Sandwich* stood in for the Little Nore, a white flag flying at her maintop. A guard of the West Yorks Militia were sent to board her and found very few men on deck. A lieutenant and a party went below and arrested the subdued 'Admiral' who offered no resistance, submitting to having his hands manacled behind his back, then taken off with Davies, his second in command. As he stepped ashore at the Commissioners' Stairs a hostile crowd pressed around him and he shouted out, "Don't shoot me; it's not my fault. I will clear myself, you see."

Other ships sailed in to give themselves up, the last of all being the *Director*, and Lord Keith was able to send a telegraph message to the Admiralty which said, "The mutiny which prevailed among the ships at the Nore seems to be quite extinguished".

By the time every ship in the fleet had surrendered its delegates and committee men there were 560 men imprisoned. The Sheerness gaols were bulging with men, as were the garrison chapel and the lower deck of the *Aeolus*, frigate. Fearing another outbreak, the Admiralty rushed through Parker's trial. It took place on board the *Neptune*, ninety guns, on Thursday 22nd June, with Vice-Admiral Sir Thomas Pasley as President and a commodore and ten captains forming the court. In spite of the great ill-feeling that had been aroused throughout the nation by the actions of Parker and his delegates, the four-day court-martial was extremely fair. The verdict, however, was inevitable. Parker was sentenced to be hanged.

The day fixed for the execution was 27th June and a large number of ships were brought into the Medway so that their crews could witness the punishment for daring to flout authority. The ships lay anchored, bow to stern − line-of-battle ships, frigates, sloops of war and armed transports − with the occasional space between them packed with yachts and boats, some perilously close to sinking from the weight of the sightseers packed on them.

At the head of this line was the gallows ship, ironically the *Sandwich*, which for a brief moment of infamous glory had been Parker's 'flagship'.

Many of the ships had had a change of officers for a considerable number − more than a hundred officers out of a fleet of sixteen ships − had been removed as being unfit to command, or because of their flagrant ill-treatment of their men. When Lord Howe studied the lists and the reasons given he stated that in a number of cases "mere removal was an insufficient punishment for some of those who were complained of".

Bligh had come out of it very well. He had stayed on his ship longer than most of the other captains and had helped his superiors whilst ashore, for which he had been brought to the notice of the King. He was formally confirmed in his command and went back to the *Director* where he found an exhausted McTaggart only too happy to welcome him aboard and to hand the ship back to its rightful captain.

On the morning of 27th, Bligh called his crew to attention at 7.45 and the ship's company with the seamen in the forecastle and officers and marines on the quarterdeck, waited in the bright summer sunshine for the whole sad business to begin. On the other ships, hundreds of officers and men were also shuffling into position, then a strange hush fell upon the scene, a hush broken only by heedless shouts from sightseers ashore or by the crying of a child too young to know that it was present at a historical occasion. In this strange silence, the sound of tramping feet echoed loudly as men of the East and West Yorks Militia and the West Norfolks, followed by walking invalids from the naval hospital, marched in single files along the south shore of the Medway to draw up on the waterfront facing the *Sandwich*. Behind them rattled a battery of horse drawn guns.

As the ships' bells began to make the hour, there came a flat boom from a single gun fired on *L'Espion*, flying the flag of Vice-Admiral Skeffington Lutwidge, who had succeeded Buckner as Port-Admiral, whilst a yellow flag — the signal for capital punishment — broke at her maintop. At the sound of the gun there was a stir amongst the ships as a boat, containing a lieutenant and a party of marines pulled away from each, and made for the *Sandwich* to attend the execution.

At 8.30 Parker was brought onto the *Sandwich*'s quarterdeck where he spent some time with the ship's chaplain then, asking for a glass of wine, lifted it and said, "I drink first to the salvation of my soul; and next to the forgiveness of all my enemies". He shook hands with the ship's commander, Captain James Mosse, and was led forward to the forecastle, passing through a double file of marines on the starboard side, then onto a platform that had been erected on the cat-head and which had a further projection that would enable the thousands of onlookers to have a better view of his last moments. The warrant of execution was read by a clerk and when it was ended, Parker asked if he might say a few words. Seeing Mosse hesitate he added, "I am not going to address the ship's company, sir; I wish only to declare that I acknowledge the justice of the sentence under which I suffer; and I hope my death may be considered a sufficient atonement, without involving the fate of others."

He then requested "a minute to collect himself", knelt for a moment in prayer then rising, said firmly, "I am ready".

The deputy Provost-Marshall stepped forward to put the noose about his neck, but being both nervous and awkward, bungled the task and finally Parker turned to the boatswain's mate and said, "Do you do it, for he seems to know nothing about it". The provost then tried to put a hood over his face but Parker protested that he would not agree to this unless it was kept from his eyes until he said otherwise. The prisoner then turned and smiled at some of the members of the crew who had been his messmates and calmly remarked to Captain Mosse, "Is the gun primed and the match lit?"

"All is ready," the other replied.

Although the noose was already about his neck, Parker stepped forward a few paces and asked some officers and guests standing near, "Will any gentleman be so kind as to lend me a white handkerchief for the signal?"

One was handed to him and bowing, he thanked the guest who had been so obliging then, walking back onto the platform, again repeated the questions about the gun, receiving the same answer. He paused, a lonely dark figure, outlined against the brilliant June sky. A group of seamen stood by with one end of the rope, another group, bent about a gun, watched for the signal but with a suddenness that took them all by surprise he leapt forward into the air and his body dropped, slowly revolving, in space. The bow-gun boomed and a gout of white smoke circled around then drifted lazily towards the still water. At the same time the gallows rope, squeaking loudly in its sheave, began to hoist the body slowly towards the yard-arm. Thousands of pairs of eyes watched as it moved upwards and then there came a sudden, indrawn gasp as halfway to the yard-arm the body seemed to convulse, jerking on the rope as if it was still alive. This lasted for only a few seconds, however, and then the dark, shapeless bundle that once had been a man, hung quietly and at peace.

As the death gun boomed, Bligh turned to McTaggart. "Dismiss the ship's company," he said, and walked slowly to his cabin, leaving many of his men on deck, staring as if hypnotized at the *Sandwich*'s fore-yard. It was exactly 9.30 a.m.

Although a large number of men were deported, many to the growing convict settlement of Botany Bay, only some thirty were executed, the Admiralty showing considerable leniency in view of the graveness of the whole affair and the jeopardy into which it had placed the nation in time of war.

Although the mutinies were over at Spithead and the Nore, other outbreaks occurred in other parts of the world when news of what had happened reached those distant parts.

There was a mutiny at the Cape which was firmly suppressed by the governor, Lord Macartney, who threatened to sink the rebellious ships which were then anchored under the guns of his batteries.

Another was off Cadiz where Lord St Vincent was bombarding the city. The admiral, however, was backed by his officers and a considerable number of loyal men and was soon able to quash the outbreak although to do so he was compelled to hang a considerable number of mutineers, especially from ships which were joining his fleet from England. Finally the blunt old seaman exploded with, "Why do they send me mutinous ships?

Do they think I will be hangman to the fleet?"

The Great Naval Mutiny, although regarded by the seamen as a failure, had an important outcome. It stimulated a full enquiry into the causes that had provoked it and this led, in time, to a considerable number of improvements in the service.

Lord Horatio Nelson
by L. F. Abbott

The Battle of Copenhagen by Pocock

Bligh's tomb in Lambeth Parish churchyard

[14]

Camperdown

BLIGH WAS WORKING in his cabin when an excited midshipmen burst in to inform his captain that the Admiral was flying a signal ordering all ships to weigh at once and proceed to sea. The Dutch were out!

Within seconds Bligh was on the *Director*'s poop deck where his first lieutenant was waiting to tell him he had called all hands to stations and that the women were being bundled out of the ship.

"Thank you Mr McTaggart," Bligh replied. "We'll get under weigh as soon as convenient."

"Aye, aye, sir," the other replied and, picking up a speaking trumpet, settled himself firmly on two stout legs to begin the stream of orders that would transform the *Director* from an assembly of wood, iron and canvas into a vibrant thing of beauty and grace, responsive to the lightest touch on her helm and to the action of wind and wave.

"Hands to the capstan. Loose heads'ls. Hands aloft to loose tops'ls!"

There was a sudden flurry of activity, the patter of bare feet on the deck planking, then the ship fell quiet again with faces turned aft, awaiting the next order. It soon came.

"Heave short!" and the capstan pawls began their clack, clack as the dripping cable began to feed through the hawse-hole.

"Hove short, sir," came from the boatswain's mate at the capstan, indicating that only a few fathoms of the anchor cable remained in the water. McTaggart paused, squinting up into the morning sunlight to make sure that the boys were properly stationed aloft to overhaul the running gear whilst the sails were set. Satisfied on this point he raised his trumpet again and bawled, "Set the tops'ls!"

There came the crack and flutter of canvas as the three yards were hoisted and the large sails sheeted home. The hands tailed onto the braces, heaving the yards around so that the sails on the main and mizzen were just filling whilst that on the foremast was aback, giving the ship sternway.

"Up and down," came the second lieutenant's shout from the forecastle to be answered by McTaggart's, "Break her out!"

To the stamp of a hundred men, the ponderous anchor was wrenched from the sea bed and, free from its restriction, the *Director* began to move, pivoting with the backed foresail, canting her bows until she was headed in the right direction, then she began to settle sweetly onto her new course, all hands at the braces hauling until the foresail filled on the port track. The time was a little after noon. She was under weigh.

"Let go all!" and the masts began to blossom with white canvas until, from courses to royals, from headsails to spankers, she was moving forward under all plain sail.

That immediate task over, Bligh automatically adjusted himself to the heel of the ship and looked about him. Some of the other vessels were still at anchor, others were ranging up alongside his own, a few were ahead. By this time a dozen or so ships-of-the-line and six smaller vessels were working through the Yarmouth Roads, their bows pointing towards the open sea. This was a critical moment for although the anchorage was a mile wide the ships had to keep clear of each other whilst picking a delicate course across the Yarmouth Sands, and Bligh called William Foote, his third lieutenant to his side, to assist him with the navigation, leaving the first and second lieutenants to range the deck and make sure that everything, below and aloft, was secure, for a hasty departure from harbour had a tendency to catch out the unwary.

With the north-east wind straining her canvas the *Director* moved on until the bobbing buoys that marked the gatways slipped astern and he could relax.

After a while he saw the tall figure of his first lieutenant amidships and called out, "Mr McTaggart. You may dismiss the watch below and send the hands to breakfast when you think proper."

Robert Lightfoot, one of his midshipmen, stood by him with the signal book whilst William Eldridge, another midshipman, also moved to his side with slate and pencil ready to write down the signals and changes of course for the log. Bligh lifted a large telescope to his eye and steadying himself against the mizen shrouds, swung it onto the flagship, away on the starboard beam.

A group of figures on the seventy-four's quarterdeck leapt into focus and he was easily able to pick out the massive six-feet-four-inch tall figure of Duncan. It had been a very frustrating time for the amiable giant. After long and hard months of blockade he had come back to harbour to find himself in the midst of the mutiny and when he had set sail for the Texel once again, only one other ship – the *Adamant* – followed. He was forced to patrol up and down with these two ships, always keeping in sight of the Dutch look-outs stationed on the Texel, and the low-lying coastline of the West Frisians, even anchoring in the Texel Channel itself, whilst making signals to a fleet that appeared to be just over the horizon – a fleet that existed only in his imagination and in the minds of the enemy.

With his own seventy-four and fifty-gun *Adamant* he flaunted his flag before a fleet that consisted of nearly a hundred stout Dutch ships including fourteen sail-of-the-line, commanded by the thirty-three-year old Admiral Jan de Winter, a fleet that could have swept aside the tiny blockading fleet with contemptuous ease. By then even the Russians had gone. Mackaroff, their admiral, had hoisted a signal and without any prior discussion with Duncan, the entire fleet of eighteen ships slipped away over the horizon and were not seen again.

By mid-June both the *Venerable* and *Adamant* were foul, leaking and 'cranky', provisions were perilously low and typhus was breaking out. But by then the recently mutinous ships were slipping back to join him and by the end of the month he was almost up to full strength again. Determined to stamp out any last remnants of insubordination, he kept the fleet at sea for nineteen weeks until strained by sudden summer gales, with the drinking water becoming green with scum and with more signs of the dreaded scurvy breaking out in some of the ships, he was forced to return to Yarmouth at the beginning of October, leaving the *Russell*, 74, *Adamant* and *Circe*, frigate, with a handful of cutters to maintain the blockade.

Inevitably, within a few days of his departure, the Dutch emerged from the harbour in which they had sheltered for two years to run down the coast. Captain Henry Trollope in the *Russell* saw them coming out almost with disbelief, then hastily despatched the *Active*, to carry the news to Duncan. It was the cutter's arrival at the back of Yarmouth Sands that brought the North Sea fleet scrambling out to sea. And now, if fate was kind, the long awaited confrontation was ahead.

Within the hour the fleet was in the prescribed two columns, the leading ships shortening sail to allow those which had been slow in clearing harbour to get up with them and take their stations. During the afternoon the *Venerable* backed her fore topsail to lose way, whilst another cutter, the *Vestal*, brought Duncan fresh news of the enemy. Realizing that every captain must be consumed with curiosity, Duncan began a series of hoists that spelled out the fact that the Dutch had quitted the Texel on the morning of the 7th with a fleet of fifteen ships-of-the-line, four frigates and some smaller vessels and when last seen had the *Russell* and *Adamant* shadowing them.

The 7th; that meant that the enemy had been at sea for two days. Time enough for them to have turned, crushed the small English squadron and got back to the safety of the Texel.

The fleet sailed on, shortening sail for the night, the ships in each column following the bobbing stern lanterns of the vessel ahead until the morning light revealed a depressingly empty horizon and no sign of the enemy. Another day crawled past and the morning of the 11th broke fine and clear but with ominous clouds banking up to the westward. Two bells in the forenoon watch had just been made when the topsails of Trollope's ships lifted above the horizon with an urgent signal flying from the *Beaulieu*, frigate; ENEMY IN SIGHT.

The Dutchmen were to the south-west, sailing close in to the shore somewhere near the village of Kamperduin, heading for the Texel. Almost as soon as their hulls became visible, the signal broke from the *Venerable*'s yard-arm ... thirteen. This time no one needed a signal book to decipher *that* order. PREPARE FOR BATTLE.

Lightfoot passed it on, nevertheless, and the three words sent a sudden thrill of anticipation coursing through Bligh's body. A battle was inevitable and he found himself remembering the last in which he had taken part at the Dogger Bank, sixteen years before. Then he had been master, one whose duty was primarily to obey. Now, as captain, of a third-rate, which carried twice as many guns as the old *Belle Poule*, to him alone was the responsibility for the decisions, the orders. How he handled his ship during the coming battle could further his career or bring him before a court-martial. It could, quite possibly bring injury or death.

But even whilst these thoughts were flashing through his mind, McTaggart was bellowing the orders through his speaking trumpet that started off young Thomas Grundy, the marine drummer, tapping his staccato rattle to the beat of "Heart of Oak" that brought the ship suddenly alive, as nearly five hundred men began to ready the ship for the coming fight. Bulkheads came down, the light wooden screens being easily knocked from their slides and hurried down to the hold together with tables, chairs, forms and anything else that, being of wood, might spread a shower of deadly splinters if struck.

At the same time the topmen swarmed aloft, reaving preventer-lifts, slinging the lower yards with chain before slipping into the tops to test their swivel guns and to lay muskets, pistols and hand grenades ready to hand. The buckets handing on the quarterdeck rail were filled, other buckets of water were placed in the chains and head, whilst pumps were rigged in case any shot came in below the water-line. Boys scampered over the deck, sprinkling sand to make the planking moist against fire and to give a better foothold.

Other men were taking up their stations on the middle and lower decks and as he stood reflectively at the rail, looking down at this orderly bustle, Bligh saw Samuel Dickson, the schoolmaster stand for a moment to stare about him as if for the last time, before descending to the cockpit where Thomas Herron the surgeon was already preparing the small space that was to receive and deal with the maimed and mangled bodies that would soon be passed down from above. As Dickson paused, he was joined by Robert Burrows the ship's chaplain, and the two men finally disappeared from sight down the first of the ladders that led to the small, airless cockpit well below the water-line.

At the same time, powder-boys were running down to the magazine, one deck lower still, to receive their 'salt-boxes' of cartridges for the first broadsides. The hatches were closed, only the small fore and aft hatches being left open with a marine posted at each to prevent anyone other than powder-boys and midshipmen trying to creep away to the deceptive safety of the darkness of the orlop-deck.

Then came the heavy rumble of the guns as the crews threw off the frappings of the breeches and heaved away at the train tackles to draw the monsters inboard so that powder and shot could be rammed home. This ominous sound had been heard many times during the years of blockade, but that was only in practice. Now it was a prelude to battle and Bligh experienced the dull pain in his stomach that always preceded violent action. But to outward appearances he was completely calm and the smile he gave Thomas Davey, captain of the marines as resplendent in red and gold he marched aft with Lieutenant Weir and a company of their men, was warm and relaxed.

Nettings were roused out and hauled into position, covering the ship's sides from bow to stern as a protection against boarders, whilst another net was slung above the deck as a protection from falling yards and other debris, a net curiously known as the *sauve tête*.

Then all this activity suddenly ceased and Bligh automatically pulled out his watch. The ship had 'cleared' in under eleven minutes, a good time. He carefully slipped his watch back into his pocket and took a turn up and down the narrow limits of the poop, the marines and midshipmen edging back to give him room. He paused at either bulwark, turning slowly, staring about him. There ahead, only dimly seen because of a thickening mist was the Dutch fleet, something less than a score of ships, strung out in line ahead with frigates and smaller ships nearer to the shore, sailing on the larboard tack, north-east by east.

The English fleet, on the other hand, was moving towards it in two groups with no semblance of order, the faster ships still moving past the slower. The *Director* was in the lee and larger division, with the *Russell* in the van and with four other seventy-fours, a sixty-four and a fifty in close company, and the *Agincourt*, another sixty-four somewhat astern. The weather division, led by the *Venerable*, had three seventy-fours, three sixty-fours and a fifty. Each division had attendant frigates which, not considered powerful enough to lie in the 'line of battle', kept well up to windward. As far as he could see, the two fleets were well matched in size and numbers and knowing the courage and tenacity of the Dutchmen, he realized that victory was by no means certain.

He stopped for a moment as through the clinging mist he saw yet another hoist fluttering at the flagship's yard-arm. He glanced back to warn the midshipmen but saw that they had already noticed it and were repeating the order: eighty-eight – MAKE MORE SAIL.

Bligh acknowledged the report and continued to stare across at the plunging *Venerable*. The admiral, he thought, must have paused before sending that message, for its execution would undoubtedly tend to split up the fleet even more; but knowing Duncan it was to be expected. The one thought in the admiral's mind was to get at the enemy; the Dutch ships would soon be in the shallows where the heavier and deeper British ships could not follow, thus enabling them to get away. This would not do at all. Duncan had waited for two years for them to come out – he was not going to let them escape now, by being held back by his slower vessels.

With a strong north-easterly wind filling their studding sails the British ships plunged straight for the enemy's line. Duncan's intention was to cut through it and then, by coming about, place his ships to leeward between the Dutch and the shore so that they would be unable to take advantage of their shallower draught. To do this he had to approach with his two irregular divisions so that the whole of the Dutch fleet could 'cross his T', enabling it to rake his ships as they bore down. But he had to take this chance – there were the enemy – let him get at them.

As the fleets drew nearer, one of the admiral's officers remarked, "How many ships do you propose to engage with this division?" and received a typical reply, "Really, sir, I can't ascertain, but when we have beat 'em, we'll count 'em!"

By now the signals were fluttering up and down, many of them not being understood because of the heavy haze. At 11.18 the *Director* was ordered to take the lead in his division but Trollope in the *Russell* preferred to ignore this signal and kept his position in the van.

At 11.25 came twenty-one:– ENGAGE THE ENEMY.

At 11.36 came the signal:– LEE DIVISION TO ENGAGE THE ENEMY'S CENTRE, to be followed two minutes later by:– LEE DIVISION TO ENGAGE ENEMY'S REAR, and Bligh was inclined to agree with a half-whispered comment from one midshipman to another, "I wish he'd stop these signals and let us get on with it."

Over in the *Bellinqueux*, Captain John Inglis was more forthright. Quite bewildered by the signals that came flowing from the flagship he finally closed his telescope with a determined snap and in his rich Scots accent shouted to his sailing master. "Hang it Jock! Doon wi' the helm and gang richt into the middle o't!"

The space narrowed between the two fleets. It was nearly

noon. Bligh now had to concentrate on his own section of the coming battle — at the moment, Duncan and the ships in the windward division need not have existed. The turn in towards the enemy had put the *Monarch* in the van, with the *Russell, Director* and *Montagu* sailing almost in line abreast of her starboard quarter, with the Dutch drawing closer every minute. It was very quiet, only the usual noises of a ship plunging forward under a press of sail and the thud and hiss of water alongside broke the silence. On board the *Director*, nearly 500 men waited tensely. A marine fidgeted with his musket until a hissed reprimand from Sergeant Leach made him freeze into immobility; William Birch, the master, stood stolidly at the lee bulwark, his eyes constantly turned aloft, watching the leeches of the sails for any tell-tale shake that would tell him that the helmsman had allowed the ship to fall away and looking at the strained, tense figure, Bligh saw himself as he must have been, sixteen years before.

Even the midshipmen had fallen silent, three of them, Lightfoot, Blaguire and Eldridge, standing close together, the former still holding his signal book although the *Venerable* was now obscured by the *Monarch* and by the haze. Down below the men were grouped about their guns, silent, waiting. They were stripped to the waist, their handkerchiefs tightly bound about their heads and ears so that they would not suffer permanent deafness from the roar of the guns, and also to keep the sweat from pouring into their eyes.

A few moments later a dull rumble sounded from ahead and two tall fountains rose on either side of the *Director*'s bows whilst there came a sharp twang from overhead as a stay parted. The enemy had opened fire and were taking advantage of being able to fire broadsides whilst the British could only reply with their lighter bow guns. But the closeness of the first fall of shot showed Bligh that they had left it too late, and had thrown away this advantage. They were nearly on the Dutch line now, ship following ship, stretching away on either side — a dozen or so to larboard, only one, the *Russell*, to starboard. Now they were close enough to pick out details of the enemy ships; the open ports with the ugly snouts of the guns, still wreathed in white smoke, emerging again after that first salvo; the occasional flash of gold on the quarterdeck; the dim figures of men in the waist and tops.

Then the *Monarch*, leading the lee division, forced her bulk into the opposing wooden wall and her first broadside erupted in smoke and flame, hurling shot into the high carved stern of Vice-Admiral Reintjes' ship, the seventy-two-gun *Jupiter*. Bligh glanced at his watch once again. It was 12.40. A few minutes later the *Director* moved into the enemy line, heading for the narrow gap between the *Haarlem*, 64, and the *Alkmaar*, 50. Her bowsprit came abreast of the former's stern, then the forecastle and Bligh, spreading his feet wide in anticipation of the shock yelled "Fire!"

Flame rippled down the entire length of the *Director*'s sides, the guns firing as they bore, vomiting round-shot and grape, whilst thick clouds of throat-rasping smoke belched from the muzzles, clung greasily, then drifted away to leeward, obscuring the suddenly wrecked bows of the *Delft*. The *Director*'s quarterdeck was now abeam of the *Haarlem*'s stern, her carronades adding their staccato crack to the deeper bellow of the carriage guns, and Bligh saw the stern windows and taffrail of the Dutchman disintegrate in an explosion of shattered glass and splintered woodwork. Then they were past, to receive in turn a ragged broadside from the *Haarlem*'s starboard batteries.

"Bring her round!" Bligh yelled, intending to lay his ship alongside the other, but the *Director* had too much way on her and he suddenly saw, looming up through a bank of white smoke, the stern of the *Monarch* which was trading broadside for broadside with the *Jupiter*.

"Larboard helm! Let her fall away!" he bawled to the master, and the *Director*'s long bowsprit just shaved the other's stern as she slid past, his men leaning out of the ports to give Onslow's ship a cheer as they went.

As all semblance of formation seemed to have been lost, Bligh hesitated for a moment then climbed the mizen shrouds to try and see for himself what was happening elsewhere. Astern, the *Monmouth* had also broken through the line and was engaging the *Alkmaar*, whilst the *Delft*, at the extreme rear of the Dutch line, was now sandwiched between the *Russell* and the *Montagu*. It was obvious that this area of the battle was going well, for Vice-Admiral Onslow had brought nine of his ships against five of the enemy. Ahead, however, things seemed more confused. A huddle of ships surrounded the *Venerable* which was supported by the *Ardent*, 64, whilst the *Powerful*, 74, and the little *Circe* were

moving to aid their hard-pressed admiral. The *Triumph* went
about as he watched and was crossing the bows of the Admiral de
Vries' flagship, the *Vrijheid*, 74, which with the *States General*, also
a seventy-four, had been pounding Duncan's ship. It was
apparent that the windward division was seeing most of the
action and Bligh ordered Birch to make for the Dutch van.

The *Director* soon left the confused fighting at the Dutch rear
astern and moved forward on a north-easterly course, passing the
Leyden, 64, and then the *Brutus*, 74, flagship of Rear-Admiral
Bloys as she went. Broadsides were traded with each, one of
which shot away her foreyard and nearly cut through her fore
topsail yard. But she was not going to engage them more closely
for Bligh had noticed that the *Vrijheid* appeared to be disengaged,
and with the early dusk of October due within two hours, he
was determined to tackle the seventy-four before it could slip
away in the darkness. As the *Director* neared the other, he ordered
McTaggart to pass the message around the ship – that he was
determined to lay his own alongside that of the Dutch Admiral.
On the way he pumped another broadside into a ship that was
being attacked by the *Veteran*, 64, saw her strike, then passed the
Hercules, 64, which was drifting away to leeward, burning
furiously.

Just after 3 p.m., Bligh opened fire on the *Vrijheid* when some
twenty yards away on her larboard quarter. The Dutch flagship
had already been in action with the *Venerable, Ardent* and *Powerful*
but was still in good condition and full of fight. Indeed, at the
commencement of what was to be her last duel she had only
thirty or so men killed and wounded.

The *Director*, heaving to the continuous recoil of her guns,
moved slowly across the other's bows with the smoke hanging
about her like an almost solid white pall, the underside of which
was lit up by the crimson flames of her broadsides. The trucks
rumbled as the sweating, choking men flung themselves at the
tackles to run out the guns, skipped out of the way of the recoil,
then heaved at the tackles once more to draw each gun inboard
to be sponged, wormed, have fresh cartridge and shot rammed
home, then run out again for the next broadside. The iron hail
crashed into the Dutchman's bows, ripping her decks, smashing
masts and rigging, whilst dull answering thuds from below and
the occasional sharp clang of iron striking iron showed that the
Director was also being hit in return.

Bligh stared at the dark bulk of his opponent, squinting with aching, smoke-weary eyes, then gave a snort of triumph as he saw that the other's shape was changing. A shot had struck the *Vrijheid*'s foremast causing it slowly to bend forward. For a moment the ship seemed to take on a drunken, tattered look then the complete foremast collapsed in a hideous welter of rigging, shrouds and spars. The supporting stays parted and the mainmast came down with a rush, bringing the mizenmast with it. Within a few moments the ship was completely dismasted. What was equally important, the raddle of canvas and spars hung over her starboard side, masking most of the guns and Bligh immediately brought his ship around, to run along the suddenly vulnerable side and pour in further broadsides.

"Back the fore-topsail!" he roared and the ship lost way, ranging alongside the other, keeping up such a fierce and rapid fire that it sounded like a continuous roll of thunder. Hardly a shot was fired in reply and Bligh saw, almost in disbelief, the other's flag flutter down from her jackstaff.

She had struck.

"Cease firing!" he cried and as this message reached the lower decks, the sound of the guns died away. For a moment there was silence then, as the men poked their blackened faces through the flame-blistered ports, there was a roar of hoarse cheering as they saw reason for the order. Grinning broadly, Bligh looked around at the cheering men about him; even the usually taciturn McTaggart was waving his hat excitedly above his head as he joined in with the rest.

The *Director* got underway again and seeing the *Venerable* half a mile away to leeward, Bligh bore up and ran alongside the flagship. As the two vessels moved forward together, Bligh picked up a speaking trumpet ready to hail the tall and unmistakeable figure on the other's quarterdeck. But he was forestalled for Duncan called across, "Well done, Captain Bligh. I have been watching you. Congratulations. Now will you take possession of her, and send the admiral over to me if you please."

Bligh waved his arm in recognition of the order then, wearing ship, he began the beat back to the wallowing *Vrijheid*.

Although the *Director*'s booms had been destroyed, a boat was found that could still float and McTaggart was sent away to board and take possession of the other ship. Bligh stalked impatiently up and down the quarterdeck until the boat returned

with the dejected figure of the flagship's second in command
sitting in its sternsheets. He was received courteously then Bligh
turned to the senior midshipman who had also boarded the
Vrijheid for a report.

The youngster who had never seen death so closely before was
plainly showing the effects of the ordeal. "It was terrible, sir," he
told Bligh. "Bodies everywhere on the deck, and when Mr
McTaggart and I boarded her we found Admiral de Winter and
the ship's carpenter trying to patch up a small boat so that he could
get away to another ship. He surrendered to us but Mr McTaggart
allowed him to keep his sword. He has been taken across to the
Venerable as ordered, sir."

"How about the captain?"

"He is a Captain Van Rossum sir, and was too badly wounded
to be moved, so we have brought the next senior officer, er,
Captain-Lieutenant Siccame, in his stead. From what I can
gather, sir, before we came up the *Vrijheid* had little more than
two dozen killed and wounded, but when she struck to us there
was over two hundred. But the admiral allowed that it was being
dismasted, and with her guns being unable to fire, that caused
him to strike to us, sir."

This mention of killed and wounded suddenly reminded Bligh
that he had not yet called for an account of his own losses and he
sent for Surgeon Herron, demanding an immediate report. To his
surprise only seven men had been wounded and but three of
those needed further attention.

The fighting was virtually over. The surrender of their
beloved admiral seemed to have knocked the fight out of those
who had not already struck and, breaking off the action, they
slipped away to the Texel, by which time the *Venerable* was flying
thirty-nine – BREAK OFF ACTION, the last signal of a signal-
bedevilled day.

The *Vrijheid, Hercules, Gelijkheid, De Vries, Jupiter, Wassanaer*
and *Haarlem* were captured, together with the *Alkmaar* and *Delft*,
both fifties with two frigates, the *Monnikendam* and *Embuscade*;
almost half the entire Dutch navy. Their losses in man-power
were also considerable, being 540 killed, 620 wounded with
nearly 4,000 taken prisoner. The British had 203 killed and 622
wounded.

Two British ships-of-the-line, the *Adamant* and *Agincourt* had
no casualties at all, whilst the *Russell* had the same number as the

Director. By comparison, the *Ardent* had suffered terribly, having at one time been attacked simultaneously by five Dutch ships.

The next task in the gathering dusk was for all hands to turn to and splice, send up fresh spars and bend on new sails, an activity which ceased for a while soon after midnight when all hands were called to bury the dead.

The prizes were also taken in tow, a difficult task as nearly all were dismasted, badly leaking or both, and the ships — victors and captured alike — had to claw their way back to Yarmouth and the Nore in the face of an autumn gale. The *Director* struggled into the Yarmouth Roads with the *Gelijkheid* in tow and with more than 200 prisoners in her hold. Two ships did not make it. The *Delft* and *Monnikendam* both foundered whilst the *Embuscade* drifted ashore on the Dutch coast and was retaken. As it happened, not one of the captured ships were of any further use to the British navy — they were too badly damaged for that.

On 13th October, whilst still at sea off the coast of Holland, Duncan wrote his report of the battle for the secretary of the Admiralty and sent it back to England by his captain, sailing in the cutter *Rose*:

After describing the action Duncan continued: "It is with the greatest Pleasure and Satisfaction I make known to their Lordships the very gallant behaviour of Vice-Admiral Onslow, the Captains, Officers, Seamen and Marines of the Squadron, who all appeared actuated with the truly British spirit, at least those that I had an opportunity of seeing."

As he wrote these words he must have been conscious that only a few months earlier, many of these gallant "Seamen and Marines" had been in a state of revolt, and that ten of the ships that had supported him so nobly had then been flying the red flag of mutiny.

[15]

England Rejoices

IN HIS REPORT, Duncan included a significant phrase — *"at least those I had an opportunity of seeing ... "*.

This was obviously done with a thought for the future for soon after the fleet had returned to port, John Williamson, captain of the *Agincourt*, 64, was informed that he was to face a court-martial. The charges were serious indeed.

Firstly: That he did not, upon order and signal of sight, and upon sight of several of the enemy's ships, do his duty, and obey such signals; and that on the 11th October last he did, in time of action, keep back, and did not come into fight and engagement, and did not assist and relieve such of His Majesty's ships as it was his duty to assist and relieve. Secondly: That on the said 11th October last, during the time of action, through cowardice, negligence, or disaffection, he did keep back, and did not come into the engagement, and not do his utmost to assist and relieve such of His Majesty's ships as it was his duty to assist and relieve.

Bligh was one of those summoned to give evidence at the court-martial held on board the *Circe* on Monday, 4th December. He did so with mixed feelings. Primarily, in common with the other ships' captains, he was disturbed that the glorious victory of Camperdown (as it was now called) should be tarnished by the suspected cowardice of one of their number. On the other hand, he was not unduly surprised that of all people Williamson should be facing such a charge. He still clearly remembered the circumstances of Cook's death, and time had not altered his conviction that it was Williamson's dilatory action that had been responsible for that tragedy. He also remembered the similar lack of initiative after the murder, when Williamson returned to the *Resolution*, leaving his captain's body with the natives, and he still had bitter memories of the latter part of the voyage when he had tangled with Williamson on several occasions.

Bligh was brought in to give evidence but was only asked two questions, one by the court, the other by the accused. To both, his answers implied that he was quite unable to determine where the *Agincourt* was or what it was doing, as he was somewhat preoccupied with other matters at the time!

His brief evidence over, he was commanded to attend a ceremony which, for him, was a further ordeal. The Battle of Camperdown had undoubtedly saved Pitt's ministry and, for the time at least, the fear of invasion receded. The King had therefore decreed that a General Thanksgiving should be held. Men who had fought under Howe off Ushant in 1794, in a battle now known as the Glorious First of June; under Jervis off Cape St Vincent; and under Duncan at Camperdown, should receive the heartfelt thanks of the Lords Spiritual and Temporal and the commonfolk of the realm.

Bligh arrived very early at St Paul's on Tuesday, 9th December and after he had shown a very awed but very proud Elizabeth into a reserved pew, along with the wives of the other captains, he moved to a position just inside the west door where he stared curiously about him. Like most Londoners, he rarely visited such places and indeed, had only been inside the great cathedral once before to look around briefly with his girls when on a visit to the royal menagerie at the Tower. Now, with time to spare, he was able to examine more closely all the magnificence of the cathedral which had opened for Divine service a century earlier, almost to the day.

As he stood alone, hands behind his back and with his head tilted upwards so that he could study the splendid sweep of the arches leading to the incredible dome, he felt a tap on his shoulder and heard a voice say, "Ah, Captain Bligh. Why not come and join us, sir?"

He turned and saw John Wells, captain of the *Lancaster*, which had been one of the ships in the windward division at Camperdown. The two men shook hands and moved across to a small group of men, all of whom had commanded ships in the recent battle – Sir Henry Trollope of the *Russell*, John Knight of the *Montagu* and William Hotham who had commanded the *Adamant* when only that ship and the *Venerable*, had kept up the blockade of the Texel. Bligh was warmly welcomed as a companion in arms and was soon as deeply engrossed as the rest in reliving parts of the action, comparing ship with ship, and lapsing into technicalities.

Inevitably the talk led to Williamson, for several had already been called to give evidence at the court-martial which was to drag on for another two weeks. Not one of them could remember seeing him bring his ship into action and they had gravely to admit that, on the face of the evidence so far, his naval career was in danger. As it happened, Williamson was to be found guilty on the first charge and sentenced to be placed at the bottom of the captain's list, which meant that he would no longer be able to serve in any ship in the Navy.

After eighteen years, Cook's death had been paid for by the man Bligh always held responsible.

Whilst they had been talking, there was a great swirl of activity in the world outside the thick walls of the cathedral. Large crowds had been collecting since dawn, to thicken and spread along the processional route, whilst the more fortunate settled down at overlooking windows determined to have their money's worth, for many had paid up to fifty guineas for the privilege. Foot Guards had been marched into the Strand to take up their positions and troopers of the Horse Guards, of the Queen's Regiment of Light Horse, and of the sixth Regiment of Dragoon Guards trotted into the Mall and Charing Cross, their cloaks giving a splash of brilliant colour to the drab streets. Between Temple Bar and St Paul's, the route was lined by men of the London Militia, the East India Volunteers and the Light Horse Association whilst batteries of guns of the Artillery Company went bumping into Hyde Park to be unlimbered.

By eight in the morning, the beginning of the long procession appeared to be greeted with cheers from the crowd. It was led by a marine division from Chatham with their band, blaring and banging away at "God Save the King", "Rule Britannia" and "Heart of Oak", in succession — stirring music for such an occasion.

Behind them came long lines of seamen, headed by lieutenants and petty officers marching with rigid swords, but with eyes that constantly moved from side to side so as not to miss any fair damsel in the large crowd. Then the first of three artillery wagons rumbled into sight on which were displayed the captured French, Spanish and Dutch flags respectively. Between these trophies were the carriages containing high ranking flag officers including Sir Alan Gardner, Sir Thomas Pasley and Sir Horatio Nelson.

Immediately behind the third wagon, bearing the Dutch flags which had been captured from De Winter, Reintjes and Lucas, came a carriage bearing the tall, unmistakeable figure of one of the heroes of the day, Admiral Adam Duncan but now Baron Duncan of Lundie and Viscount Duncan of Camperdown, wearing the two hundred guinea sword that had been presented to him by the City of London. Seated next to him was Rear-Admiral Douglas, representing Vice-Admiral Lord Keith to whom the Dutch Admiral Lucas had surrendered in Saldanha Bay.

They were followed by a phalanx of carriages bearing members of the House of Commons and the cheers became interspersed with boos and jeers as the crowd recognised William Pitt who had become very unpopular of late because of his foreign policy and his insistence on vast sums of money being poured out to foreign princelings.

But the cheering soon regained its former volume when, after members of the House of Lords had moved past, the first carriages of the royal cavalcade came into view.

They carried King George's four sons — Their Royal Highnesses the Dukes of Gloucester, Clarence and York and Prince Ernest — together with their considerable retinues, and were followed by a number of carriages containing maids of honour and ladies of the bedchamber. Then, to great enthusiasm, the royal couple came into view at last, the King in blue and gold in honour of the occasion, Queen Charlotte in mazarine blue with a diamond head-dress. Both were obviously enjoying the occasion, smiling and bobbing from left to right, acknowledging the cheers of the vast crowd, although both recalled that the last time they had driven in state to St Paul's was eight years earlier when they had gone to give their thanks for George's temporary recovery from insanity.

Their painted and gilded coach was followed by a glittering array of Marshalls, State trumpeters and "a numerous body of Life Guards" then two more coaches, containing in one the Princesses Augusta and Elizabeth, and in the other the Princesses Sophia and Mary. Another detachment of Life Guards trotted in the rear to close the procession.

Within the cathedral a tabarded herald came forward to push and cajole the captains into line and Bligh, taking his place with the rest, looked across and saw two other groups of captains who had fought at St Vincent and on the Glorious First of June. He was still picking out some he knew when the great west doors were flung open and the hitherto muffled cheering of the crowds outside rolled into the cathedral, to send a wave of anticipation amongst the people in the packed pews, most of whom had been patiently sitting on hard wood for more than four hours! Peeping sideways, Bligh was able to see the head of the procession swinging up the hill, then the stolidly tramping seamen and marines wheeled to form a guard of honour on either side of the cathedral and up the wide steps. As each of the following artillery wagons slithered to a halt at the foot of these steps, the escorting lieutenants moved forward, took the captured flags and marched up to the west door with them where they ceremoniously handed them over to the captains to whom the various enemy ships had struck.

Bligh was one of the last to move forward, for the Dutch colours were in the third wagon, and he solemnly received a staff bearing the tattered flag that had flown over the stern of the *Vrijheid*. He turned and moved back into the cathedral, to take his place with the others and then, to the burst of martial music and the cheers of the congregation, marched down the aisle to form up beneath the great dome. He stood there, embarrassed by the hundreds of inquisitive eyes that were turned his way, then became conscious that the centre of attraction had suddenly changed. Looking towards the entrance he saw that a great throng was pressing in at the west doors, to resolve itself into a double lane, one side of which was formed by the royal dukes and by the princesses, easily recognisable by the tall white feathers that bobbed above their elaborate wigs; the other by the admirals and the Lord Mayor with his sheriffs and aldermen.

There was a sudden, expectant hush within the cathedral in contrast to the increased frenzy of cheering from outside, then the whole building shuddered with noise as there came a blast of trumpets and the choir burst into a great melodic outburst of welcome as Their Majesties began to progress down the aisle.

The rest of the royal party, together with the admirals and the civic authorities, fell in behind them, passing through a rigid line of marines and men from the First and Second Coldstream Guards. At last they took their seats, settled themselves, and the service began.

At the close of the first lesson the captains, flanked by junior flag officers, walked two by two to the great altar where on bended knees, they presented the colours to the Dean and

Chapter, who arranged them on either side of the altar. The winter sunlight touched the shot-torn and ragged colours of a score or more of captured enemy ships. They lay there, the vertical and horizontal tricolours of France and Holland, the gold and red of Spain, flags that had once fluttered bravely but now lay limp and dejected, tokens of surrender ... and of victory.

After the last captain had handed over his colour the Bishop of Lincoln entered the pulpit and began to read from the Second Book of Samuel: "And he said, the Lord is my rock, and my fortress, and my deliverer. The God of my rock; in him will I trust; he is my shield, and the horn of my salvation, my high tower, and my refuge, my saviour; thou savest me from violence ... ".

The sonorous voice droned on, filling the great cathedral with eloquent rounded phrases that spoke of Divine aid, of courage and of sacrifice, immensely stirring to the civilians amongst the congregation. To Bligh and his fellow seamen, however, they bore little relation to the actuality – to the smoke and noise, the blood and sudden horrible death – that were the main part of any victory, however glorious.

By 2.30 the service was over and easing their cramped bodies, the congregation thankfully rose to cheer as once again bowing to left and right, the royal party moved slowly up the aisle to arrive at the top of the steps at the precise moment that a twenty-one-gun salute commenced banging away in St James's Park. The first of the State coaches was drawn up waiting, and the procession, in reverse order this time, clip-clopped smoothly away, down the hill, heading for home.

The lesser people, including the officers and seamen who had mainly been responsible for the whole occasion, were left to fend for themselves. Bligh managed to prize Elizabeth from the jostling crowd and escort her to the hired carriage waiting at the rear of the cathedral, where the driver had an amusing story to relate. A group of ruffians, hoping to indulge in some lucrative pocket-picking had brought along an ox which they had turned loose in the crowd. A number of people were thrown down in the initial panic but the beast was chased along the route, to hoots of laughter from the rest, to be cornered and captured in St Paul's Churchyard.

The carriage was a long time getting through the press of people which had now spilled across the road, and it was frequently brought to a standstill, allowing many of the excited townsfolk, on seeing Bligh's naval uniform, to come alongside with cheers and congratulatory remarks – to his further embarrassment. Not all had such a reception, however. Pitt was one of those who did not leave with the rest, having had enough insults for one day. He stopped to dine with Mr Speaker and others in Doctor's Commons and was finally escorted home, later in the evening, by a party of the London Light Horse.

Bligh was glad when the day was over for it had been a tiring occasion. Also, for some weeks past, he had been troubled with a rheumatic complaint which at times rendered his left arm practically useless. Indeed, he had been compelled to write to the Secretary of the Navy, asking for leave of absence from the *Director* of which, once the verdict of the court-martial had been announced, he was expected to resume command.

The arm was stiff and painful and the long hours of waiting, together with the strain engendered by the thought of doing something wrong under the eyes, not only of the King, but of his superior officers, had quite exhausted him. He was too tired even to take advantage of a pair of seats offered by the management of Drury Lane for that evening's performance where in addition to the main attraction – *Romeo and Juliet* – the theatre was staging a tribute to the country's seamen entitled *Britain's Brave Tars* or *All For St Paul's.·*

1797 was nearly over. It had proved a momentous year for Britain. It had seen the two great victories of St Vincent and Camperdown. It had also lived through the shattering experience of the mutinies at Spithead and the Nore. Also, in February, the same year, it had seen an invasion of British soil. Four armed vessels, containing about 1,400 men, appeared in the British Channel and standing in to the Welsh coast, had landed them at Llanwnda near Fishguard. They were commanded by an American, Colonel William Tate whose soldiers were a ragged, undisciplined crowd of men, the scum of every jail in France, and who soon showed their worth when they came up against an army of 3,000 men commanded by Lord Cawdor. The 'invaders' laid down their arms without firing a shot and a story was later circulated that one reason for this sudden capitulation was that they had sighted a group of Welsh women in their red coats and tall black hats and immediately assumed that they were a regular Guards battalion!

In Europe, however, Bonaparte was moving from triumph to triumph. Austria had suffered several defeats and in October was compelled to sign an humiliating peace treaty, to break her alliance with Britain, and to cede a great part of her territory. Before this treaty was actually signed, Pitt endeavoured to make peace with France, sending Lord Malmesbury to Lille with authority to restore all of his country's recent conquests with the exception of Ceylon, the Cape of Good Hope and Trinidad. But the negotiations dragged on and when the internal struggles in France ended with the triumph of the Republican army on 4th September, the whole scheme was abandoned. The war party in France was now in full power and the weary struggle which had begun four years earlier continued.

Once again the threat of invasion spread throughout the land and in the autumn of that year Britain's first Loyal Volunteer troops were formed. An old shipmate of Bligh's, Captain James Burney who had commanded the *Discovery* after Cook's death, had a great deal to do with the formation of what was, in effect, an early 'Home Guard'. He wrote a pamphlet entitled "Plan of Defence Against Invasion" which recommended the creation of a volunteer force of men, "between the ages of eighteen and fifty-five, capable of bearing arms", who should be required to attend one afternoon a week to be trained in military matters.

He also went on to recommend that "all workmen in His Majesty's Dockyards should be exercised under their own officers" and that "the masters of all merchant-vessels should be required to have their men instructed in the use of small arms".

The response to Burney's pamphlet was immediate, men flocking to volunteer. Indeed, within six years the Loyal Volunteers had grown to nearly half a million, a great achievement considering the size of the population of under twenty million, and that Britain already had a large number of men already under arms. The scheme produced the inevitable crop of patriotic songs which included:

A New Song – Written and Sung,
with the greatest applause by a MEMBER of the South East District
OF LOYAL LONDON VOLUNTEERS,
and respectfully DEDICATED To THEM, and every
VOLUNTEER in GREAT BRITAIN.

Even so, many in Britain felt a chill of apprehension at the news that Bonaparte had taken command of the 'Army of England' and had arrived in Paris on the 5th December to begin plans for the invasion. On his arrival the Directory declared, "It is at London that all the misfortunes of Europe are manufactured, it is in London that they must be terminated ... ".

Consequently the threat of invasion was ever-present. It was known that large numbers of ships had assembled in Genoa, Civita Vecchia and Bastia, held there by the Mediterranean squadron under Nelson, and there was tremendous consternation in Britain when it was learned that a gale which had briefly taken Nelson's ships off station, had allowed the French fleet to slip out and disappear over the horizon – to where, no one knew. Bligh, in the *Director* which, with every other available ship of the Channel and North Sea fleets was constantly at sea, heard the news and realized how badly Nelson must be feeling at that moment, and the tremendous strain it must have entailed. The responsibility of having to decide where to take his fleet in pursuit of an enemy that might be sailing to the Middle East or India, to the West Indies or even to Ireland, knowing that a wrong decision would place him on the other side of the world, must have been almost unbearable. But after months of frustration Nelson found the enemy at last, at anchor in Aboukir Bay near Alexandria.

The news of his victory of the Nile electrified the whole of Europe. It was the first major reverse that Bonaparte had experienced, the French army was isolated in Egypt and dreams of a march on India were ended. The bells rang, Britain went wild with joy and Lord Spencer, Head of the Admiralty, fainted away when the news of the victory reached him – having been so keyed up for so long with understandable anxiety.

1799 was a year of successes and reverses. The French occupied Naples, only to be thrown out again six months later. Bonaparte invaded Syria, stormed Jaffa but was repulsed at Acre. British troops attacked Seringapatam, caused the death of the tyrant Tippoo Sahib and thus freed the British possessions in India from their most formidable enemy. Bonaparte defeated the Turks at the Battle of Aboukir and then, returning to France, overthrew the Directory and had himself made First Consul, with the prosecution of the war entirely in his hands. With this chilling news from abroad came something that caused grumbling and distress nearer home. At the end of the year Pitt introduced a new form of revenue. It was called Income Tax!

During 1800, Bligh was detached for special duties, including a voyage to St Helena to convoy home a squadron of East Indiamen and also — shades of the past — to bring back a number of plants for the Botanical Gardens at Kew. His reputation as one of the leading hydrographers in the country also sent him to Dublin to prepare a complete survey of the harbour, a task which was so well performed that he was also ordered to do a similar survey of Holyhead. The *Director*, which he had commanded for four and a half years, was paid off in July 1800, and most of his surveying work was done whilst on half pay. Although he thoroughly enjoyed the work, he felt out of things, doing leisurely, peace-time tasks when his country was at war, but international events were moving towards a situation that would soon see him in violent action once more.

When the King addressed Parliament on 2nd February, 1801, his speech contained little that was encouraging. There had been a series of French victories on the Continent and the Baltic States now seemed intent on causing trouble. The mentally unbalanced Paul I of Russia, until recently an ally of Britain which had been subsidizing him at the rate of £112,000 a month, had become captivated by the military genius of Bonaparte. Wishing to flatter the Tsar, Bonaparte, without any authority, made him Grand Master of the Knights of Malta whilst convincing him that the conquest of that island by Britain, some two months earlier, had deprived him of something that was rightfully his.

For centuries, Britain had exercised the right of searching neutral vessels for contraband of war and using this as an excuse, Paul ordered all British merchant ships in Baltic ports to be seized, thus immobilizing some 300 ships whilst their officers and crews were taken ashore and imprisoned. He then revived the old Armed Neutrality which consisted of Russia and Denmark and a somewhat reluctant Sweden and Prussia in a coalition which had first been created by Catherine II, twenty years before.

Britain immediately accepted this as a challenge to her rights and on 12th March, a huge fleet cleared the Yarmouth Roads and headed north for Denmark.

With it was Bligh in his new command — the *Glatton* of fifty-four guns.

[16]

Prelude to Battle

"BOAT COMING alongside, sir."

Bligh looked up from the chart he had been studying and brought his blue eyes to bear on the midshipman who had come with the news.

"Thank you," he said. "I shall be on deck presently."

When the other had gone, he draped a heavy cloak about him and pulled on thick gloves, for March in the Baltic, was always cold and for the past week, the snow-laden wind had been bitter. He came out onto the quarterdeck, glanced around at the three score British warships anchored six miles from the Danish stronghold of Kronenburg before walking to the rails to see for himself who was in the approaching boat. His arrival coincided with the coxswain's hail, "*Amazon!*"

Bligh smiled with genuine pleasure as the tall, elegant figure of the frigate's captain stood up in the sternsheets, waited whilst the boat surged upwards against the *Glatton*'s dark sides, then sprang across the gap, scrambling up until he emerged through the entry-port. Bligh stepped forward, hand outstretched. "Ernest Riou. It is good to see you."

They walked below to Bligh's cabin where, glass in hand, they chatted with the ease of old friends. They had first met when Bligh was master of the *Resolution* and Riou one of the midshipmen. Their next encounter was under strange circumstances. Bligh, homeward bound after the *Bounty* mutiny arrived in Table Bay to meet Riou who, outward bound, was in command of the transport *Guardian*, taking cattle and convicts to the new settlement of Botany Bay. They spent a considerable time together for Riou, a magnificent seaman himself, was enthralled by the other's account of his adventures in the open boat. They then parted, Bligh for England in the *Vlydte*, Riou for New South Wales.

He was destined not to complete the journey, however, for whilst to the south-east of the Cape of Good Hope his ship struck an ice-berg 1,000 miles from land, and after a long, heart-breaking battle against the rising water, Riou ordered most of the men away in the boats and when the survivors arrived in Table Bay they reported the *Guardian* as a total loss. Yet Riou, with some sixty companions — and this number included twenty-one convicts — managed to keep the ship afloat and finally, after a nightmare experience during which he had managed to carry the men along with him, even crushing an incipient mutiny, the battered, waterlogged *Guardian* arrived back in Table Bay. When she was beached it was found that her survival had been little short of a miracle. There were enormous breaches in her bow and stern but the lower deck had held the strain, a large number of casks in the hold had floated up to give her buoyancy, whilst the iron and shingle ballast had fallen out or had been washed through the gaping holes in her hull.

On his return to England, Riou was promoted to commander and when in London, always called upon Bligh if he happened to be near Durham Place.

This time he had come to inspect Bligh's ship, for the fifty-four-gun *Glatton* was unusual. In 1779 carronades were introduced into the Navy, but it was not until two years later that another friend of Bligh's, that Henry Trollope who had commanded the *Russell* at Camperdown, prevailed upon the Admiralty to allow him to arm his ship, the *Rainbow*, with an unusually heavy gun, the sixty-eight-pounder carronade. He had hoped to prove its superiority when he engaged the French *Hebe*, but within a few moments, and after getting away only one broadside, his opponent hauled down her colours. In 1795 the Admiralty purchased several East Indiamen, amongst them the *Glatton* of 1,256 tons, and when Trollope, who had been appointed to command her went on board, he was delighted to find that the armament included no less than twenty-eight sixty-eight-pounders on the lower deck.

There were drawbacks, however, to this arrangement. There were no bow-chasers and the broadside carronades were so large that their muzzles nearly filled up the ports, so that they could not be trained fore or aft. Still a carronade 'fanatic' and determined to prove its superiority, Trollope put to sea and whilst cruising off the coast of Flanders sighted a squadron of four French ships. As the *Glatton* approached, four more appeared until he found himself opposed by four frigates, two corvettes, a brig and a snow. But Trollope, remembering the row of sixty-eight-pounders on his lower deck was ready to take the risk. He fought them all day and under cover of darkness repaired the damage to his spars and rigging. The next morning the enemy were still in sight and Trollope prepared for battle once more, but the Frenchmen had had enough; they presented their sterns to him and sailed away to Flushing.

There was great enthusiasm when he returned, for the odds of eight to one were phenomenal, even in those days of brilliant exploits. Trollope was knighted for this action and the Navy, impressed by such a practical demonstration, had no second thoughts about the carronade which, from then on, became standard armament.

The conversation of the two friends turned to the present. There was considerable feeling amongst the captains at what they considered the dilatory methods of their admiral, Sir Hyde Parker, son of old "Vinegar" Parker under whom Bligh had fought at the Battle of the Dogger Bank. He had even delayed sailing from Yarmouth, being occupied with arrangements for a ball for Lady Parker and it needed an urgent and private message from Nelson, his second-in-command, to Jervis at the Admiralty to get the fleet under weigh and to bring it off the Skaw, the most northern tip of Denmark by 19th March 1801.

Still procrastinating, Parker waited for the return of Vansittart, an envoy who had gone on ahead of the fleet, and then sent a message to the Governor of Hamlet's Castle of Elsinore asking him what he intended to do if the fleet passed the stronghold on its way up the Sound from the Kattegat to the Baltic. The reply was obvious – the Danish guns would open fire. These delays allowed the Danes more than a week in which to strengthen the defences of Copenhagen and to moor floating batteries and ships to complement the powerful Trekroner fort which, with other batteries, commanded the approach to the harbour.

With the large fleet swinging at anchor within sight of the Danish coast there was an increasing irritability, brought about by nervous tension and annoyance at Parker's apparent tardiness. Nelson, always one for immediate and violent action, found the situation particularly galling but out of deference to a man many years his senior, endeavoured to hide his feelings as much as he could. Even so, his occasional caustic comments were passed from ship to ship and savoured by officers and men alike.

A typical one of these was provoked when he saw Vansittart

return from his abortive diplomatic mission, "I hate your pen and ink men; a fleet of British ships of war are the finest negotiators in Europe!" Nelson had exclaimed.

Later, when Parker had asked him which of the two approaches to the city the fleet should take he had replied, somewhat testily, "Let it be by the Sound, by the Belt, or anyhow; only don't let us waste any more time!"

Whilst the two captains had been talking, Parker had at last made up his mind, in part at least, for early the next morning the signal was made from his flagship, the three-decker, ninety-eight-gun *London*, for all ships to weigh and make for the Sound in line ahead. By six o'clock the fleet took station and moved majestically towards the Start. The van was led by Captain James Mosse in the *Monarch*, 74, and commanded by Nelson who had shifted his flag from his own *St George*, 98, to the *Elephant*, 74, as being a lighter and handier ship for the tricky navigation that lay ahead. More than dangers from the torturous course awaited them, however. The mouth of the Strait was less than two miles wide and commanded on the Danish side by Kronborg Castle and the defences of Elsinore, and on the Swedish by the batteries defending the city of Helsingborg.

Standing at his battle station on the *Glatton*'s poop, Bligh felt a great sense of relief that something was happening at last as, with a steady topsail breeze from the north-west, the ship moved ponderously forward, her blunt merchantman's bows dipping in the wake of the ship ahead. The ships made a truly magnificent sight in the pale morning sunshine. There were eighteen line-of-battle-ships, with Nelson in the van, Parker in the centre and Rear-Admiral Thomas Graves commanding the rear in his seventy-four-gun *Defiance*, five frigates commanded by Riou, sloops, bomb-vessels, gun-brigs and even two fire-ships.

Very soon the green fields of Elsinore and the white Gothic pile of the castle came into view, with the fortress of Helsingborg and the steeples and high roofs of the Swedish city beyond. As the leading ship, the *Monarch*, came abreast of the Castle, there came the flat boom of a gun, then others, as the batteries and some bomb-vessels anchored near the shore opened fire. One or two British ships returned the fire then realizing that they were wasting ammunition, fell silent again. There were some casualties, however, for a twenty-four-pounder blew up in the *Isis* killing and wounding seven of its crew. The guns on the

Swedish side did not open fire and the fleet moved closer to that shore so that the shot from the Danish fort splashed harmlessly at least a cable's length from the smaller ships which fringed the rest.

By noon the fleet had come to anchor again in the lee of the lovely green island of Hven and during the afternoon, Nelson and Graves with William Domett of the *London*, set out in the lugger *Lark* to have a look at the Danish defences. What Nelson had feared was now very apparent. The Danes had made full use of the extra time allowed them and the defences they had prepared were quite formidable.

Copenhagen, situated mainly on the large island of Zealand and partly on the small island of Amager, was protected on one side by the guns of the Citadel and on the other by the Trekroner (or Three Crowns) batteries perched on two artificial islands. Ships had also been warped into position and anchored line ahead along the whole sea-front of Copenhagen so that their broadsides presented an unbroken line of fire. There were eighteen ships, third and fourth Rates, East Indiamen, transports specially pierced with gun ports, frigates and sloops. Only a few of them were fully rigged, most had their masts removed so that they were, in effect, floating batteries.

As if that was not enough, all the buoys that marked the labyrinth of shoals had all been removed, making a passage extremely hazardous for anything larger than a rowing boat!

That evening all captains were called to a council in the great cabin of the *London*. After the cramped conditions of the *Glatton*, whose fifty-four guns were not enough for her normally to be considered powerful enough to be in the line of battle, Parker's cabin seemed enormous. It was carpeted, elegantly furnished, and with rich damask curtains that shut out the cold Baltic night on the further side of the huge stern windows, whilst hanging silver lamps cast pools of light onto a long table which sparkled with silver and cut glass.

Despite excellent food and wines the dinner was eaten in comparative silence and when a dozen stewards in white had placed the port on the table and moved quietly away, the atmosphere had become even more depressing. Parker, as president, sat at the head of the table and first called upon Nelson and then Vansittart to describe the defences of the city. When both had finished telling of the batteries, the forts which had provision for firing red hot shot, the moored ships and the rest, he immediately declared that the whole project seemed impossible. But Nelson, impatient as ever of anything that savoured of irresolution, rose and began to pace the length of the cabin, all eyes following him as he walked. He kept throwing back his head, where the lank hair fell over his forehead, revealing his emotion by continually moving the stump of his right arm.

Some of the other captains brought up the question of the Russian fleet, stating that even if they passed the formidable Danish defences they would still be faced with an enemy that was reputed to have as many as eighty ships-of-the-line, to bring a snort from Nelson and the reply, "So much the better; I wish they were twice as many. The easier the victory, depend on it!"

The arguments went back and forth across the table and Bligh, watching Parker with interest, realized that the admiral was a very worried and irresolute man. In the face of the formidable defences an attack could easily end in disaster. If he did nothing and waited for the combined fleets to attack, the outcome could be equally disastrous. If he withdrew his fleet, in the face of such odds, his career was ended. It was a decision that Bligh was glad he was not called upon to make. It was then that Nelson stopped his pacing. Walking to the side of his commander-in-chief he outlined a plan which he had obviously been considering for some time.

There were two ways of approaching Copenhagen. One was by the passage known as the King's Channel; the other by the Outer Deep. Between them was a three-quarter-of-a-mile long shoal, the Middle Ground. The main Danish defences were concentrated along the King's Channel and Nelson's plan was so simple that like most simple plans, others around the table were annoyed at themselves for not thinking of it also.

Whilst two captains held up a large chart between them, Nelson pointed out the route he suggested they should take. "Here is the main concentration of fire, here, at the northern end. I propose that we take in a fleet and sail due south, through the Outer Deep, then double back at the top of the Shoal ... here. This will permit us to approach the city from the south instead of the north as they seem to expect. By this means we avoid having to sail under the guns of the Trekroner Batteries and we can hit their line where it is weakest, here, at the southern tip."

Parker was half-turned in his seat, eyes narrowed, studying the chart and the route that Nelson had suggested they take. After a long pause he said, "That passage between the southern end of the Middle Ground Shoal and the coast of Amager Island is very narrow. What's more it's full of rocks and shoals and with the marks removed, half our ships will be aground before you know it."

"That is a risk we'll have to take, sir. In any case you will see from this chart that there *is* a way through — if we can find it. Of course, this will be impracticable for the *London* and *St George* who require six fathoms, but just give me ten of the smaller line ships and some frigates and I'll do it!"

The cabin became very still, all eyes turning to Parker for his decision. The admiral stared down at the glass he was holding, then suddenly jerked up his head and exclaimed, "We'll do it!" then, swinging back to the other he went on, "You can have your ships, Nelson. You can have the *Isis* and *Glatton* as well; *and* all the frigates."

He paused for a moment then added with a twisted smile, "That should be enough, even for you!"

Nelson's pale face flushed, then he smiled broadly. He had made his point and got what he wanted, but, as if something else had just struck him he added, "With your permission, sir. I suggest that you keep the heavier ships at the north of the Middle Ground Shoal — here — ready to deal with the Russians or Swedes if they decide to join with the army."

There was still much work to be done and during the night boats were out under Nelson's supervision, charting a passage through the shoals and putting down new buoys. The next morning, Nelson was out again, this time in the *Amazon*, with Riou, whose "gallant and good" qualities he had quickly recognized. After a final examination of the area he gave the order to weigh and to a cheer from every vessel in his squadron, and with a light and favourable wind, the ships moved along the Outer Channel between the island of Saltholm and the Middle Ground. Riou's *Amazon* led the way, the whole squadron following along the outer edge of the shoal, to go about at its farthest extremity, reaching Draco Point, some two miles from Copenhagen, at 5 p.m. as the last rays of the sun faded from the tall spires of the city. Whilst it was still light enough to be seen, Nelson had hoisted the signal to prepare for action and as the bunting ran aloft he said, "I will fight them the moment I have a fair wind".

Later that evening, Bligh was rowed across to the *Elephant*, having been invited to dine with Nelson. Looking round him as he went he felt uneasy, for the thirty-four ships, huddled together as they were, made a tempting target for the mortars and larger guns on the shore, but the Danes were too busy manning their ships and strengthening their own defences to take advantage of the situation. With Thomas Foley, captain of the *Elephant* acting as host, Nelson, Graves and the other captains spent a pleasant and relaxed evening together. The light of the lanterns picked out the tanned, eager faces of Fremantle of the *Ganges*; Hardy who, though captain of the *London* had volunteered to accompany Nelson; Riou; Fancourt of the *Agamemnon* and Colonel the Hon. William Stewart, commanding 600 men of the forty-nine Regiment and the Rifle Corps, and Bligh felt a thrill of pleasure at being in such company. The excellent food was eaten, the wine drunk. Then before the captains returned to their ships, Nelson stood and, glass in hand, said, "Gentlemen, I give you a final toast. To a leading wind and success of the morrow!"

[17]

Copenhagen

AS BLIGH WAS rowed back to his ship he saw that the night had brought a heavy mist, and as he took a final turn on his quarterdeck he wondered what the wind and weather would be like on the following day, the day of battle. Even as he walked up and down, Hardy was out in a small boat, taking soundings in the channel that lay between the fleet and the enemy, the mist allowing him to go as far as the end of the long line of anchored ships, whilst he sounded with a pole, for the noise of a lead being cast would have given away his position.

Hardy returned to the *Elephant* at eleven o'clock, insinuating his huge frame into the small space in front of Nelson's cot which the admiral had ordered to be placed on deck so that he could dictate whilst lying down, for he had not slept for several days. Hardy told him that there was adequate water for the ships and that if they followed the line he had marked on his chart, not one would go aground.

At one o'clock in the morning of 2nd April, Nelson had finished his orders and half a dozen clerks were busily transcribing with their admiral urging them to hurry, for the wind was becoming fair. Instead of attempting to get a few hours sleep he constantly called for reports on this important point and by daybreak, as the clerks were completing their work, he was told that the wind had gone round to the south-east, a wind that would take him into battle and out again when it was all over.

When it was light enough for them to see the signal, all captains were ordered to the *Elephant* to be given their orders. The line-of-battleships were to anchor by the stern, abreast of the vessels forming the enemy's line, the leading ship not to drop anchor alongside the first, but the fifth, so that the tip of their right wing might be crushed by the others sailing past. The ships which were eventually to anchor there would find their work half done and on its completion would act as a reserve force, moving on to the assistance of those ahead.

The frigates *Amazon, Blanche, Alcmene, Arrow* and *Dart*, with the fire-ships *Zephyr* and *Otter* were placed under the command of Riou with orders to act as circumstances might require; the bomb-vessels were to station themselves outside the British line so as to lob their shells over it; and the frigates *Jamaica* and *Desiree*, with the brigs and gun-vessels, were to take up a position to rake the southern end of the Danish line. It was also intended that the soldiers under Stewart and some 500 seamen under Captain Fremantle should storm the main Trekroner battery as soon as the ships had knocked out most of its guns.

At the same time, Parker with the two ninety-eight-gun ships, four seventy-fours and two sixty-fours would be in support at the northern end to prevent reinforcements reaching the city.

The captains returned to their ships passing their pilots and masters who had been summoned for 9 a.m. This time, however, a tired and irritable Nelson met with opposition, for the pilots who for the most part had been mates in Baltic traders, refused to follow the line that Hardy had so painstakingly laid out during the night. Nelson and Hardy argued with them but the pilots stubbornly refused to change their minds and in the end Nelson agreed to follow the alternative route they put forward. As it turned out it was one of his gravest errors of judgement and he was later to write: "I experienced in the Sound the misery of having the honour of our country entrusted to a set of pilots, who have no other thought than to keep the ships clear of danger, and their own silly heads clear of shot."

At 9.30 the signal went up for all ships to weigh and to proceed as ordered. The *Edgar*, 74, moved off first, heeling to the morning wind, heading for the channel. The *Agamemnon* should have gone next but when she attempted to leave her anchorage she was unable to weather the edge of the shoal and Nelson, staring bleakly at her, saw the ship in which he had gained so much glory immobilized at a time when her seventy-four guns were desperately needed. The *Edgar* was unsupported for a while and had to bear the concentration of the enemy's fire, and the *Polyphemus*,·64, which should have been at the end of the enemy's line where their strength was greatest could not get into her proper position.

The *Isis* followed and took her berth as did the *Glatton*, Bligh dropping anchor "precisely abreast of the Danish Commodore". This was Olfert Fischer, flying his flag in the *Dannebrog*, 62. The *Ardent* also took up her correct position, then there came further

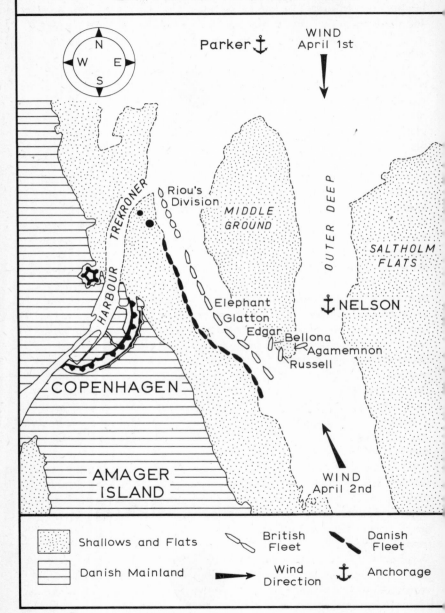

BATTLE OF COPENHAGEN

Parker ⚓

WIND
April 1st

N
W · E
S

TREKRONER

HARBOUR

Riou's
Division

MIDDLE
GROUND

OUTER DEEP

SALTHOLM
FLATS

⚓ NELSON

Elephant
Glatton
Edgar
Bellona
Agamemnon
Russell

COPENHAGEN

AMAGER
ISLAND

WIND
April 2nd

| | Shallows and Flats | | British Fleet | | Danish Fleet |
| Danish Mainland | | Wind Direction | | Anchorage |

tragedy. The *Bellona*, in spite of the fair wind and ample room, hugged the Middle Ground too closely and ran aground some 450 yards from the rear of the Danish line. The *Russell*, following in her wake, grounded too, with her jib-boom almost over the other's taffrail.

Nelson, bringing in the *Elephant* saw what had happened and ordered his ship's helm to starboard, leaving the agreed order of sailing but guiding those who were astern of him, thus saving others from going aground also. But his carefully worked out plan of attack had failed, for he had been deprived of a quarter of his main strength with three of his twelve largest ships virtually out of the fight. The gun-brigs too were almost useless, only one getting into action, the rest being prevented by the currents from weathering the eastern end of the shoal, whilst only two of the bomb-vessels could use their mortars on the shore defences.

These unfortunate circumstances forced Riou to take his frigates into the vacant station opposite the Trekroner, attempting with his lightly armed ships, to perform a task which three sail-of-the-line had been directed to do.

From the outset, the battle was nothing more than a slogging match, ship against ship, with the shore batteries joining in. Bligh soon realized that the action was the hottest in which he had ever fought. His ship constantly reeled and shook to the crash and recoil of her broadsides, whilst smoke clung thickly about her decks so that the low outline of her opponent could barely be seen. His gun's crews were loading and firing, loading and firing, the *Glatton*'s heavy armament smashing iron into the *Dannebrog*, punching great holes in her sides, digging deep furrows in her decks and hurling her guns about as if they were made of wood and not, as in the case of the thirty-two pounders, monsters that weighed three and a half tons each.

But the *Glatton* was taking a great deal of punishment in return. At half-past eleven, Bligh looked up as an ominous crack came from overhead and saw the fore-topmast totter and fall, enveloping the crews manning the carronades on her forecastle. Soon afterwards the clanging sound as of a giant's anvil came from amidships and a few moments later midshipman John Williams came running aft to report that seven of the upper-deck guns were out of action. Bligh acknowledged the news and watched as the lad ran forward again, then momentarily shut his eyes as the other suddenly stopped, spun around and pitched forward, to lie still and twisted on the deck.

Meanwhile Parker, with the heavier ships, was still more than four miles away, beating up against the south-west wind. He was desperately anxious about the turn of affairs for despite three hours fighting, the Danish fire seemed to be as strong as ever and he could see that three of the ships – the *Agamemnon, Bellona* and *Russell* were flying signals of distress. He had men posted at his mastheads to report, but the thick smoke concealed what was happening. After a great deal of agonising thought he finally ordered signal number thirty-nine – DISCONTINUE ACTION – to be hoisted.

What followed was to become legend. When the order was reported to Nelson he put his glass to his blind eye and said, "I really do not see the signal", followed by a petulant, "Damn the signal! Keep mine for close battle flying! That's the way I answer signals. Nail mine to the mast!"

Rear-Admiral Graves in the *Defiance* repeated the signal, but only allowed it to be hoisted to his lee maintopsail yardarm and still kept number sixteen, the signal for close action, flying at his maintopgallant masthead. But the frigates and sloops which were being pulverized by the heavy guns of the Trekroner saw the repeat signal and began to haul off. Fearing that he might run down another ship, Riou ordered his guns to stop firing so that the smoke could drift away and allow him to see more clearly. It was a fatal order, for it also allowed the Danes to get a clear sight of their enemy.

Riou, with a bandaged head, was sitting on a gun and encouraging his men when the *Amazon* swung into mid-channel, showing her stern to the Danish guns. Men were falling about him as the ship was raked and as he ran forward to help some of his men hauling on the main-brace he called out, "Come then my boys, let us all die together!"

Those were his last words. The next moment a chain shot cut him in two.

The battle seemed to be growing in fury and intensity. The Danes fought bravely and stubbornly, having several advantages, for reinforcements from the shore kept moving into the ships as the fire of the British ships knocked out the guns' crews. Some were replaced five times.

The *Dannebrog*, which had been receiving the broadsides of both the *Glatton* and *Elephant* had lost nearly all her original crew and flames were beginning to stab with yellow tongues from her battered ports. Then a hoarse cheer came from the British as her flag fluttered down, Fischer shifting his pennant to the neighbouring ship, the *Holsteen*, 60.

Thinking she had struck, Nelson sent across a boarding party but the boat was fired on by those who had remained at their posts, despite the flames which were leaping and crackling around them. Both British ships began to pound her again and shortly afterwards her cable was cut by a shot and she began to drift before the wind, blazing furiously, with the survivors leaping frantically from her portholes.

The noise of the battle was tremendous. More than 2,000 guns of all calibres were creating a continuous drumroll of sound that deafened and stupified. To this was added the staccato rattle of small arms, the shrieks and cries of the wounded, the thud and crash of shot striking home and the crackle of burning timber. To Nelson, it appeared as if the struggle had reached a stalemate and he was undecided what to do next. He wanted to take prizes but the enemy obviously preferred to let their ships sink underneath them rather than surrender. Even if he demolished the whole fleet — as he was steadily doing — he was still faced with the prospect of having to pass beneath the still undamaged guns of the Trekroner batteries on his way out of the channel.

He finally called for pen and paper and without leaving the deck, wrote a letter in which he said:

TO THE BROTHERS OF ENGLISHMEN, THE BRAVE DANES.

Vice-Admiral Lord Nelson has been commanded to spare Denmark when she no longer resists. The line of defence which covered her shores has struck to the British flag. Let the firing cease, then, that he may take possession of his prizes, or he will blow them into the air along with their crews who have so nobly defended them. The brave Danes are the brothers and should never be the enemies of the English.

He finished writing, waved the letter to dry it, then shook his head as a wafer was offered with which to seal it. "This is no time to appear hurried and informal," he said. A man was sent below for a candle and some sealing wax but was killed on the way, and another had to be sent. The letter was firmly closed with the wax and imprinted with Nelson's largest seal, then was sent ashore under a flag of truce to be opened and read by the

Prince Royal of Denmark who was stationed in one of the batteries.

A little after 3 p.m. another boat with a flag of truce put off from the shore bearing a Danish envoy, Adjutant-General Lindholm. When it was sighted, the guns of the Trekroner stopped firing, the ships followed suit and a sudden, blessed quiet fell over the whole area. Lindholm asked for an explanation of the first letter and received another in which it was stated that Nelson consented to a cessation of hostilities and that the wounded Danes might be taken on shore. The envoy returned to his prince for a further consultation and during the waiting period, Bligh was surprised to learn that the *Elephant* had made a signal, requesting him to report on board. He climbed down into his gig and was rowed across to the other ship, making his way aft. Nelson, Foley and Hardy were talking together on the quarterdeck as he came up and saluted and the admiral turned, a warm smile on his white, drawn face, to step forward and hit him affectionately on his shoulder.

"My dear Bligh," he said. "You have supported me nobly as my second throughout the action. I could not want for better support from anyone. Please receive my own personal thanks which, in turn, I would be indebted if you would pass on to your gallant crew."

Bligh stumbled through his thanks, almost overcome by this generous and unexpected gesture, and returned to his ship where soon afterwards, three loud cheers showed how his tired, smoke-blackened but triumphant crew had received the admiral's message.

He had barely returned when Nelson made the signal for his ships to weigh in succession, the *Monarch* leading. As the seventy-four moved ponderously past it was seen what a terrible mauling she had undergone. She had been stripped of all her shrouds and her masts were in such a tottery state that a sudden gust of wind would have sent them all over the side. As she moved forward she touched upon a shoal, but the *Ganges*, in her wake, took her amidships and nudged her free.

Seeing what had happened, Bligh stood rigidly at the rail as the *Glatton* moved over the same ground, but his ship went clear and he was able to breathe again. Then there came a titanic explosion which caused the deck to shake and tremble beneath his feet. The fire had reached the *Dannebrog*'s magazine at last and as he looked back he saw parts of the shattered hull hurtling downwards to drop with sullen splashes into the icy water. He saw too that the *Elephant* had also run aground a mile or so from the Trekroner and had stuck fast, whilst at the other end of the line the *Desiree* had gone to the assistance of the *Bellona* and was also fast on the same shoal that had held the seventy-four prisoner throughout the battle.

The spires of Copenhagen slipped astern and Bligh sent Robert Tom, his first lieutenant, to find out what the action had cost in lives. He was appalled by the reply. The *Glatton* had lost her pilot and seventeen seamen and marines had been killed; a lieutenant, master's mate, midshipman and thirty-four seamen and marines seriously wounded — one sixth of the ship's complement. Even so, the ship had not suffered as heavily as others, the worst hit of all being the *Monarch* with fifty-six dead and 164 wounded, including her captain, James Mosse, whom Bligh had first met when captain of the *Sandwich* during the Nore mutiny. Altogether the British losses in killed and seriously wounded were not far short of a thousand. The Danes, it was estimated, had lost in killed, wounded and prisoners nearly 6,000 and Nelson had been very sincere when he remarked, "I have been in one hundred and five engagements, but today's was the most terrible of them all".

With the Danish navy well nigh obliterated Nelson was now anxious to take his ships against the Swedes and Russians, but Parker began to exercise his authority again, declaring that he would not move further into the Baltic whilst the Danes were still under arms. A fourteen-week armistice was agreed upon during which the "treaty commonly understood as the Treaty of Armed Neutrality, as far as related to the co-operation of Denmark" was to be totally suspended.

Two weeks later, as the fleet was moving north, a lugger appeared bringing peace terms from Russia. That country now had a new Tsar, for the crazy and despotic Paul I had been murdered a week before the battle and Alexander, his successor, was violently opposed to Bonaparte and anxious to form a coalition with the British.

Had news travelled as quickly then as today, the slaughter at Copenhagen need never have taken place.

[18]

The Constant Blockade

BLIGH STEPPED onto the *Warrior*'s quarterdeck and with his hand still holding his salute, looked about him with extreme distaste. Any ship undergoing a complete refit was an offence to a seaman's eye but this seemed worse than most. Her topmasts and topgallant masts had been sent down to give her a stumpy, bottom-heavy appearance, shrouds, stays and running rigging lay scattered in untidy heaps whilst the decks, that had formerly been of a satisfying whiteness created by hours of stolid labour with holystone and sand were now stained with paint, dirt and mud.

When his gear had been swayed up from the boat alongside, Bligh walked aft to the cabin which was to be his home for a year. It was as impersonal as a vacated hotel room. A small desk, a few chairs, some cupboards with their doors wide open to reveal empty interiors, a cot. And that was all except for the canvas-shrouded shape of a pair of twenty-four pounders taking up a considerable amount of deck space. Over everything hung the sickly smell of fresh paint. For a while Bligh busied himself about the cabin – putting a few books on a shelf, hanging up his sword and some articles of clothing, suspending a miniature of Elizabeth from a small hook near the head of the cot, a hook that, no doubt, had served the same purpose for many previous captains. That done, he stood irresolute, wondering what to do next. He almost called out to see if the captain's servant had yet reported for duty but decided that could wait. For the moment he preferred to be alone.

He walked to the cot, lay down upon it and stared with unseeing eyes at the deck-head above. Although he felt physically tired after the coach journey from London, his mind was too filled with conflicting emotions to allow him to sleep. The main feeling was one of relief – relief that he was again in command of a ship-of-the-line after fretting on the sidelines of war for a year, whilst his fellow captains were busily winning honour and fortune at sea.

War with France had come to an end with the Peace of

Amiens in March, 1802, and within two months Bligh was back on half-pay with hundreds of other officers. This had caused much disappointment, for Harriet had chosen this time to be married to Henry Aston Barker, a son of the well-known Robert Barker, whose 'Panorama' in Leicester Square was one of the attractions of London, and he was not able to provide as generous a reception as he would have wished.

In March 1803, the King's speech at the opening of Parliament was virtually a declaration of war and whilst it sparked off his own countrymen to fresh efforts, it also prompted Bonaparte to revive his invasion plans, to create a new 'Squadron of the North' and to order hundreds of gun-vessels and flat-bottomed boats to be built along the Dutch coast. There were also disturbing stories circulation about Britain of 'secret' invasion weapons — monster barges, some six hundred feet long worked by windmills, and Montgolfier balloons capable of carrying an army across the Channel.

With all this activity obviously directed against her very existence, no one was greatly surprised when Britain declared war on France in May, 1803.

Within hours of the declaration, Admiral the Hon. William Cornwallis — "Billy Blue" — in the *Dreadnought*, 98, and with ten sail-of-the-line, was back on the old familiar blockading station off Ushant, watching the French fleet in Brest. Other units under Moore, Pellew and similar dashing frigate captains commanded the 'flying squadrons' that patrolled the approaches to other French ports, whilst Nelson prowled the Mediterranean outside Toulon.

When Bligh took command of the *Warrior*, 74, on 12th May 1804, the invasion scare was at its height. Bonaparte had given orders for an army of 160,000 men to be mobilized and for 2,000 invasion boats to be constructed ready for the dash across the twenty-odd miles of water that had always proved such a formidable barrier. The enthusiasm in France for the project was tremendous. Every department in the State voted to produce a ship-of-the-line; each of the larger villages a frigate; and every commune one or more of the gun-vessels, boats or prams of the invasion fleet. These smaller ships were to assemble in seven ports — Ostende, Dunkerque, Calais, Ambleteuse, Vimereux, Etaples and with Boulogne as the main depot.

But Britain's seamen were not prepared to wait. They sailed

into the harbours and roadsteads of Havre and St Valery and brought out ships and gun-boats; they attacked Dieppe and destroyed its batteries; they bombarded Granville under the eyes of some of Bonaparte's most distinguished officers. The British Navy now possessed more than six hundred ships and in addition to activities in home waters, began to recapture the colonies which had been tamely surrendered at the Peace of Amiens. St Lucia, Tobago, Guadeloupe, Demerara and Essequibo were taken, together with St Pierre and Miquelon on the Newfoundland coast.

Also, in India, Sir Arthur Wellesley's small army had beaten more than a quarter of a million men in four pitched battles and eight sieges and thereby ended the power of France in that country.

During much of this time Bligh was desperately anxious to return to sea and join the Channel fleet, but was compelled to watch the leisurely progress of the shipwrights and riggers working on the *Warrior* and whilst more fortunate ships were constantly arriving and sailing, his own remained firmly lashed alongside a sheer hulk in the Hamoaze.

As the work finally neared completion he was faced with another problem — shortage of men — and in a letter to Elizabeth he complained that he "had not yet above 241 men and only forty of them seamen". The navy had become desperate for crews and the press was out every night scouring the villages of Devon and sweeping the most unlikely candidates into their net.

Still undermanned, the *Warrior* sailed from Cawsand Bay on 16th July and as her bows dug into the chop of the Channel, Bligh read the Articles of War to the assembled ship's company. During the following morning he sighted the bulk of the 110-gun *Ville de Paris*, Cornwallis's flagship, and made his number, but did not approach the scattered fleet too closely owing to fog. On the next day this had thinned and the *Warrior*'s boats were out distributing cattle, vegetables and hay to those ships which had not been able to return to harbour to provision. When that was done, the boats were hoisted inboard again and at last Bligh felt that he and his ship were an integral part of the Channel Fleet.

It was not a 'happy' ship, however; the echoes of the mutinies still rumbled about the crowded mess decks and as his log shows, Bligh was constantly having to order punishment for "insolence and contempt" and for "disobedience of orders and neglect of duty". Sergeant Hinton and Corporal McLeash of the Marines were reduced to the ranks for "insolent and mutinous expressions", Seaman John Brannon had two dozen at the gratings for "improper conversation, tending to lead the people astray" and Marine Walford, three dozen for "mutinous expressions".

Naturally sensitive on this subject, Bligh was determined to stamp out disaffection at all costs and also paid his usual careful attention to the cleanliness of the ship, never having forgotten the lessons of hygiene he had learned from Cook. In consequence he ordered seventeen separate lashings for "filthiness", "uncleanliness" or "neglect of person".

During the eleven and a half months of Bligh's captaincy of the *Warrior*, a hundred or so punishments were ordered, some men collecting three separate lashings. Marine Thomas Crase, for example, had a dozen for insolence, a dozen for sleeping on his post and ten for enticing another marine to neglect of duty; Seaman Pat Donally who also had run the gauntlet for theft, later had a further ten lashes for the same offence and a dozen for being off the deck during his watch; and Seaman T. Harris, who appears to have been a 'hard case', had two dozen for disorderly conduct, two dozen for insolence and neglect, and a further dozen for uncleanliness.

The worst breach of discipline, however, came from an officer, Second Lieutenant John Frazier. He was a bad-tempered, morose man who had previously been in the Merchant Service, during which time he had broken some bones in his ankle, but who protested that he was fully recovered when he joined the Navy. During the voyage he again hurt his ankle and came to Bligh with a letter in which he requested to be sent ashore for a medical "survey". Bligh had considered him something of a malingerer but passed on the request to the admiral who replied that as the *Warrior* was soon to put back to port, the matter should wait until then. Frazier was examined by Mr Cinnamond, the ship's surgeon who found no swelling and discharged him as fit for duty. The next day and again on the following day, Bligh sent the lieutenant a message, ordering him to relieve the officer of the watch, but when he refused on both occasions to do so, Bligh was finally compelled to have him arrested for disobedience.

On 8th November the ship returned to Cawsand Bay and

Frazier was summoned to appear before a court-martial on the 23rd and 24th of the same month. Surgeon Cinnamond spoke up in favour of the accused, however, swearing that he had only removed Frazier from the sick list because Bligh had ordered him to do so. Principally because of this evidence Frazier was acquitted and Bligh had to take him back into his ship, an embarrassing experience for them both.

Back on blockade, the *Warrior* ran into the bad weather that was typical of that winter of 1804-5. There was continual rain, sleet and wind, with waves that threw the ships onto their beam-ends, straining their timbers so that the water seeped in to slosh about the mess decks and keep the men incessantly at the pumps, putting out the galley fires so that they were deprived of the comfort of a hot meal, making life a misery for everyone. Bligh's log continually includes such comments as "Employed about the necessary duties of the ship to enable us to stand the bad weather – Under close reefs – Top gallant masts struck".

During November the *Warrior* limped back into port with ripped sails, broken spars and sprung masts and one of the first ashore was Frazier in whose pocket was a letter to Lord Cornwallis which said:

SIR

I beg to state to you that William Bligh Esq., Captain of His Majesty's Ship Warrior, did on the ninth October last, publicly on the quarter deck on his Majesty's Ship Warrior grossly insult and ill treat me being in the execution of my office by calling me a rascal, scoundrel and shaking his fist in my face and that at various other times between the ninth of July and the thirtieth Day of October, 1804, he behaved himself towards me and other commissioned, warrant and petty officers in the said ship in a tyrannical and oppressive and unofficerlike behaviour contrary to the rules and discipline of the Navy and in open violation of the Articles of War. I have, therefore, to request that you will be pleased to order a Court Martial to be assembled to try William Bligh Esq., Captain of His Majesty's Ship Warrior.

I am, etc.,
JOHN FRAZIER, LIEUTENANT

This was a serious accusation and although Bligh received a sympathetic letter from Cornwallis in which he said, "your conduct since you have been under my orders has always been perfectly to my satisfaction", the request having been made, things had to take their course.

Back at sea the *Warrior* plunged into the hard gales, one of which swept several of the blockading ships from their station to be greeted on their return by a signal from the *Tonnant* saying that six French ships-of-the-line and two frigates had broken out of Rochefort but where they had gone was never discovered. A week later, during another violent gale, the *Dreadnought* was taken aback and the *Warrior* sailing in her wake, struck her high ornamented stern, and damaged her own bowsprit. She kept with the fleet, and the bowsprit was repaired at sea.

On 17th February 1805, Bligh read the funeral service over the body of Seaman James McDonald who had died of "a fever". The log goes on to say that, with typical thoroughness, Bligh had then "washed the sick bay". This was the second death in the *Warrior*, a seaman having been washed overboard during the previous year "who, notwithstanding every effort made to save him", was unfortunately drowned. There was to be a third, just before Bligh left the ship, when Seaman David McKee died "of a sudden decline".

The main problem, as always, was water, but new arrivals would send their boats around the fleet, supplying those whose supplies were running low. Something akin to a trading organisation went on amongst the hard-pressed ships. Bligh writes of receiving fresh beef from the *Nero* and a topsail yard from the *Montagu*, whilst he supplied the *Dreadnought* with blank cartridges and the *Tonnant* with tea.

On 23rd February the *Warrior* was back in Torbay and Bligh was ordered to appear at the court-martial instigated by the revenge-seeking Frazier. It lasted for the two days of 25th and 26th February. Bligh dismissed it briefly in his log as: "went on board the *San Josef* to attend a court martial, as did all the officers", but he was naturally worried as to the outcome. He knew that Frazier was a vindictive and spiteful man and he was not sure what mischief he would introduce during the trial, well knowing that the other would be prepared to let his own career suffer if he could damage that of his former captain. He was also acutely aware that there were now nearly seven hundred captains in the Naval List, and he had the uneasy feeling that one of them, more or less, would not be missed.

Vice-Admiral Sir Charles Cotton presided at the Court-martial and the charges which Bligh had to face were those stated in

Frazier's letter, and which dragged in as witnesses nearly every officer and petty officer in the ship. The evidence most of them gave was very confusing, the majority agreeing with what Frazier put to them regarding Bligh's temper, then qualifying their statements by additional comments which cancelled out what they had already said. Most agreed that Bligh was inclined to shout and swear when things were not going well or when work was not up to standard, but hastily added that when that particular moment was over he immediately calmed down. Many of the witnesses called for the prosecution admitted that they would as soon sail with Captain Bligh as any other captain.

Bligh sat for two days listening to this conflicting evidence until the afternoon of the second day, when he was called to speak in his own defence. He stood up in his place, facing the President and the court and spoke up firmly, denying all the charges, especially that of tyranny and oppression.

The verdict of the court, as printed in *The Times* on 1st March was:

> On Monday a Court Martial was held on board the fleet at Torbay, on Captain Bligh of the *Warrior*, on charges of tyranny, unofficer-like conduct, and ungentlemanly behaviour, preferred against him by one of his Lieutenants (who was tried some time since for disobedience of orders and acquitted). After a trial which lasted two days, Captain Bligh was reprimanded with an admonition from the President, and restored to his command.

Bligh was back in his ship and Frazier disappeared from history. He had been discharged from the *Warrior* on 13th December of the previous year and does not appear to have served after that date.

The next time the *Warrior* came into harbour, Bligh found an interesting and exciting letter from his old and valued friend, Sir Joseph Banks. Dated 15th March it informed him that the present Governor of New South Wales was anxious to retire and that a successor was needed. Sir Joseph felt that Bligh would be ideal for a post that required integrity, firmness of discipline and self-reliance. It offered an income of £2,000 a year, opportunities to collect legitimate 'perks' and as Sir Joseph pointed out, the opportunity of his daughters meeting more rich and eligible young men than if they remained in England. Bligh read this letter through several times then walked out onto the quarterdeck where, deep in thought, he walked slowly up and down for a long time. The offer was a very tempting one, but the decision had to be considered with the utmost care.

He had not made up his mind when the *Warrior* returned to her station, but on 25th March, he wrote a letter to Sir Joseph asking him for further details. He explained that his reasons for not immediately accepting such a kind and generous offer were personal ones, for he dreaded the thought of a long separation from his wife, yet he knew that she would never accompany him as she had an inherent fear of the sea.

After further letters had passed between them Bligh finally agreed to accept the offer, especially as he had been informed that he could take Mary's husband, Lieutenant Putland R.N. as his *aide* and that Mary, his second daughter, could go too.

That decision taken he knew that for the time being at least, his days as a captain of a ship-of-the-line were ended. On 23rd April he brought the *Warrior* into Cawsand Bay for the last time. A week later he wrote: "Captain S.H. Linzee came aboard and superceded me", then closed the log firmly and with finality.

He was now in his fiftieth year and despite the tremendous pressures and hardships which he had experienced, was in good health. The service as governor was for only a few years and during that time he would, as he had already promised Elizabeth, manage to "procure a little affluence". His naval service would still continue and whilst in Australia he would also have the rank of Commander-in-Chief of His Majesty's ships on the New South Wales station. When he returned to England there was every chance of him attaining flag rank.

He smiled as the thought crossed his mind. It would seem on the whole, that the Bounty Bastard had not done so badly after all!

[19]

The Governor

AFTER RELINQUISHING command of the *Warrior*, Bligh was on half pay until 23rd May 1805 when he was confirmed as the next Governor of New South Wales. He spent the next few months with mixed feelings for although he was anxious to sail and take up his new appointment, he was loathe to leave Elizabeth who was remaining behind because of her great dread of the sea. Even the thought of such a long passage was enough to make her feel ill.

Bligh spent a great deal of time writing and visiting and was actually at the Admiralty on the morning of 6th November when the news arrived that Trafalgar had been fought and won and that his former commander, Horatio Nelson, had been killed during the battle.

Suitable transport was available at last and Bligh sailed from England during February 1806 with his daughter, Mary Putland, in the *Lady Madeleine Sinclair*. This transport, together with three convict ships, were under the convoy of H.M.S. *Porpoise*.

There was trouble from the start due mainly to ambiguous wording by the Admiralty which caused both Bligh and Captain Joseph Short of the *Porpoise* assume that they were in command. Short, who had commanded his ship for a year, had been instructed to take the course from Bligh, otherwise he would be in command until they reached Australia. Bligh, on the other hand, was the senior naval officer and having hoisted his Commodore's broad pennant, assumed that he was the commanding officer from the outset.

This state of affairs led to furious arguments. On one occasion, when Bligh altered the course of the *Lady Sinclair* without advising Short, that irate captain fired a shot across her bows and another across her stern and threatened that the next would be amidships. Ironically, Short ordered Bligh's son-in-law and A.D.C, Lieutenant Charles Putland R.N. to supervise the firing.

After a passage of some six months, including a run from the Cape of Good Hope of fifty-one days, the *Porpoise* and *Lady*

Sinclair dropped anchor on 6th August 1806 and Bligh was able to study the capital of the colony he had arrived to govern.

His old mentor, Captain Cook, had discovered New South Wales on 28th April 1770, the first settlement being established during January 1788 when H.M. Ships *Sirius* and *Supply* reached Botany Bay with store-ships and transports which had carried 568 male and 191 female convicts with thirteen children, together with 206 marines with forty-six wives and children and some twenty officials. The passage took just over eight months, twenty-three convicts dying *en route*. Captain Arthur Phillip, who had commanded the squadron, soon realized that Botany Bay was unsuitable territory for a settlement, being flat and barren and with little water. Consequently he sent the *Supply* to examine the coast to find somewhere more agreeable.

Her captain found the ideal place, Port Jackson, a few miles to the north, an almost land-locked harbour with deep water for his ships. Phillip chose a cove a few miles within the harbour naming it Sydney Cove after the Secretary of State for the Colonies, the British flag was hoisted over the site on 26th January 1788 (now celebrated as Foundation Day) and work began on building the new settlement of which he was to become the first governor.

In the years that followed other convict ships arrived and then, in 1793, the first group of free settlers arrived and were given grants of land. Although the area of New South Wales was enormous, settlement was slow and by the turn of the century there was only one white person to every 300 square miles.

Captain Hunter became the second governor and the colony expanded, a number of townships being built between Parramatta and the banks of the Hawkesbury, a steady growth which continued during the term of the third, Captain P.G. King.

King was still governor when Bligh stepped ashore on Friday 8th August to be received with full military honours and an address of welcome signed by the three most important men after the governor. They were:

> George Johnston, for the Military
> Richard Atkins, for the Civil
> John MacArthur, for the free
> Inhabitants

He was then escorted to Government House where he stayed as King's guest until assuming the governorship. Before leaving,

King made Bligh a grant of three large tracts of land at a peppercorn rent. Bligh named them Camperdown and Copenhagen after the two battles in which he had fought, and Mount Betham after Elizabeth's family.

Even before King sailed for England, however, Bligh realized that a formidable task was ahead of him. The colony was virtually controlled by a group of army officers who had established a monopoly on most imported goods, especially spirits, which they resold at great profit to themselves. Nearly all of them had neglected their soldiering to farm as well, using free convict labour to rear cattle and sheep which produced the largest returns instead of agricultural produce which was desperately needed by the colony. Complaints made by civilians were brushed aside by the all-powerful army clique and their men. Their regiment, which had developed from the original 200-odd marines, had become the New South Wales Corps, but because it was mainly engaged in the sale of liquor, was known as the Rum Puncheon Corps.

This traffic in rum was to be the prime cause of Bligh's headaches in the years ahead. His orders were to break the monopolistic power of the army and to abolish the sale of rum, but he soon ran into trouble. Rum, he discovered, was the main currency of the colony. Cattle and sheep, crops and payment for services, were all made in rum and the more Bligh saw what was happening — for the trade had been going on since the days of the first governor — the more appalled he became. After a quick tour of the country districts he returned to Sydney and issued a General Order which prohibited the bartering of rum and other spirits in lieu of coin. Anyone flouting this law would be liable to severe fines and even imprisonment. It was a declaration of war.

Realizing that their new governor was about to hit them in their most tender spot — their pockets — the army officers immediately closed ranks and prepared to resist. A trained diplomat, perhaps, would have used the skill and finesse of his profession to handle such a situation but Bligh, used only to the harsh discipline of an exacting service and to the instant and unquestioning obedience of the captain of a ship, was utterly unsuited to the task.

One contributory factor was a deep-seated, inter-service jealousy. Since the founding of the colony, the governors had always been naval officers, whilst the day-to-day task of keeping order was left to the military. Hunter and then King, especially, had run into difficulties with the arrogant, profit-greedy officers of the New South Wales Corps but had been forced to compromise, for it was the same corps which was supposed to carry out their commands. Yet the officers were the principal offenders in the rum scandal. They rallied round their leader, Major George Johnston who had signed the welcome on behalf of the military but Bligh had more trouble with another of the signees, Lieutenant John MacArthur, a tough, wealthy and far-seeing Scot and a man with immense power. He had seen that the future of the country lay in the raising of high quality mutton and wool and started a flock of merino sheep in 1797 which flourished. He also had a finger in everything else that seemed profitable. Hunter had called him a "busybody", yet much of Australia's subsequent wealth stemmed directly from MacArthur's pioneering efforts.

At one of his first meetings with Bligh he tried to get him interested in sheep but the new governor flew into a rage in which jealousy of the other's success probably played a part. When he accused MacArthur of owning 5,000 acres of land in the finest situation in the country, MacArthur, not one to brook opposition, reminded Bligh that the land had been given him on the recommendation of the Privy Council and the Secretary of State.

"Damn the Privy Council and the Secretary of State too!" Bligh shouted in reply. "What have they to do with me?"

This was the first of many such bitter arguments. It was singularly unfortunate that such an antipathy existed, for in their own way both men genuinely had the welfare and future of the colony at heart. Had they settled their differences and worked together, great things would have undoubtedly been accomplished.

The climax was reached when MacArthur, defying Bligh's authority, was arrested for sedition and placed in custody on 25th January 1808. Later the same day a furious Bligh learned that MacArthur had been released from gaol on an order signed by Major George Johnston as 'Lieutenant-Governor'. It appeared that MacArthur had been brought before a court presided over by the third signee, Richard Atkins, the Judge-Advocate, who had been an enemy of the prisoner for many years. MacArthur naturally protested at being tried by such a man and was finally 'rescued' by officers of the Corps and escorted back to the barracks in triumph.

The next day Johnston sent some officers to Government House demanding that Bligh surrender his governorship. They were followed by Johnston himself leading nearly 400 troops who marched with fixed bayonets behind their band playing "The British Grenadiers" and also a crowd of excited townsfolk, all making for Government House where Bligh and a few of the men still loyal to him were at dinner.

The soldiers were confronted at the gate by Bligh's recently widowed daughter, Mary Putland, who stood at bay with a parasol in her hand, defying them to enter her home. Ignoring their bayonets and loaded flintlocks she demanded that they "stab her to the heart, but to respect the life of her father".

Her gesture was brave but unavailing. She was bundled to one side and the troops poured into the house, noisily searching the downstairs rooms. Bligh meanwhile, refusing to submit to force, ordered a servant to saddle his horse whilst he ran upstairs to put on his uniform. He then went into a small room to select some papers which would prove useful if he was arrested. He knelt on the ground on the far side of the bed to sort them out when the door burst open and some of the soldiers entered. Bligh rose to his feet and was trying to stuff some of the papers into the waistcoat pocket of his tight-fitting uniform when one of the soldiers, thinking he was about to produce a pistol, thrust his bayonet forward and cried, "Damn your eyes; if you don't take your hand out of there I will whip this into you immediately!"

Bligh cried out that he was unarmed and eventually he was taken below where a letter from Johnston was handed to him. It ordered him to resign his authority "and to submit to the arrest which I hereby place you under, by the advice of all my officers, and by the advice of every respectable inhabitant in the town of Sydney".

Later, on that eventful day, Johnson declared Martial Law and assumed the duties of governor. The next day bills were posted around the town which stated, somewhat theatrically:

Soldiers!
Your conduct had endeared you to every well-disposed inhabitant in this settlement. Persevere in the same honourable path and you will establish the credit of the New South Wales Corps on a basis not to be shaken. God Save the King.

and Bligh was put under close arrest.

For some months Johnston governed the colony without any trouble. MacArthur was tried, acquitted and made Colonial Secretary and in every way became the most powerful man in the territory.

Bligh was unable to tell Lord Castlereagh, Secretary of State for the Colonies of his predicament until May and even then his despatches had to be smuggled on board a homeward bound ship. Johnston had already sent his version of the trouble back to England but as the days passed he and his associates became increasingly disturbed. Their report had never mentioned the word 'mutiny', a word so closely associated with the deposed governor who, now that he was out of office, was gaining a great deal of support. The worthy citizens of Sydney, for the most part, came round to thinking that he had tried to carry out his orders to curb the power of the army and eliminate the rum traffic, but that Johnston and the military self-seekers had been too strong for him. The news of his daughter's gallant action at the gate was much repeated and counter-balanced the reports of the soldiers, encouraged by Johnston, who claimed that they had discovered Bligh hiding beneath a bed. Their individual reports were very conflicting and Bligh, furious at the slur on his manhood, did everything possible to refute the slander.

As the months passed, Bligh remained in custody but it became apparent that Johnston's successors — Lieutenant-Colonel Foveaux and then Colonel Paterson — wanted him out of the country, on board ship, sailing home to an enquiry, especially as his supporters were growing more vociferous as time went by. Finally Paterson agreed that Bligh should return to England in H.M.S. *Porpoise* of which, officially, he was still captain. A document was prepared in which Bligh agreed to sail "with the utmost despatch" but when he boarded her, instead of returning directly to England, he took the ship to the settlement on the River Derwent in Tasmania where he was cordially received by the Lieutenant-Governor, David Collins. Bligh explained this apparent breach of faith by saying "by getting possession of the ship I was enabled to remain in or about the territory, which was all I had in my power to do for the good of my country".

It was not long, however, before relations between the two men became strained. Bligh was finally banned from coming ashore so he began a one-ship blockade of Storm Bay Passage and when his provisions ran short he stopped some of the ships entering and leaving Hobart to commandeer supplies for his crew.

Back in England Lord Castlereagh had finally decided that the actions of Bligh's opponents had been unconstitutional. He also decided that Bligh must return to England, for reinstatement in the post of governor after the indignities he had suffered would make his position intolerable. A new governor was appointed – a soldier this time. He was Lieutenant-Colonel Lachlan Macquarie, commanding the 73rd Regiment which had been selected to replace the mutinous New South Wales Corps. Castlereagh informed Bligh of his decision but hastened to assure him that he still retained the fullest confidence of both the King and the Government.

Macquarie arrived in New South Wales on 28th December 1809 and assumed the office of governor four days later whilst Bligh, learning of his arrival, sailed to Sydney from Tasmania to greet his successor.

Bligh's return to Sydney was bitter-sweet. On the one hand he was received with honour by his supporters and with the knowledge that all his former enemies had been called to account for their mutinous conduct but his stay in Sydney was short for Governor Macquarie was obviously anxious to get him out of his territory.

Bligh returned to England in the *Hindostan*, flying his Commodore's pennant, to arrive on 25th October 1810. This time he travelled alone for Mary Putland, widowed two years earlier, had fallen in love with Lieutenant-Colonel Maurice O'Connell, Macquarie's second-in-command. She married him before Bligh sailed, then stayed on in the colony.

In May of the following year, Major Johnston appeared before a court-martial. The trial dragged on for nearly a month, with almost another month before the verdict was announced. Bligh was completely exonerated. Johnston was found guilty of the act of mutiny and cashiered; a light sentence under the circumstances. MacArthur, who was merely called as a witness, was ordered not to return to Australia for eight years.

The confidence that his superiors had shown in Bligh was reflected immediately after the trial when he was raised to flag rank, being promoted Rear-Admiral of the Blue. He remained on the active service list but did not return to sea. Instead, he was happy to live in retirement with his family, although he suffered a great blow in 1812 when his beloved Elizabeth died after a long illness. With her passing, life at Durham Place, with all its happy memories, was unthinkable and after a sojourn at Sydenham, he finally moved to the Manor House, Farningham in Kent where he lived with his daughters and where he was promoted to his final rank — Vice-Admiral of the Blue.

In February 1801 he had been made a Fellow of the Royal Society for his work in the South Seas and he frequently went to London to attend their meetings. The last visit he paid was for the wedding of thirty-two-year old Elizabeth, his third daughter, who was married to her cousin Richard Bligh in December 1817. He had been suffering from an internal complaint for some time and soon after the wedding, when staying in Bond Street, he became ill and a few days later passed away.

He was buried in the family vault in the churchyard of St Paul's, Lambeth, where Elizabeth Bligh, the day-old twins William and Henry and also William Bligh Barker, the three-year-old son of his eldest daughter Harriet, were buried. The square monument topped by an urn can still be seen, bearing on one side an inscription which reads:

SACRED
TO THE MEMORY OF
WILLIAM BLIGH, ESQUIRE, F.R.S.
VICE ADMIRAL OF THE BLUE
WHO FIRST TRANSPLANTED THE BREAD FRUIT TREE
FROM OTAHEITE TO THE WEST INDIES
BRAVELY FOUGHT THE BATTLES OF HIS COUNTRY
AND DIED BELOVED, RESPECTED AND LAMENTED
ON THE 7TH DAY OF DECEMBER, 1817
AGED 64

But Bligh has even more permanent memorials. They are situated far away from the little Lambeth churchyard, amidst the great oceans on the other side of the world.

Here, where the Trade Winds rustle the fronds of the tall palms and where the swell of the blue Pacific beats incessantly on white coral reefs, are the landmarks that still bear his name; tangible evidence to remind us that here sailed a man who for all his faults was a great Englishman, a gallant officer and one of the most brilliant navigators the world has ever known.

Sources

Various logs in the Public Record Office and Admiralty covering Bligh's career from Midshipman in H.M.S. *Hunter* to Captain in H.M.S. *Warrior*, especially H.M.S. *Glatton*, his ship at Copenhagen and H.M.S. *Director*, his ship during the Nore mutiny.

Gentleman's Magazine, 1792-1835. London
Bligh of the Bounty, E.A. Hughes, J.M. Dent and Sons, 1936
Log of the *Bounty*, Golden Cockerel Press, 1934
Log of the *Bounty*'s Launch, Golden Cockerel Press, 1934
Naval History of Great Britain, E.P. Brenton, London, 1837
The Royal Navy, (7 vols) W.L. Clowes, London, 1897
The Great Mutiny, James Dugan, Andre Deutsch, 1966
The Naval Mutinies of 1797, C. Gill, Manchester, 1913
Life of Capt. James Cook, A. Kitson, London, 1912
A Book of the Bounty, G. Machaness, London, 1938
Mutiny, Nordhoff and Hall, London, 1933
Pitcairn's Island, Nordhoff and Hall, London, 1935
Nelson, Carola Oman, London, 1947
The English Circumnavigators Purves and Cochrane, Edinburgh, 1882
Bligh of the Bounty, Geoffrey Rawson, London, 1930
The Life of Vice-Admiral William Bligh, George Mackaness, Sydney and
     London, 1951
Turbulent Journey, Owen Rutter, London, 1936
Life of Nelson, Robert Southey, London, 1881
A Portrait of Lord Nelson, Oliver Warner, London, 1958
History of the British Navy, C.D. Yonge, London, 1963

Index